Travail in an Arab Land

JUDAIC STUDIES SERIES

Leon J. Weinberger
General Editor

Travail in an Arab Land

Samuel Romanelli

Translated from the Hebrew
with an Introduction and Notes
by Yedida K. Stillman and
Norman A. Stillman

The University of Alabama Press
Tuscaloosa and London

Publication of this book has been assisted by a grant from
the Publications Program of the National Endowment for the
Humanities.

Library of Congress Cataloging-in-Publication Data

Romanelli, Samuel Aaron, 1757–1814.
  Travail in an Arab land.

  Translation of: Maśa ba- ʿArav.
  Bibliography: p.
  Includes index.
  1. Jews—Morocco.   2. Morocco—Description and
travel.   3. Romanelli, Samuel Aaron, 1757–1814.
4. Morocco—Ethnic relations.   I. Title.
DS135.M8R6613   1989   964'.0004924   88–3931
ISBN 0-8173-5135-3

British Library Cataloging-in-Publication Data available

To Our Beloved Children

Mia and Enan

אל תקרי בניך אלא בוניך

Berakhot 64a

Contents

Preface

The traveler's account has had a popular place in Hebrew literature, as indeed it did in European non-Jewish literature as well.
The *Massā'ōt* (Travels) of Benjamin of Tudela and the *Sibbūv* (Tour)
of Rabbi Petahya of Regensburg, both written in the twelfth century,
enjoyed numerous editions from the early days of Hebrew printing.[1] Like many, if not most, of the Hebrew travelogues that came
after them, these works dealt in part or in whole with a pilgrimage
to the land of Israel and an itinerary of its holy places. This was
usually coupled with some information on the various Jewish communities along the way. Many of the Hebrew travelers' accounts
read like little more than catalogues of places, names, and statis-
tics.[2] But rarely were their authors artists with any pretensions to
producing works of literary merit.

One of the most original and, from the literary point of view,
satisfying works in this genre is Samuel Romanelli's *Massā' Ba'rāv*
(Travail in an Arab Land). This is a book of travel by a gifted artist
and professional man of letters who knows how to entertain as
well as inform. The work has enjoyed an enduring success with
the Hebrew-reading public and has appeared in no fewer than
nine editions beginning with its first publication in Berlin in 1792,[3]
but it had never been translated into any European language. Excerpts and brief summaries of Romanelli's account have appeared
in Italian, German, and French.[4] The only thing available in English
was a brief passage cited by Hirschberg in his *A History of the Jews
in North Africa*.[5] The Hungarian-born British scholar Solomon

Schiller-Szinessy had planned an English translation as the second part of his Hebrew edition (1866), and its scheduled publication for 1887 was announced (hence its inclusion in some bibliographies), but never appeared.

Ever since we first became familiar with Romanelli's masterpiece some fifteen years ago, we felt strongly that it deserved an English translation and have on occasion said so in writing.[6] We eventually decided to do the translation ourselves, after years of frequent recourse to the book in teaching and as a primary source for our research on North African Jewry.

Our translation of Romanelli's *Massā' Baʿrāv* has been done from Jefim Ḥayyim Schirmann's well-annotated edition of 1968.[7] This is the closest thing to a critical edition since no original manuscript is extant and all of the seven editions that appeared between 1834 and 1926 were based upon the Berlin edition of 1792, which although overseen by Romanelli himself, is full of typographical errors. We have referred occasionally to several of the earlier editions (especially, the original Berlin edition and the Warsaw edition of 1926) in order to clarify readings that were obscured by a rare misprint here and there in Schirmann's text or where we wished to see how other editors had punctuated certain passages.

Because Romanelli's account is both a historical document and a literary work of the first order, our aim in translating it has been twofold; namely, to achieve a result that maintains scholarly accuracy, and at the same time is compatible with the guiding principle of modern translation theory that literary acceptability has priority over literal accuracy.[8] The extensive notes with which we have annotated the translation highlight the dual character of the book. They are, therefore, historical and cultural on the one hand, and literary and linguistic on the other. With regard to Romanelli's wide-ranging literary sources and many of his biblical allusions, we were deeply indebted to the very thorough work already done by Schirmann in the notes to his edition of the Hebrew text. We have by no means noted every single scriptural allusion since this would entail, in effect, annotating almost every single line.

One of the primary difficulties, or rather challenges, of translating Romanelli is conveying to the English reader the flavor of his language. We have tried to maintain the balance between the archaism and classicism of the biblical Hebrew medium with the innate liveliness of the author's style. In rendering certain biblical passages or expressions, we have attempted to give them as Romanelli would have understood them in the eighteenth century, rather than as we would understand them today in the light of modern biblical criticism and Semitic philology.

Biblical names are generally given in their accepted English form, such as Abraham, Jacob, Moses. One major exception is Eliahu, rather than Elijah Levi. His name appears in numerous European documents from the period as Liahu and Liaho (the Moroccan Jewish variant of the name), and Eliahu was chosen by us as a compromise form. Arabic personal names are given in the Classical Arabic version, but many words and phrases are rendered in Colloquial Moroccan, as Romanelli himself has given them. The Arabic and Hebrew words for "son of" (*ibn* and *ben*, respectively) in the middle of names is always abbreviated as b. When they are part of a family name, however, they are spelled out and capitalized. R. before a name indicates the Hebrew title of respect "Rabbi."

In addition to providing modern paragraphing and punctuation, the only major liberty we have taken with the text is to change direct discourse to indirect discourse in some of the conversations where we felt that this made for better reading in English.

Acknowledgments

It is our pleasant duty to acknowledge those individuals and institutions whose kindness and support greatly facilitated our work.

Heartfelt thanks are due to our dear teacher and friend, Professor Svi Rin. Himself a noted translator, he painstakingly went over our entire manuscript line by line, compared it with the Hebrew text, and offered numerous corrections and suggestions.

Our colleague, Professor Marilyn Gaddis Rose, also read our original translation and made valuable stylistic comments.

Throughout the course of our work, we received helpful suggestions and words of encouragement in conversation and correspondence with Professors Arieh Newman, Moshe Pelli, Haïm Zafrani, Harvey Goldberg, the late Hayyim Schirmann, and our late mentor S. D. Goitein. It was Professor Goitein who suggested that we make the translation a collaborative effort. Professor Anthony Pellegrini kindly went over several of the Italian literary sources with us.

We were given considerable food for thought by the students in a seminar on Romanelli that Yedida Stillman had taught several years ago at Binghamton.

As always, the staff of the State University of New York at Binghamton Interlibrary Loan Office was most helpful, cheerfully tracking down and processing our many requests for recherché items. The staff of the University Manuscript Center provided the invaluable service of preparing the typescript.

Last, but by no means least, we must acknowledge our great indebtedness to the National Endowment for the Humanities which generously provided Yedida Stillman with the grant to undertake the initial translation of Romanelli's masterpiece.

Y. K. S. and N. A. S.
Binghamton, New York

Travail in an
Arab Land

Introduction

Samuel Romanelli: The Man and His Work

Samuel Romanelli[1] was a free spirit, a son of the Enlightenment and the Age of Revolution. He spent much of his life traveling in search of knowledge, adventure, and patrons for his literary endeavors.

He was born in Mantua in Austrian-ruled Lombardy on September 19, 1757, the son of Moses Ḥayy and Consola Romanelli. His father's family included several rabbis, schoolteachers, merchants, and minor officials, but no very distinguished figures. His mother, however, belonged to the renowned Portaleone family, which for about four hundred years produced some of Italy's leading rabbinical scholars, physicians, and men of letters.[2]

Little is known of Romanelli's youth. It is clear from the mastery of Hebrew, the Scriptures, and both early and late rabbinic sources exhibited in his writing that he received a superb education in the Italian Jewish tradition. (Like the Sephardi curriculum, Italian Jewish education placed a strong emphasis on Hebrew grammar and poetry as well as on the written and oral Torah and their commentators.) He probably studied in the Talmud Torah of Mantua which also included Italian and arithmetic in its course of studies.[3] Although there had been a marked decline since the height of the Renaissance, his native city was still at that time one of the leading centers of Jewish culture in Italy. There was a major Jewish communal library attached to the Talmud Torah, and it was here that Romanelli by his own account went beyond the required school reading. In the introduction to his play ʿ*Alōt ha-Minḥa* (The Time of Offering), he mentions that it was in this library that he became acquainted with dell' Anguillara's *octava rima* version of Ovid's *Metamorphoses* and its Hebrew translation by Shabbethai Marini.[4]

Romanelli also acquired an impressive secular education that went far beyond the instruction available in the Talmud Torah of that time. He may have had private tutoring in some of the secular subjects—something not uncommon in Mantua at that period. But much of his wide erudition must have been gained autodidactically. This erudition frequently appears in philosophical asides and cross-cultural notes that crop up in *Travail in an Arab Land*.

He was an accomplished linguist. According to Steinschneider, he was fluent in ten languages, and according to an anonymous detractor, the author of a vituperative polemic against the Jews of the Enlightenment, he was proficient in twelve.[5] Romanelli wrote poetry in both Hebrew and Italian and translated works from one language to the other.[6] In his writing, Romanelli shows that he was well read in the classical and contemporary literature in French, Spanish, German, and English. He appears to be the first Hebrew writer to mention Shakespeare and Milton. He was particularly fond of the poet Alexander Pope, and translated his *Essay on Man* into Hebrew under the title of *Massaʿal hā-Ādām*, although only brief passages from the translation have survived.[7] In many of Romanelli's surviving poems there is an elevated religiophilosophical tendency that reminds one of the spirit of Pope. Indeed, it is interesting that despite Romanelli's waggish and at times fiery temperament, his sharp tongue, and an apparent taste for women, there are relatively few satires or love poems in his poetic legacy.[8] The majority of his poems were occasional pieces written for patrons on joyous or sad occasions.

From passing remarks made in *Travail in an Arab Land*, it would appear that as a young man, Romanelli may have traveled to France, Holland, Germany, and Poland.[9] Lelio della Torre, who had met Romanelli personally and knew one of his intimate pupils, mentions that he had traveled through "a great part of Europe."[10] Sometime during the 1780s, the young Romanelli made his way to England. London at that time had a small circle of Maskilim, or Jews of the Enlightenment, and patrons of Hebrew culture. Romanelli's countryman, Ephraim Luzzatto, to whom he referred as the "Hebrew Petrarch," had already been living there for two decades at that time.[11]

Perhaps unable to earn a satisfactory livelihood or because he was merely homesick, Romanelli sailed from England in 1786, intending to return to his native Italy. But after being stranded in Gibraltar for an indeterminate period of time which left him strapped for funds, he accepted an offer from a local merchant to accompany the latter on a business trip to the Sherifan Empire of Morocco. After losing his passport, Romanelli had to remain in the Maghreb for the next four years, living by his wits and going from adventure to adventure. He found a livelihood as a preacher in synagogues, as a Spanish teacher, as a translator and factotum for foreign mariners in port, and as a secretary and accountant for European consuls and for Jewish courtiers and merchants. He lived through the turbulent interregnum that followed the death of the Sultan Sīdī Muhammad III in 1790. He finally escaped from Morocco on June 13, 1790, stripped of almost all his savings, but grateful for being able to leave. As he says in his own words, "I left . . . and never looked back." It is this period of his life that is colorfully preserved in *Travail in an Arab Land*.

Romanelli made his way from North Africa to the Netherlands, where he arrived on August 18, 1790, "strolling peacefully and safely in the streets of Amsterdam." For a while, the penniless poet found patrons in Amsterdam and the Hague,[12] but then made his way to Berlin, the capital of the Haskala, or Jewish Enlightenment. There, he joined the intellectual circle of the Me'assefim, whose Hebrew journal *ha-Me'assef* had been founded by disciples of Naphtali Herz Wesseley and Moses Mendelssohn and had become the very symbol of the Haskala movement. Romanelli had been an admirer of the German Maskilim long before his arrival in Prussia and had even written a lament in sonnet form in 1786, while still in London upon the death of Moses Mendelssohn, whom he called "the light of the Exile."[13]

In Berlin, Romanelli was patronized by such leading figures as David Friedländer and Daniel Jaffe Itzig. Friedländer is respectfully mentioned in a note at the end of *Travail in an Arab Land* as one of the principal subscribers to the book's publication, and it was to him that Romanelli dedicated his religiophilosophical meditation *Rū'aḥ Nākhōn* (The Right Spirit).[14] For the marriage of Itzig's daughter Henrietta to Mendel Oppenheim, Romanelli composed a three-act allegorical drama based upon classical myth entitled *Ha-Qōlōt Yeḥdālūn ō Mishpāṭ Shālōm* (The Voices Shall Cease, or the Judgment of Peace).[15] It was in Berlin, too, that Romanelli published his *Travail in an Arab Land* at the press of the Jüdische Freischule in 1792.

The following year, he was off to Vienna where he was invited by Anton Schmid to be a literary consultant, editor, and proof-reader for the Hebrew department of the court printer Joseph Edler von Kurzbeck. It was at this press, where a number of leading Maskilim were employed, that Romanelli published his second allegorical play on a mythological theme *ʿAlōt ha-Minḥa ō Ḥāvēr Me'ushshār* (The Time of Offering, or A Happy Friend). Like his previous theatrical work, this one was composed on the occasion of a wedding uniting two leading German Jewish houses. This time, in addition to the Hebrew text, Romanelli published an accompanying Italian version of the play (*Il Pomo Traslato ossia L'Innesto felice*).[16] Romanelli spent between five and six years in Vienna. He is reported to have worked also for the printer Josef Hraszansky at some point, but no details of his activities during this period are known.[17] However, he seems to have made enemies while in the Hapsburg capital, and they later spread the rumor that he had embraced Christianity and died there in 1801.[18]

Romanelli in fact left Vienna sometime in 1798 or early 1799. He stayed for a while in Trieste which had a small but active community of Maskilim who maintained contacts with the Jewish intellectuals of Berlin and Vienna. Here Romanelli published his Hebrew grammar *Grammatica ragionata italiana ed ebraica con trattato, ed esempj di poesia* (1799), the first Hebrew work printed in that city.[19]

In 1799, Romanelli left Austrian-controlled Trieste for northern Italy which had come under the sway of Napoleon. Likey other Jews at this time, he became an enthusiastic supporter of Napoleon, whom he viewed as the emancipator of European Jewry, although only a few years earlier, he had written a patriotic poem in honor of Franz II and his brother Archduke Karl as they were about to go to war against the young Bonaparte.[20]

It is difficult to trace Romanelli's movements during the next decade. He seems to have wandered about a great deal. He tried to settle down in many different Italian Jewish communities, but his frequent disrespect for the wealthy, for religious leaders, and for communal norms of behavior earned him many enemies. He was even expelled from a number of communities.[21]

Romanelli had visited Nice sometime around the end of the eighteenth century and prepared a rhymed inscription for the inauguration of a Jewish school there.[22] In 1802 he was in Genoa, where he was commissioned to compose a literary Hebrew inscription for the gateway of the new Jewish cemetery.[23] He was back in his native Mantua in 1807. There he brought out a volume of hymns and elegies (*Ossia Raccolta di inni ed odi*) to Napoleon by the rabbis of the Great Sanhedrin which had been convened in Paris during February and March of that year. The Hebrew poems were accompanied by Romanelli's own Italian translation. It is not known whether Romanelli had been in Paris at the time the Sanhedrin met—or at any time for that matter. However, it is known that he had spent the holiday of Shavu'ot in Lille, some two hundred kilometers north of Paris, during some unspecified year, and composed a poem on the occasion of the festival at the request of members of the Jewish community.[24] It is most likely that this visit followed the meeting of the Sanhedrin.

In 1808 we find the peripatetic Romanelli in Turin, where he published his second lengthy metaphysical poem *Maḥazē Shadday* (A Divine Vision). This work recounts the ascent of the poet's soul to the celestial spheres, where it discourses with an angel on the nature of the universe. Accompanying the 273-verse Hebrew text was a somewhat longer Italian version entitled *Illusione felice*. This opus shows a considerable maturing of Romanelli's poetic skill since the time he wrote *Rū'aḥ Nākhōn* sixteen years earlier in Berlin.[25]

The last six years of Romanelli's life were spent in the Piedmont region in and around Alessandria, where he published inter alia an Italian translation of the Yom Kippur liturgy with an introduction and literary analysis (*Ordine cerimoniale del Sacro Ministero*).[26] The translation of Jewish liturgy was something that was apparently dear to Romanelli's heart. He had already translated the Sephardi prayerbook to Italian in 1802 (*Orazione ebraiche di rito spagnuolo cotidane dal sabbato e de' noviluni*).[27] Years earlier, while in the Hague, he had written a sonnet in praise of "a dear group" of young Sephardim who were then engaged in a Dutch translation of their prayer rite.[28]

Romanelli's final place of residence was in Casale Monferrato on the Po River about thirty kilometers north of Alessandria. The town had a good-sized Jewish community at that time which had been established several centuries earlier. Here the wandering poet was befriended and looked after by the son of his landlord who was his pupil and confidant.[29]

Romanelli died suddenly at the age of fifty-seven from some sort of seizure while at supper on October 17, 1814. Because of his Bohemian life-style, his neglect of minor religious laws (and perhaps not so minor ones), and especially his sharp and at times mocking tongue, his death seems to have been passed over in silence by his contemporaries. The only record of it is in the register of deaths of the Jewish community of Casale Monferrato.[30] Indeed, he was totally ignored in the early works on Italian Hebrew poets and poetry. A considerable body of his writing remained in manuscript when he died,[31] and much of his work and his contribution to modern Hebrew literature was forgotten for the next half century with the sole exception of his *Travail in an Arab Land*.

Romanelli's Classic: Travail in an Arab Land

The lasting popularity of Romanelli's *Travail in an Arab Land* is due both to its content and its style. As we noted in the Preface, the book differed from most of its predecessors in Hebrew travel literature in that it did not deal even in part with a pilgrimage to the Holy Land, nor was it a description of the countries adjacent to it. Rather, it dealt with the Jews of Morocco, about whom little was known among their European coreligionists, a fact that Romanelli himself emphasizes in his introduction.

Morocco seemed to have a particular fascination for Europeans generally in this period. Perhaps this was due to the fact that it was so near geographically and yet at the same time—with the exception of a few limited points of contact along the coast such as Tangier and Mogador—so thoroughly inaccessible and exotic. A few Europeans who had visited the Sherifan Empire in the late eighteenth century wrote books about the country. These men were mainly former consuls who had served in Morocco, such as Georg Höst, Louis Chénier, and Franz von Dombay.[32] The latter, in fact, had been Romanelli's employer and benefactor during the early stages of Romanelli's stay in Tangier.[33] None of these men, however, traveled throughout the country as widely as Romanelli; nor did any of them live on such intimate terms with the native population at all levels, and particularly with the Jewish community, whose inner life—at home, in the synagogue and the yeshiva, and in its relations with the Muslim majority—he shared.

Romanelli states at the very outset that he had written this work for Jews, about Jews, with some treatment—by no means negligible—of the Gentiles living alongside them. Furthermore, the book is first and foremost a personal account of his own adventures experienced in the context of Moroccan daily life and current events at a particularly turbulent period.

Throughout the pages of his account, Romanelli candidly shares with the reader his hopes, his fears, his successes and failures. He relates, for example, how he talked his way into trouble with a government official in Mogador, and then how he conned his way out of it (Chapter 13). He tells how he almost was enmeshed in the snares of love with his landlord's beautiful daughter (Chapter 8), and how he and a Gentile companion got drunk at a wedding party and almost caused a scandal in Meknes (Chapter 10). Although Romanelli never suffers from false modesty and enjoys telling the reader how his wit and erudition impressed people, he nevertheless possessed the ability to make fun of himself even as he did of others. Reflecting upon the vagaries of his fate, Romanelli ironically exclaims "When I say that I am wise, I am treated as a fool, and when I say I am a fool, I am treated like a wiseman!" (Chapter 13). When he finally succeeds in getting out of Morocco after being stripped of all his savings, he notes thankfully, but wryly, "As in the days of our exodus from Egypt, God showed me wonders—except I did not go out with great wealth since they despoiled me, rather than the other way around" (Chapter 14).

Romanelli's aim is to present an honest, but at the same time entertaining picture, even if it is at his own expense. As he informs the reader in his introduction, he has tried to show "no partiality to anyone, not even to myself".

In addition to being a witty raconteur, Romanelli possessed a keen eye for detail. As befits a good travelogue, his narrative is liberally interspersed with colorful images of native scenes—the marketplace with its sights, sounds, and smells; the house with its distinctive Moroccan appointments and furnishings; wedding festivities; funerals; royal court ceremonials; and military maneuvers. Food and clothing as well as other aspects of local material culture are vividly and accurately described. As the historian of modern Hebrew literature, Joseph Klausner, has noted, it was not until the late nineteenth century that we find other Hebrew writers exhibiting such an ability to use the language for such lucid and detailed description.[34]

Romanelli's ethnographic interest extended to native Moroccan customs, superstitions, and folklore. Although as a rationalist product of the European Enlightenment, he frequently mocks what he considered to be foolishness (a trait that caused him trouble with Orthodox Jewish circles in Europe), he nevertheless faithfully records such typical customs as the propitiatory *'ār* offering, the use of spittle for medicinal purposes, divination practices, and the veneration of marabouts. Romanelli frequently makes comparative observations, drawing parallels between the Moroccan customs he is describing and folk practices of antiquity or of contemporary Catholic Europe.

Language was another one of Romanelli's abiding interests and the dialogues in *Travail in an Arab Land* are laced with colloquial Arabic words and phrases for local flavor. He was, as already noted, a gifted linguist, and during the first year of his stay in Morocco he learned Moroccan Arabic. Just how he went about systematically teaching himself a dialect for which there existed no grammar book at that time,[35] he explains to the reader in a passage (Chapter 4) that, by the way, also shows his respect for the language. He also offers valuable insights into the Moroccan pronunciation of Hebrew at that time. He described consonants and vowels using his broad knowledge of languages to draw philological comparisons. He even discusses stress and cantillation, contrasting the Moroccan style with the Ashkenazi. After completing this description (Chapter 2), he puckishly challenges the reader to try and pronounce a biblical phrase with the Meknasi pronunciation which would render it hilarious to the ears of Ashkenazi or Sephardi Hebrew speakers.

No other writer in Hebrew travel literature up to that time—and indeed few since—have presented so intimate, so vivid, and so accurately detailed a portrait of a Jewish community as did Romanelli. He not only gave a remarkable ethnographic account, he also conveyed much of the texture of Jewish life in traditional Moroccan Muslim society. He portrayed both the good and the bad—the generosity, hospitality, and piety of so many Moroccan Jews on the one hand, and the widespread ignorance and superstition on the other. The hardships endured by a subject people are poignantly depicted in Romanelli's description of Jews being pulled away from Sabbath services by the Sultan's guard for corvée labor and in his reporting of the horrific persecutions that were visited upon the Jews with the accession of Mūlāy Yazīd to the throne in 1790.

Perhaps the most original and memorable vignettes in the book are those depicting the *Shāb as-Sulṭān*, the Jewish courtier class in Morocco that Romanelli came to observe firsthand through personal service. There is none of the tendency to idealize here that can frequently be found even in modern historical treatments of the Jewish courtier phenomenon.[36] Although a few decent individuals like Rabbi Mordechai de la Mar shine through as glaring exceptions to the rule, most of these men are shown to be vicious and venal abusers of power like the sinister Eliahu Levi. These men, in Romanelli's damning indictment "would disown their father and mother . . . would not recognize their brother, or even their own children." Such people "would befriend another in word and win his heart, present him with a gift, and then return to plot his murder" (Chapter 9).

These depictions of the court Jews in *Travail in an Arab Land* are masterly studies in malevolence and power. When Eliahu with his low voice quietly threatens Romanelli, the reader too trembles. It is a tribute to Romanelli's artistic skills that these men continue to haunt the reader even after their violent and unlamented downfall in the final dramatic chapter. By the same token, the reader breathes a sigh of relief as Romanelli at long last strolls the streets of Amsterdam as a free man.

It is Romanelli's skill as an artistic narrator that carries the reader smoothly through the book from start to finish. Each of the fourteen chapters is carefully crafted, usually beginning and ending with the author philosophizing on the capriciousness of Fortune. Within this framework is the episode or series of episodes that confirm the philosophical observation. Occasionally, Romanelli breaks into the narrative for some additional reflections of a philosophical or academic nature. These excurses, however, are judiciously placed in the descriptive sections and are never long enough to break the flow of the story. From time to time, Romanelli addresses the reader directly in a personal tone as if he had suddenly divined the reader's thought at this particular point. He might tease the reader, admonish or cajole him. He sometimes advises him to keep a name or detail in mind because it will reappear in a later chapter.

Romanelli was an elegant stylist in the biblical Hebrew favored by the early Haskala writers. Although his language could be flowery at times, it is surprisingly vital and fluid. Because of his thorough mastery of the biblical text and its commentators, he was able to use its archaic forms and relatively limited vocabulary to the fullest. He seems to have particularly favored the Prophets and Hagiographa. In Chapter 14, for example, there are no less than eleven borrowings from Psalms, ten from Job, seven from other books of the Hagiographa, twenty-two from various prophets, as against only ten from the Pentateuch. Romanelli frequently cites biblical passages in clusters, so that in a single paragraph, or even in a single sentence, he might use two or more quotations or paraphrases from the same book. Sometimes, he employs a concatenation of related images from different biblical books.

Indeed, it would not be an exaggeration to say that almost every line of *Travail in an Arab Land* is rooted in the biblical text.[37]

However, Romanelli had such a command of the language and its grammar that he was not limited to taking biblical words and phrases in calque form, but could change tense, gender, number, and word order to suit his needs. He could break up and combine phrases into new combinations, and he did not hesitate to use words in accordance with a particular exegete or his own personal interpretation in order to expand the parameters of meaning. Neither did he hesitate to create neologisms for certain modern words, such as: *kelī shā'ōt* for clock, *qenē mattekhet* for cannons, *āvāq sōrēf* for gunpowder, and *qenē mabbāṭ* for spyglass. He made use of a very small number of foreign loanwords such as *pāspōrṭ* (for which he also employs *mikhtav yeṣī'a*). In some instances he uses foreign forms for European nationalities and languages, as for example, *īṭālī'ānō* for Italian, *īnglīsh* for the English language, and *īngīlīndīr* for the English. In one instance, he combines a biblical and a foreign vocable coining *tappūḥē ōrāniyyē* for oranges.

Romanelli was extremely fond of puns and other forms of evocative wordplay. When the wandering Italian finds employment in the counting house of Jesse in Mazagan, he writes, "Jesse's home was a breadwinning house for me" (*bēt Yishay ḥāyā bēt laḥmī*), a delightful play on Jesse the Bethlehemite (*Yishay bēt ha-laḥmī*) of I Samuel 16:1.

The title of this book is one of the best examples of wordplay. The word *massā'* evokes the same association of images in Hebrew (*massā'/massā'*) as does the English combination *travail/travel*. The Hebrew, however, has the additional meaning of a prophetic vision or pronouncement which is clearly evoked here as well since the entire phrase is taken from Isaiah 21:13, where it is part of a series of dire prophecies. There is, therefore, in addition to the various meanings suggested by the words of the title, an element of ominous foreboding that adds to the tension created throughout the narrative and prepares the reader for the disasters that occur in the concluding chapter.

Samuel Romanelli's *Travail in an Arab Land* is more than a well-written and accurate travelogue. It is gripping drama and artistic literature. Little wonder that the nineteenth-century Jewish literary historian Leopold Dukes mistakenly suspected the book to be an imaginative fabrication.[38]

Travail in an Arab Land

It Being the Account of the Events
And the Travail That I Witnessed in the Provinces
of Morocco, Their Ways and Deeds, Their Laws
and Customs,
Among the Jews, the Arabs, the King, the Courtiers, and
the People

by

Samuel Romanelli of Mantua

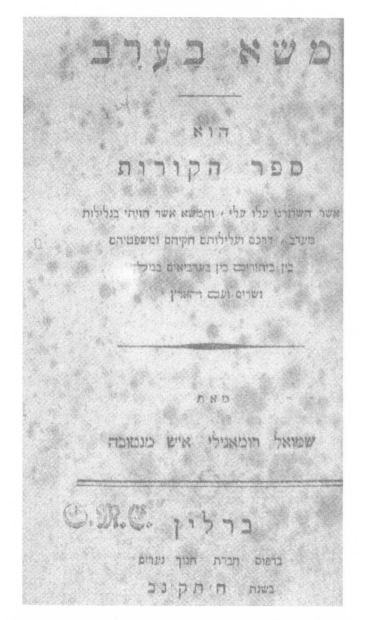

Title of the first edition of *Travail in an Arab Land* (Berlin, 1792).
Courtesy of the New York Public Library

הקדמה

מוֹשַׁב בְּנֵי יִשְׂרָאֵל הַשּׁוֹכְנִים לָעֵת חַמַּת בִּגְלִילוֹת הָעַרְבָאִים
הַחֵרֶד מֶמְשֶׁלֶת קֵיסֶר הַמְאֻרִיטַאנְיָאה בְּאַפְרִיקָא
הַנִּקְרָאת מִיּוֹם טַיִּרְעָקשׂ בִּלְשׁוֹן עֲרָבִי אוֹ מַגְרָב בִּלְשְׁגוּתֵ׳נוּ
בִּגְלִלוֹת בְּאַרְבַּאדְרְ׳אַם · כְּמוֹ שֶׁם כְּלִי נַעַל מֵעֵינֵי כָּל הָעָנִים
הַיּוֹשְׁבִים חֵלֶם נָרְעוֹת הַעִיכָנִפֹת לִוְבָאֵמֹת אֵיוֹה דֶרֶךְ תֵּגַע
שְׁמֹעַתֶם עֵינֵינוּ ? דְבַק הֲלֹכְדִּר מִלֹא בּוֹעֵר הוּא וְכָאֵין נֶחְשָׁבְתָּ
שְׁלֹשָׁה אוֹ אַרְבָּעָה סֹחֲרֵי יִשְׂרָאֵל בְּתוֹךְ מְנֻאָדוֹר וּמְעֵיחַל מִקְצָן
אֲשֶׁר בֵּין אַנְשֵׁי מַיּוֹטְרַאֵן טַאגֵעֵר וּלְשַׁרְאָצֵ׳י וּבֵין אַנְשֵׁי הַהַבְּגֵּד
נֵבְרֵיאשְׂמָאֵר בְּכָל זֶה אֵי׳וֹ שִׁיחַ וְלֹא יִפְדַּח לְהָקִיק אֶת נֶפְשָׁם
מֵתּוֹרְדֹמֶת עַצְלוּתָם וּלִשׁעוֹרֶה תְּשׁוּקָה לְבוֹתָם לְהַשְׂכֵּל · וְאָף
אִם מֵדַבֵּר בָּם בַּסְּפָרִים אֲשֶׁר חֻבְּרוּ בִּלְשׁוֹנוֹת חֲנֹוֹם עַל עֵנִין
קוֹרוֹת הַמַּעֲרָב הֵן לֹא נִזְכְּרוּ שָׁם רַק כַּחֵלֶק כְּעֵרָן לַהֵכָּל · אַךְ
מִי זֶה יִפְתֶּה לְדַבֵּר עַל בֵּיהוּדִים בַּל יֵדַע לְשׁוֹנָם וֹ — הַמְּדִינָה
הַיּוֹשֶׁבֶת רְאֹשׁוֹנָה וּקְרוֹבָה לַגְּלִילוֹת מַעֲרָב הִיא כֹּתֹּרֵ׳ מִיּכָבֵּר
צַדְּ רֹחַ׳אֵם מַהְלֵךְ שִׁשָּׁה אִי׳פֹ׳ אֶמֶה מְבַרֵיחַ בֵּין קָדְ שַׁאגֵרִי לֹא
עַם קָצֵה טַאֱאַגַּנִ׳יַא׳׳א · עִיר מַבְצֶר שְׁאַוּ׳שָׁא עוֹמְדֹרָה בְּגְבוּלָה
טִיטֹרְאַן · הָעֲמֻנַם מַעֲמָה מַחֲקִירָה חֲדָשָׁה יָנִיחַ לְעֵנִיּוֹ
עֵמִוּעַת הַיָּהוּדִים בְּאַרְצוֹתָו וְהַפְּלֵכוֹת בְּמֵנְדֵּי הַפְּתִיחָה) בְּכָל
רַשָׁע מִסָּאם בְּנֵפֶשׁ לְהוּצִיאֵאֹהוֹסְפַל וְהַשְׁמֵרוּ לַהַשְׁרֵף ? הַעֲלָת
זֹאת עַל לֵב אֵשׁ מִסְבָּרִי בַּל וְרָאָה הַשַׁחַת הַבְּקַע תַחַת רַגְלֵי
לְנָדוֹת אוֹתְנוּ וְאֵת כָּל אֲשֶׁר לוֹ חֵי שְׁאוֹלָה ? מִי זֹאת אֵיפֹוֹא
יֵכָא לֵנוּ ? וְהִשְׁמְעֵאלִי הָרוֹבֵץ עַל הָאָרֶץ כָּל חַיּוֹם / נִרְחַף
וְנִבְעַר מִדַעַת · וֵיתֵק בּוֹיֵק רֵתוֹ הַנְבוֹהַרָה · וְשׁוֹנֵא לְכָל אֲשֶׁר
כְּשֵׁם יִשְׂרָאֵל יִכָּנֶה ? וְהַמֵּוֹקֵשׁ הַעֵלַח עַל כֻּלָם הוּא הָעֵדֶר
הַדְּפוּס כִּי עַד הַיּוֹם לֹא חֻבַּא שָׁמָּה (וְלֹא תֻבָא לְעֹלָם) ·

רי[ן]

First page of Romanelli's Introduction to *Travail in an Arab Land*
(Berlin, 1792). Courtesy of The New York Public Library

The Author's Introduction

The Israelite community presently living in the Arab territories of Africa's Barbary Coast under the rule of the Emperor of Mauretania, which is called nowadays *Marrākesh* in Arabic and *Maroc* in our languages, is almost entirely hidden from the eyes of the peoples living here in the countries of Europe. How indeed would word of them reach us? Commercial intercourse is small and of no account. There are three or four Jewish traders at the port of Mogador,[1] and all the trade in goods between the people of Tetuan, Tangier and Larache on the one hand, and between the inhabitants of the fortress of Gibraltar on the other, is not worth very much, neither is it sufficient to arouse them from their slumber of indifference, nor incite their hearts with any desire to take note of them.

Even though the Jews are mentioned in books on the history of the Maghreb written in Gentile languages, they are only taken into account there as a small part of the whole.[2] For who would be tempted to speak about the Jews without knowing their language?

The nation that is situated closest to the Maghrebi territories is Spain. A narrow strait of only 6,000 cubits extends from the tip of Tarifa to the shores of Tangier. The fortress town of Ceuta lies on the very border of Tetuan.[3] However, does the evil Office of the Inquisition allow any report on the Jews to pass through its lands which are afflicted with the blindness of folly? Does it not contemptuously condemn anyone publishing such information, burning both the book and its author? Would any Spaniard consider such a thing without seeing the pit yawning beneath his feet ready to swallow him alive together with all that he possesses into the netherworld?

Who then will prophesy for us? Will it be the Ishmaelite who squats on the ground all day lazy and ignorant, spellbound by his fanatic religion, hating everything that is called by the name of Israel?

Finally, the obstacle to disseminating information about Moroccan Jewry that surpasses all others is the absence of printing. For to this day, it has not been brought there, nor will it ever be.[4]

These, therefore, are a few of the reasons that prompted me to publish these accounts which honestly treat the subject of my brethren and coreligionists in detail. They may also deal in a general way with the foreigners who are with the Jews; however, this is not their object.

What follows is all of the complex events that befell me in the course of my travels and brought me to this point. For some four years, I lived there and had the opportunity to mingle with all kinds of people great and small, learning their doings, knowing their comings and goings and almost all their ways. Nevertheless, I have been careful to report only that which I witnessed, and in relating my own personal history at length, I shall tell their history, which is like the branches growing out of the tree trunk. Pay no heed to those who think that every wayfarer minimizes or exaggerates the truth as he wishes so long as the proof of his testimony lies far away. Whatever I have said can be checked and will be found true. Know, dear reader, that the truth alone is a lamp unto my feet and a light unto my path. I have shown no partiality to anyone, not even to myself.

Now go read my book and judge it fairly. Whether it be on the positive or the negative side, weigh every word in the balance of justice, and may God be with you!

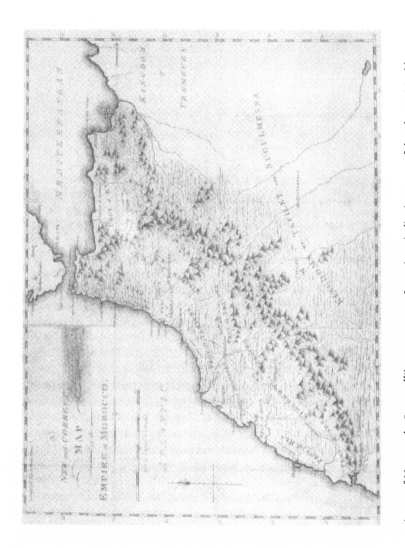

A map of Morocco by Romanelli's contemporary Lempriere, indicating many of the places visited by Romanelli. William Lempriere, *A Tour from Gibraltar*, (London, 1791)

1

Due to the turns of my fortune and the contrivances of the times in which I lived, I happened to be in Gibraltar's citadel heading toward Italy, my native land. Surely many designs are in a man's mind, but it is what the Lord devises that will be accomplished.[1]

This fortress, now under the rule of Great Britain, stands at the foot of a high mountain at the extremity of Europe. It has nothing to do with anyone by land or by sea, except for its provisions which arrive by ship. It is only an observation post guarding the mouth of the narrow strait that divides the two Pillars of Hercules. It should not surprise you, therefore, that I was anxiously pre-occupied in my thoughts of getting out of this closed-in place. Where was I to go? Via Spain overland? No one comes in or goes out that way. Besides, how could a Jew dare to pass through there without renouncing his faith? You know that it is not in a person's power to really change a religion that he has suckled with his mother's milk any more than it is within his power to change his birth. Were I to disguise myself and pretend to be someone else, my life would be hanging precariously against the possibility that I might be recognized. Finding a ship to leave by sea was rare. This last difficulty weighed heavily upon me. How was I to go? If I were to keep on like this until a ship arrived, even if it would be ready to sail the following morning, the money in my purse would be exhausted by then.

Into my perplexed and dejected mind a chance thought suddenly flashed with a ray of hope. Hope! The imagined good, a support for the humbled spirit, a crutch for the downtrodden heart. A person drowning in the roaring seas will grasp at anything that comes to hand, and he who is pursued by Fate will place his trust even in a spider's web.[2]

One of the respected merchants of the place hearing me bemoaning my ill luck, called me aside and asked if I would be willing to go to Barbary with him. In my haste, I replied that I would go. "Very well," he replied, "but take care not to reveal my secret, for you know how fierce is the merchants' jealousy. Know that I am going to the Sultan of Morocco to plead for his permission to settle in the city of Larache and from there engage in overseas trade in wool and wax. If I obtain the permission, you can be steward of my house. If I do not succeed, you will have lost nothing."

I was pulled by the cords of hope and by his assurance that he was an honest man. I had been enticed. He went and obtained an exit document (passport) for himself and his servant from the city registrar. I got a letter for myself which a Genoese sea captain who was friendly with me requested on my behalf. We had planned it this way, lest the secret become known to all.

One day a sailing vessel arrived heading for Tetuan.[3] The merchant paid its passage. We boarded and set sail. We passed the fortresses of San Roque and San Felipe and the town of Algeciras which stand one next to the other facing Gibraltar. We cut through the waters of the strait, whose current is swift at the sides, and within four hours we were between the mountains on our way to Africa.

We reached the river that leads to the city,[4] but did not come to the city itself because the Sultan had commanded sometime before that no Christian or Jew should enter wearing Christian attire on account of an incident that had taken place.[5] The consuls of the European monarchies who had been stationed there to look after their nations' merchants, had to leave and go to Tangier. The only exception was the French Consul who, at the Sultan's direction, went to Rabat. In their stead, they left behind Jewish deputies in Tetuan. They were four in number—one for France, one for Spain and Portugal, one for England, Sweden, and Denmark, and one for Venice, Genoa, and Ragusa.[6]

After receiving a permit from the Arab coast guards, we came ashore to take lodging in a house that lay 2000 cubits[7] outside the town at a place called Martil.[8] We spent three days there.

Were it not for the fact that Barbary's geography defends it with steep cliffs along the seashore enclosing the points of entry and providing natural guard posts, I have no doubt that 100,000 brave soldiers skilled in European warfare would in a short while capture all the provinces of Morocco from one end to the other, if they could find some way to penetrate it and space wide enough to maneuver. It was because of this geographical factor that the proud forces of Don Sebastian, the Duke of Braganca, were ensnared in a trap at the Battle of El Qsar in 1577.[9]

We found an English merchant at the lodge who had come to buy high quality horses and mules which abound in that country. As a matter of fact, the horses are not fit for anything other than riding since there are no carriages to pull in the country. Furthermore, since they graze in the pasture all day long, eating and drinking their fill of the fat of the land, work is difficult for them, and they are not very good for labor—just like the natives.

The merchant brought his own bed and tent with him as is the custom of all travelers in Morocco, because there is not an inn or a bed to be found wherever you go. The following morning, a Jew from Tetuan came to us to be our guide and interpreter, for in this town, as in Tangier, Larache, El Qsar, Arzila, and throughout the Rif region, there are many descendents of the Jews who fled Spain.[10] On the third day, we set out on our way with a guard of six Arab warriors mounted on horseback to protect us from the highway bandits who lie in wait to murder any passersby in foreign dress. We went behind the city wall until we reached a paved road.

Now when I say "paved," you should not imagine that their roads are like ours—running straight, comfortable for traveling, and in good repair. Nature's handiwork is gloriously manifest throughout the Maghreb, whereas all the human hands are weak. Nobody lifts a stone or removes an obstacle.

As we proceeded on our journey, I considered how I might get to know the people and their speech so that I might win their favor as I followed on at their easy pace. For I did not know how the matter would turn out. With the Jew, I debated points in the

Torah, and I was able to incline the hearts of both Jews and Gentiles toward me in a kindly way.

The sun was at midday when we sat down to break bread in green pastures under the shade of some trees of the field by a brook whose water flowed gently with a plaintive grace. The interpreter spread a blanket on the grass and set out a feast for us of food from his own house which was quite sufficient to refresh us. The foreigners became Jews (so-to-speak) during the meal, since it was kosher food and there was plenty to drink—a flagon of *eau de vie* which the Jew had sealed with his personal signet and with a twisted cord.[11]

Those who slander us with lies and say that the table of God's people is defiled were the very ones who joined us to eat our victuals and drink our beverages. What a contrast to the man Daniel and his companions who refused to defile themselves with the King's delicacies and with the wine he drank, choosing instead pulse to eat and water to drink.[12] The Ishmaelites, however, took their bread alone since they are not allowed to eat with either Hebrews or foreigners, as it is an abomination for them.[13] Afterwards, they loaded up the mules and we traveled on.

At dusk as the evening shadows lengthened, before it became dark and we might stumble on the dark mountains, we pitched our tents on a plain shaded by hilly crests. The merchant and the interpreter went inside the tent together, while I stayed outside with the servant, for he said it cannot be "as with the servant, so with his master."[14] The drivers of the mules tethered their feet to a stake in the ground as is their custom, because just as there are no inns for travelers, so there are no pens for sheep, no stalls for cattle, no stables for horses. Everyone lies down to sleep in their tents or under the canopy of heaven.

As soon as the eyelids of dawn began to part and the expanse of space stripped off their covers of darkness, we got up each one from his place. I raised my eyes and saw the stars in their orbits. And behold, they were surrendering the sparks of their brilliance and retreating before the dawn. As I looked at them, I said in jest that perhaps even as I peek at the faces of these entities, their inhabitants are likewise gazing at my planet.[15] The servant, who was a simpleton, mocked me thinking that I was insulting the

View of Tangier from the bay. Oskar Lenz, *Timbouctou: Voyage au Maroc, au Sahara, et au Soudan*, Vol. I (Paris, 1886)

cosmos of the Living God. The merchant, however, confirmed what I said, and he too laughed at the servant's gullibility.

While we were speaking the Gentiles got up and said that we should set out because everything was ready. Each man mounted his mule, and we pushed on. When it was time to eat, we chose—as we had done the day before—the splendid setting of mountain and plain to set our table. After having rested there a while, we continued on our way. Arriving at a great rock, there appeared before our eyes the city of Tangier rising above the shore, standing out among the sand dunes that encircle it up to its very entrance. There were crowds of Arabs spread over the open country who had come to buy grain, bread, and other foodstuffs, for it was market day. They looked to us like a herd of camels or a flock of goats. But we could not lose time staring at them, and so we passed on to the city.

No one can describe our amazement when we arrived there! Our eyes beheld an exotic tumult. There were blacksmiths and farriers on all sides. They looked like torches wrapped in the filthy web of their beard, the sweat of their brow dripping onto their chest, naked to the middle of their buttocks, their legs uncovered, and their feet bare. They were doing their work in caves or right out on the roadway. I thought that I was in the depths of the underworld. We were taken to the home of a Jew (since no one could stay in an Arab house), and the baggage was brought after us. And so we found some repose after all of the hardship of that we had experienced along the way.

When night blanketed the earth, we still did not know what we were going to do. Suddenly, the noise of a crowd of merrymakers reached our ears. The servant who had been playing a lute asked: "What is the noise of this crowd in my ears? Do I hear the sound of drums?" The people of the house responded that their neighbors were inviting them to a wedding celebration and that if we should wish to see it, it would bring back the joy to our faces. Then without even waiting for our reply, they led us there.

There were young girls performing. One was holding a kettle full of whitewash in one hand, and in her other hand some tattered rags. She dipped these in the whitewash and made designs on the floor and on the doors of the entranceway, like David when he altered his manner at the court of Achish.[16] One girl with her head bowed to her shoulder and a scarf in both hands—one raised over the shoulder, the other down against her belly—was turning slowly with a loose hand motion. I thought she was insane, but they informed me that this was how they dance in their cities. All this was amidst young women beating clay drums that resembled a bottle open on top and closed with a skin on the bottom, or like the drums used on the comedy stage in the story of Axur.[17] However, any resemblance between this and music was purely coincidental. Could any person control himself and not break out laughing at such a sight?

But then man is vanity. The children of man are a fallacy on the face of the earth. Just as the practices of the North Africans seem strange to our eyes, so our practices seem strange to theirs. The truth is that all is vanity. We scoff at a child when we know his crying is for some immaterial reason,[18] and the heavenly hosts above laugh at us because we are like infants until the time we become old and gray.

The following morning we went out to see the town, which is one of the Pillars of Hercules. It had been under Portuguese rule

A gate of the Casbah of Tangier.

until 1661, at which time they gave it over to the people of England.[19] When the latter too saw that the expense of administering
it was greater than the benefit, they razed and abandoned it.

Now I shall turn to describing for you the house and its contents.
This house was built of pebble chips and thick, hollow plaster.
The bare whiteness over all its surface strained the eyes of the
onlooker. The plan of the house is a square built around a courtyard.[20] On each of the four sides is a long, narrow room. Most of
the doors of the court and the living quarters are closed from the
inside without any key—just a wooden bar, one end of which leans
on the ground while the other is propped against the closed door.

There are no real windows, but only two or three holes the size
of a brick on the doorway of each room. These are not for light
since they are too small for the sun's rays, they are just a passage
for air.

The bed is spread on boards quite high from the ground. This
platform is set into the wall beams.[21] Under it, they store household utensils. From the rafter to the edge of the bed, or even past
the bed down to the floor, hangs a red silk or white linen curtain.
Sometimes the poor keep this curtain drawn to cover up the absence of a bed. The bed described here is the one used by a
husband and wife. The young boys and girls are simply wrapped
in a mantle in which they sleep.[22]

Small mirrors hang on the walls, as well as glass lamps that are
lit on the Sabbath eve. Their table looks like a stool, and there are
no chairs, for they sit on the floor like the Arabs. They place a pot
of porridge on a washstand or a clay oven. The ceilings and the
floors of the rooms and the courtyard are plastered over with
mortar like a wall. The walls of the house are covered with a mat
of soft reed up to the standing height of a man.[23] No graven image
may be seen on the walls. In their view, however, this is so as not
to turn to false gods. In my view, however, this is either because
they are simpletons, or because they are neither able nor willing
to bend their shoulders to bear the yoke of the sciences. Under
no account will you see the image of a female nude, the likeness
of a male organ, figures with bare buttocks, or any human nudity.[24]

Their roofs have parapets and are connected to one another in
such a fashion that by way of the rooftops, one can go from house

A Moroccan tailor sitting in the kind of traditional shop described by Romanelli. Photograph by Yedida K. Stillman

to house and courtyard to courtyard. The entranceway to the court is small and low so that even dwarfs would have to bow down their head like a bullrush in order to pass. Near the entranceway of the courtyard are the privies stinking with excrement. Most of the houses have only one story, but a few have two or three. On the uppermost floor a balcony runs along the courtyard.

This then was the layout of the house in which we were staying. Nearly all the houses were of this plan. Only the homes of the Christian consuls were laid out in the manner of European houses. The homes of the poor were filled throughout with filth and excrement, whereas the dwellings of the leading citizens, though without elegance, seemed to me to be worthy of admiration.

The shops are like holes in the wall, like the caves I saw when I arrived. They were raised half a man's height above the ground level so that a man sitting on the floor inside them can reach whatever he wants just by stretching his arm without having to stand up, as these shops are not even big enough to hold two people.[25] The door of the shop is locked with a wooden key. In these "caves" every type of ware is sold. The smallest group of merchants are those dealing in textiles. A larger number sell spices, and the large majority are vendors of foodstuffs. Just one look at the latter was enough to churn my innards. Roast meat, oil, soap, butter, olives, and all kinds of comestibles—everything goes into one of the straw pans of the scale and is handled with their fingers and is passed from the seller's hand to the buyer's. The balance weights are stones from the market. Arab tailors are only able to make their own style of clothing, while Jews make their own clothes, and some of them also make Christian-style garments. Arabs make shoes for both themselves and the Jews. The latter make their style shoes as well as footwear for Christians.

On Sunday, the merchant, accompanied by his servant and the interpreter, journeyed to Larache to discuss his business with the brother of the Genoese Consul, Francesco Chiappe, who resides there and has close connections with the royal house.[26] He left me in Tangier to look after his capital and goods. My meals were taken care of daily by the master of the house until the merchant's return.

2

F ree of any preoccupations, I allowed myself to seek out and
investigate the Jews, their manners and customs. They are
good-hearted folk, charitable and hospitable to strangers. They
honor the Torah and study it. They hold the European Jews who
come there in high esteem and call them "freemen."[1]

The lack of books and news mires their hearts in the mud of
ignorance and superstition. They tend to view all new and
mysterious[2] things previously unknown to them as miracles. The
sciences are too lofty for them.[3] Their ignorance is bliss, for they
say that many victims have been thrown into the pits of heresy
and atheism by science. The light of knowledge does not shine
upon them, nor has it even reached them until now to eradicate
their moral failings and their immature vanities. A veil of obscur-
antist faith corrupts their hearts and blinds their eyes. They cling
steadfastly to their ancestral customs even to the point of trans-
gressing the laws of God, rather than violating their own laws. One
of the proverbs they are fond of quoting (which befits them as do
legs on a cripple)[4] is "the customary practice of our forefathers
is Torah."[5] They will not examine who their forefathers were and
what were their customs, if they have something on which they
rely—even if it is like the customary practice of Jehu b. Nimshi.[6]
They do not understand that in so doing they have gone against
the intent of the Torah which seeks to set us apart by its laws from
the practices of the other nations. With the Moroccan Jews it is the
opposite, because they follow their ways completely. Either they

interpret rhetorical hyperbole in Scripture literally, saying that under no circumstances should it be taken in the abstract, or they imagine secrets and read mysteries into matters that are as clear as day. They lean upon the dictum that "for every thorny point mountains upon mountains of laws may be derived."[7] They are awed by dreams and terrified by visions. They will fast on account of bad ones and feast as a consequence of good ones. They are besotted by dread apparitions[8] and by fear of night. No man would dare sleep alone in a room at night, nor would any woman dare to go alone from house to house. They swear by a burning lamp and say: "By this angel," thinking that the lights of a fire are celestial angels, an error that has come to them from a misinterpretation of the verse "He makes the winds His messengers, fiery flames His servants."[9] The end result is that the might of even an intelligent man is dried up, and they become like light-minded women.[10] Despite all this, their minds are not entirely blocked from reason,[11] because they comprehend other matters perfectly well. In fact, sometimes their intelligence emits flashes of insight that reveal that it is not thick by nature, but only held down and mired in thick muck, like the sun when it is covered by a very dense cloud.

The women are good looking and have a robust build.[12] However, they are rather like dumb beasts, having no part in science, understanding, or knowledge. They do not know how to speak, read or write Hebrew, Arabic, or Standard Spanish. The women, like the men, speak a mixed language as is common among all Jews in their various diaspora communities who do not make a point of learning properly the language of the peoples among whom they live. Their language is Spanish with a Portuguese accent.[13] The women do not even pray, despite the fact that this was imposed upon them by the sages of the Mishna.[14] The Moroccan Jews counter this by citing the Mishnaic dictum: "Whoever teaches his daughter Torah, it is as if he teaches her wantonness."[15] They also counter that a woman is impure during her menstrual infirmity and the days of her menses can fall quite suddenly.[16] This ancient custom has its roots in olden times and was adopted by them from gentile practice, for indeed the Arab women do not pray either.

I was taken to the school where the Talmud is taught.[17] Their method of teaching is clearer than that of the Polish Jews and resembles more closely that of the Oriental Jews. They are also greatly involved in Kabbala—the escape for those who affect wisdom without any solid grounding in scholarly enquiry. "O villain! You covet mysteries because there is no need for evidence."[18] If they were really wise, they would understand this science in its true context and be able to remove the separating curtain and to extract the precious hidden thing from its treasures. Their eyes would surely see that it is all a seed of truth that goes to, and is intertwined with, the depths and breadths of natural philosophy and that it is cloaked in a mantle through which the eyes of the beholder will not penetrate without the sacred gems being spilled at every street corner.[19] But they cannot imagine this, neither can their mind think in this way. Since they fear approaching the glorious princess within the palace,[20] they prefer to tie knots with letters and to forge links between words, and to pretend to prophesy from them without understanding.

Philosophy books, such as *The Guide*[21] and the like, are highly esteemed by them. When they mention their names, it is almost as though recalling marvelous things. They read little in the way of legal decisions in the rabbinic juridical literature and even less Bible. They recite the Torah by heart with its cantillation, as well as the books of Job, Proverbs, Psalms, Isaiah, and Daniel.

On Tuesday, I had an urge to see the seashore. It looks rather like the shore at Gibraltar. The latter, however, shows the creative hand of England which adjusted and perfected its beauty. The former expresses the ignorance of the Arabs. For although the hand of Nature is with them to help them and show them the way, they kick its offering[22] and are too lazy to even put one stone next to another. There is not a single ship on the shore, only fishing boats. They have no warships, only pirate vessels on the high seas.

As I walked to the beach, I passed the Arab mosque during prayer time.[23] I stood looking at the towering structure from a distance, for no Hebrews or Christians may enter its gates without renouncing their faith. The sanctuary consists of a long chamber with straw matting on the floor. The courtyard in front of it has colonnades around its sides. Inside the courtyard is an ablution font where they wash their feet before entering. The roof of the prayerhall is covered with overlapping green tiles, and the minaret stands alongside it. It is not their custom to have bells. Instead, a man ascends the minaret at seven set times a day and prays in a loud voice, calling the people to come to prayer at dawn (*el-mwod-den*), in the morning (*el-ṣabāḥ*), first noon (*ḏhor el-luwlī*), second noon (*ḏhor al-tānī*), evening (*el-ʿāsar*), night (*el-maghrib*), and midnight (*el-ʿashāʾ*).[24] This perhaps explains why in Hebrew the words *ṣohorayīm* (noon) and *ʿarbayīm* (dusk) are dual forms.[25] While watching this take place, I recalled the *halakha* in Tractate Yoma concerning the meaning of "cockcrow," viz.—"Rav said: 'It was a man that called out.' But Samuel said: 'It was a rooster that crowed.'"[26]

On the Sabbath day, I walked to one of the synagogues of the Jews. They have four in Tangier—small conventicles without any decoration or ornament.[27] They sit on wooden seats and not on the synagogue floor, except on the day of Tishaʿ Be-Av.[28] They follow the rite of the Sephardim. They pronounce the letters of the Holy Language correctly. They make a clear distinction between geminated and ungeminated consonants, between /h/ and /kh/, and between /k/ and /q/. However, the *ṣade* as pronounced by the Sephardim of Amsterdam is more correct than the Moroccan pronunciation.[29] The Moroccans pronounce ʿ*ayin* like the Arabs, even stronger perhaps. The spirantized *gimel* is like "g" in Dutch.[30] Shewa takes on the sound of the following vowel with the laryngal letters *alef*, *hē*, *het*, and ʿ*ayin*. They do not place any stress on it, and in fact, the mobile *shewa* is almost quiescent in their pronunciation. At a *meteg*, they read it as *patah* which is like the view expressed in *Minhag Shay*.[31] The Ashkenazim read ultimately stressed words with penultimate accent, whereas the Moroccans do the reverse when chanting. The *vav* they pronounce as "w" in English, and thus differentiate between *vav* and spirantized *bet* (= v). On the other hand, they make little distinction between the vowels *shūreq* and *hōlam*, and between *sērē* and *hīreq*.[32]

A rabbi from Meknes delivered a sermon in Arabic, citing the scriptural verses in the Holy Tongue. I could hear that he swallowed the *patah* in the definite article and with the other consonants at the beginning of a word and that he pronounced the *patah* as *hīreq* and *hīreq* as *patah*. I was puzzled and inquired about this, but no one could solve it for me. He pronounced *tav* as "ch" in Spanish or English, or "ci" in Italian, or "cz" in Polish.[33] Now try to pronounce as he did the verse that was the subject of the sermon—*tōv tittī ōtāh lākh mit-tittī ōtāh le-īsh aḥēr*[34]—and just listen to how it will grate in your ears!

They sway while praying like the Jews of Poland, except that the latter do it moving forward and back, while the former do it from left to right. But who is to say which is correct?

On Sunday I went roaming through the market, which I had not been able to examine upon my arrival. Its general appearance did not change as far as I could see—an army of countryfolk whose faces resemble the blackened bottom of a clay pot.[35] They are half covered by a hooded, old tattered robe[36] and sit helter-skelter on the ground selling all sorts of foodstuffs, even camel meat. It looks very red and lean, and they say it makes very good eating. However, it is not an appetizing sight. Another exotic item is *el-kermōs dn-ṇsāra* (that is, "Christian figs"). These are figs surrounded by a pod covered with thorns on the outside, and called in Spanish *cosiombos*.[37]

Around that time, the Sultan of Morocco sent three ships to the district governor of Gibraltar for repairs because the Arabs are good for nothing and whatever work they do is entirely fortuitous.[38] The governor, however, refused. The Sultan was infuriated and angrily dispatched missives to Tangier ordering the expulsion of all English subjects within three days with the exception of the consul who would remain as a hostage. On the very same day that the merchant returned with the good tidings that he had been successful, the Sultan's directive also arrived and, in an instant his hopes were dashed. The merchant, at the direction of the consul, sailed by himself that day on a vessel to bring the news to the people in Gibraltar. He left everything he had in our keeping until such time as his business was settled. We entertained the hope that perchance the two monarchs would make peace, and he would return. But it was a vain hope. The consul himself secretly fled via the garden adjoining his house and did not return for several days. The entire city was in an uproar at his disappearance and at his return.

On the first night after the merchant left, I had a falling out with his servant. In order to understand the circumstances surrounding our quarrel, you should know that he was Catholic. He had been seeking to turn to his own benefit the merchant's bringing me to Morocco, thinking that he could tempt me to go from there with him to Spain (because he was running away) and then change my religion. In the beginning, I allowed him his hope in order to turn his foolishness to my advantage.

Once in Morocco, I no longer paid any attention to his absurdities, and this vexed him greatly. He thought that I had had a change of heart and tried to compel me every moment to keep my word. But while he was scheming against me in Tangier, his wife was spreading a net to ensnare him back in Gibraltar. When she had seen that he had not come home for dinner on the day we departed, she knew that he had absconded. So she went to the commanding officer of the garrison and implored him to get her husband to return to his home. The warrant came to the consul in Tangier unbeknownst to the servant.

It happened that while he was bothering me that night with his arguments, I pulled the veil of deception away from his eyes and told him that his deluded mind had led him astray[39] if he believed I would trust his worthless protection,[40] or that I would betray my parents' religion which was an inheritance from the mountain of God for them and their descendants forever, and that I would forsake the Fount of living waters to hew out for myself cisterns, broken cisterns![41]

He was dumbstruck and torn between anger and shame. He had no spirit left in him. After being silent a moment, he began to curse the day he had spoken to me. He demanded that there be punishment and requital.[42] He assaulted me with verbal blows. He grabbed the merchant's sword to kill me, but I jumped up and wrested the weapon from his hand, throwing him to the ground, for the strength had gone out of him. Having heard the noise, the people of the household came and separated us.

The next day, his wounded spirit calmed down, and he was no longer downcast. He tried again to press me concerning our journey. Stupid misjudgment, how mighty are you! Religious fanaticism, how foolish you are! On the day the consul returned, he had the servant summoned and told him that he was giving him two choices—either to return home or go to jail. The servant was overcome with terror in the consul's presence, for suddenly Nemesis had overtaken him. Shamed, he submitted and agreed to return to Gibraltar. When he regained his self-control, he came back to the house. He kept hidden from me what had occurred and did not relate his conversation with the consul, telling me only that he had examined his ways and had seen that it was best for him to return to his country. I told him to do as he saw best and go back to his homeland. He quickly got out his wardrobe and the merchant's trunk and left with the other English subjects. No foreigner accompanied them—for this was the Sultan's decree. He did not return—not he, or the merchant, to this very day.

3

How many wandered far from the straight path
Who were considered great men in their time.
Foretell the signs before they come to pass!
By the seashore I reside.
One moment I am hopeful,
The next—I am in the midst of the sea.[1]

O treacherous Fortune, fickle and intriguing! How you have cheated me and with a mocking hope delivered me from bad to worse! What have I done to you, and how have I wearied you that you give me bitterness to eat, wormwood to drink, and wear me out with your deceit? Who will bring me again to the fortress city of Gibraltar? Who will guide me now to the land of Edom?[2] Lonely, wandering, lost! An alien among the fierce Arabs on the one hand, among the wretched, oppressed Jews on the other. Where was I to turn? From whom was I to seek help? What did I have here? Whom did I have here that You should dig a grave for me here?[3] These distressing thoughts tormented me the entire night, so I could not sleep. I got up the next morning in a state of grief and panic. I racked my brain for a scheme, and not finding any that could restore me, I abandoned my thoughts to the will of Chance. I made an effort to put on a good face and to cool my temper.

I recalled the Meknasi's sermon of the preceding Sabbath and could not forget that after he had finished, the cantor got up and blessed each man so that he would give as much as his heart would prompt.[4] I asked whether anyone was allowed to do this and was told that I could and should do it, because they did this with any visitor in their midst. Furthermore, they had heard from the interpreter[5] who had brought me that I was fully capable of preaching. I prepared myself[6] to preach in Spanish. Their style of sermon is like that of the Polish Jews and all who are hasty in their studies, becoming entangled in profundities whose meaning they do not know and whose context they distort. They neither realize nor understand that only by keeping the words in order along with the arrangements of the subject matter and in accordance with norms, does learning stand, just as a building stands on the construction of its parts.

Senseless questions, meaningless answers, stammering, and distorted language—and after all that Kaddish![7] This then is their wisdom and discernment in the eyes of the nations! Woe unto us that we have had our fill of disgrace instead of honor! Some learned speech,[8] an apt moral, a rhetorical flourish—albeit not a very embellished one—was all I needed. These seemed to them like astonishing wisdom, sweet as honey. They gave me their approval, sang my praises, and contributed generously.

After four sermons in four synagogues, there was no one left to preach to and no one to request it. I deeply regretted that there was no consul there representing the Hapsburg Emperor.[9] My distress was increased by the fact that in my haste I had lost my travel document. I said to myself that I was doomed, my hope for getting out was gone. I consulted an acquaintance who told me: "Listen to my advice. There is a man from Vienna who has been here for five years.[10] He is living in the home of the Spanish Consul. He is honest, wise, and sincere. He is the most affable of people. Write him a letter. There may be hope yet." I did just that, sending an epistle in French with his Arab servant. The latter returned with a summons for me to come.

The man's countenance reflected his innate integrity. His kind words bespoke his honorable character. He encouraged me with his words[11] and promised to help me as long as he remained there, in exchange for which, I would take care of his correspondence in English. That very day he began to show me his honor

A Jewish circumcision ceremony in Mogodor as depicted in an early nineteenth-century engraving. James Riley, *An Authentic Narrative of the Loss of the American Brig Commerce* (Hartford, 1847)

and magnanimity. I kissed his hand and took leave of him happy and confident.

Feeling relieved, I took a leisurely stroll with my friend. While we were on the beach, the governor of the city arrived on foot, followed by his attendants. The soldiers quickly formed a semicircle. They bowed and called out in a loud voice together: *Allāh ibārek f-amr sīdī,* meaning "may God bless you, Sir, with success."

When we returned home, my friend's mother, who was pregnant, was already in labor on the birth stool and bore a son. They quickly hung scrolls inscribed with two overlapping triangles called David's Shield, with scriptural verses, and with the names of angels, in order to protect the mother who had just given birth from Lilith.[12] With their fingers, they drew signs on the thresholds using clay and pitch to ward off the demons. On the entranceway, they hung bits of rags and pieces of matza as an offering of food and clothing for them.[13] This is their custom in all its foolishness.[14] They claim that this is comparable to the scapegoat ritual for Azazel.[15] And so they make their sacrifices to the demons, clinging fast to the superstitious customs, as I have already noted.

Eight days later, the boy was circumcised. After the ceremony, a table was set for the men by themselves. There was a bowl for every two persons, and a single knife for everybody. They would take the stew from the plate with small pieces of bread to lift it into their mouth. They drank water from a clay jar, covering its opening with the sleeve or hem of their tunic to seal it against magic spells. They normally drink a glass of *eau de vie*[16] before eating, for they have no wine. The first dish was couscous, the choicest food in all of Barbary. It is flour mixed with water to form grains resembling millet. They dry it in a double boiler on the burning fireplace and cook it with meat or with butter and milk. It is a wholesome and tasty delicacy. The Arabs sit in a circle on the ground and a big basin full of couscous is set in the middle. Each man digs into it from his side with his hand, takes a handful, rolls it in his hand, and throws it into his mouth. Having no napkin to clean their hands, they rub them on their shoes, on their weapons, or on the wall. People send portions of couscous as a gift to friends.[17]

Their manner of eating, sitting, and standing is also described in Maréchal Richelieu's book in the section dealing with Muhammad Reza Beg, a Persian ambassador who was sent to King Louis XIV in Paris (volume l, chapter 7, p. 186).[18]

After the couscous came *el-khlī*, a specialty in Morocco. These are pieces of meat mixed with oil in a pan or skillet, and conserved from year to year. Since there are no inns on the roads, they carry it with them for sustenance.[19]

Roasted grain and nuts and another glass of *eau de vie*, this completes the feast. And so it was at almost all of the festive meals that I was to experience later.

On Sabbaths, holidays, and festivals, they eat *skhīna*[20] (which is *ḥammīn*, and is from the same root as *yissākhēn bām* in Ecclesiastes 10:9, following the interpretation of Abraham b. Ezra).[21] This dish consists of Spanish beans baked in an oven with whole eggs, which they serve in memory of the destruction of the Temple to anyone who comes to say hello.

On the weekdays, they have no set menu, no feasting or banqueting. When they are hungry they do not go in for quails and spicy delicacies which pinch our pockets and cause our bodies distress.[22] Rather, they eat what is proper for satisfying their hunger and maintaining their health—bread, honey, butter, fish, and fresh produce.

The men went out after eating, and the women came in. However, I as a foreigner remained standing there. They ate in the same manner as I have already described. They did not draw back or avert their eyes from me. Whatever they asked me, I answered fully, refusing nothing, and thereby won their affection. Most of them are fat and sleek,[23] but one of them was as fair as the moon that dwells amid the host of shining stars. On a day when I was calling upon my acquaintances, I happened to go into her home. She was seated on a down cushion in front of a loom on which was a colorfully woven tapestry. With her skilled hands, she designed a variety of lifelike images on it. The moment she saw me, a blush as red as roses appeared upon her cheeks, revealing her heart's embarrassment. She rose to her feet and covered her hands with the sleeve of her caftan. She took my hand and kissed it. This is the customary behavior of the Hebrew women toward whoever comes to ask after them. "She opened her mouth with wisdom,"[24] showing me that she rose above her peers as the phoenix rises over other birds.[25] She also proved the equal of a man, writing Spanish and Arabic in Hebrew characters. She eloquently recited by heart passages from Don Lope de Vega.[26]

Her husband was also delighted by my visit. He showed me great honor by saying to me in the Holy Tongue (for he was a Meknasi)[27] that he had heard of my reputation, and if it would please me, I should not hesitate to call at his house, so that he would have the pleasure of my engaging conversation, for I was considered a scholar. I could see from his flattery that he was a smooth-tongued and cunning fellow. I was not mistaken by what I had perceived, albeit he was being sincere with me. He had two wives (for they are not prohibited from having more than one wife). The beloved one lived in Tangier, while the despised one resided in Meknes. It so happened that the unloved one had children, but the favored one had none. Once when they quarreled, she distressed him by saying, "Give me children, or else I die."[28] Having done some research in matters such as this, I would say that as a rule a wife is not jealous of her friends, but only of her rival wives. Sarai's maid Hagar was given by her mistress to Abram as a co-wife. Once Hagar is Abraham's wife, she runs away from her mistress Sarai. Rachel waited seven years in her father's house to be Jacob's wife and is silent when her sister Leah takes her place. Once in Jacob's house, Rachel becomes jealous of her sister and stirs up a quarrel over the mandrakes. Hannah and Peninnah in Elkanah's house is another example. One upsets her rival, and the latter weeps and refuses to eat.[29] Our sages showed great wisdom when they abolished polygamy and kept us from this trouble.[30]

Occasionally, when I came to his house, I saw Arabs coming to ask about the future and its secrets in the auguries he divines for them. They still believe in the follies of astrology. The inquirer whispers his question over the pen, and the person who is being consulted, on the basis of the sum of the points which the pen makes at random, looks for the answer in a chart in his book in which is inscribed the signs of the zodiac and the names of the stars. Many Arabs also mislead the people in this way.[31] The Israelites, too, believe in divination as being akin to the Urim and Thummim.[32]

The Arabs are an ignorant people. They have no printers and no authors. The text of the Koran is all they study.[33] Even with regard to far-fetched ideas, it is the Divine Spirit that spoke them all. It is all true, and anyone who questions them risks his life. Only the schoolmaster has the book, and he writes for each pupil his passage on a wooden tablet. The following day he erases it and writes another in its place. This is in order not to desecrate the words of the scripture by throwing them away. Thus Muhammad barred the door of science and investigation to them in order to maintain them in their faith. One of their fundamental principles is: "Woe unto those who invent falsehood and say it is the word of God."[34] The wisdom of their sages in astronomy, medicine, and mathematics is lost, and they have only inherited the occult offshoots of these sciences. Far removed from all the genuine sciences, stripped of any knowledge, it is no wonder that they sank into the mire of stupidities, which I shall recount for you.

The unruly, the half-wit, the violent, and anyone struck with madness or dazed, are considered to be like saints. They honor them, kiss their foreheads, receive their blessing, feed them, swear by their names, venerate them in death, and seek their assistance when they are in distress. Their graves are a refuge for the oppressed. A woman (who veils her face before men) considers herself fortunate if she succeeds in sleeping with one of them.

When I left the diviner's house, one of those so-called holy men passed by, roaring like a young lion. He was playing with small pebbles in his hands. His saliva was running down his beard. He was eating raw meat and fish. I looked and wondered, "You call that a saint?" I was told that was because they are not subject to sin. To which I rejoined, "But they are not subject to righteousness either, for it is because of this that we exempt them from the observance of the commandments. By the same token, wild beasts are also not subject to sin. Should we, therefore, offer sacrifices and worship beasts or insects as did the inhabitants of Noph and Tahpanhes?[35] And even they did not follow them blindly, but only according to their priests' instructions." Then they stood silent and offered no further explanations. It was a miracle that they did not deliver me up for execution before the ruler or the qadi (he who is in charge of the religious law, that is a magistrate).

Judging anything is always a matter of perception: Thus, the Arab believes in his saints according to the degree of his imbecility; the Christian venerates his saints in accordance with their supposed miracles; while the holy man who is honored in Judaism is he who walks in the path of wisdom and fear of God.

All of the Arabs' laws are in accordance with their faith. Whatever happens under heaven is a decree ordained by the will of God Almighty, and no one questions the why and wherefore. Is this man insane? Does the ruler issue a mistaken command? *Amr Allāh huwa* (this is God's decree). And they are happy that God has chosen them to work His will. Therefore, they do not mourn the dead or cry over the slain. For this reason, they do not study the art of warfare, nor do they call on physicians. Is the death of this or that man significant in the sight of God? Or did He decree that he should fall in battle? It is futile for a man to take a lot of medicine. His stratagems are illusory, and all his wisdom is for naught. If God wills it, he shall live. If not, he shall die in the carnage. God can sustain a person even on his deathbed and can be like a rampart around him in the pitch of battle. Why then should anyone take the trouble to study the powers of herbs in order to prepare potions or know how to arrange battle lines?

He who dies in town goes directly to Muḥammad's bosom to enjoy the sensual pleasures of Paradise which is filled with the love of the heavenly maidens. He who dies on the battlefield will emerge from the ground and awaken in another place. They see a good omen in a stork. Every household on whose roof a stork builds its nest will prosper. Thus, no one who cherishes life would dare to hunt it for what would spoil the good fortune of the person who owns the house.[36] As with the Catholics, deceitful demagogues stir up the mob's emotion in the marketplace, telling them of the wonders of Muḥammad and his saints. Whenever such a man mentions their names, the audience kiss their hands.[37]

If a mad fool is a holy man for them, the sectarian gangs of ruffians and tricksters among them are considered demons. The women and children are afraid to go near them. They go from town to town to trap the gullible by their cunning. Their faces have a demonic mien, for whereas the Arabs all shave their heads, these men leave their hair in a tangled, filthy braid. They turn and move their heads around and around in order to terrify onlookers—"as Eastern priests in giddy circles run, and turn their heads to imitate the sun."[38] They devour stones and serpents before people's very eyes. They are what we would call mountebanks. Among them, they are known as the ʿĪsāwiyya, or "the sons of Esau."[39]

Along with the latter, mention should be made of the Būjlūd ("the man in skins"). He is someone covered in a bearskin costume. Such individuals will do anything for a penny or a loaf of bread.[40]

The Arabs will not debate matters concerning their religion, neither among themselves, nor with anyone else, lest they be defeated and weakened in their faith. They do not urge anyone to adopt their religion, but if a person is heard saying the words *Sīdī Muḥammad rasūl Allāh* (My Master Muḥammad is God's messenger),[41] whether in jest or in error, he has to convert or be burned alive. There is no way out.[42] They reason that whoever mentions him, God's spirit is driving him on;[43] he cannot retreat. I could not tell whether their ways are based upon those of the Catholics.

The latter tempt with blandishments and are quick to offer rewards for conversion, but they are punished, because anyone can make a fool of them. The former rule with a firm hand and will not let anyone take the name of their Prophet in vain. Both of them have strayed from the path of common sense, because a true and honest religion will neither incite nor entreat. Let Wisdom raise its voice, and the heart will judge and choose.

The Jews stand when urinating, while the Arabs squat. During a famine, a Jew disguised himself in Arab clothing and began to emulate the foolish behavior of their holy men. His real identity was not recognized and so he was fed and stayed alive. Once, however, he urinated and forgot to squat. They were planning to put him to death, until he abjured his faith. They will not whistle in their homes; neither will the Jews. This is not for the sake of decorum or proper conduct, but on account of the bad omen, for perhaps the house will be plundered and never be filled again. When they count, they begin from the small finger, bending each into the palm, and they always say: "One is God, two, and so on."[44]

I witnessed all these things during the time I was in the service of the gentleman from Vienna. It was a period of perfect calm and tranquility. But immunity does not last forever, and the joy of the oppressed is woe. Their happiness is short-lived and of the moment.[45] While I was writing letters in his house, he gave me a decree of the Sultan to copy.[46] The translation of the proclamation was to be given as an order to the consul of each nation, and they in turn were to write to their respective rulers not to dare give aid, comfort, or refuge to his son Mūlāy Yazīd, because he had rebelled against his father.[47]

The Hapsburg Consul told me the particulars about his rebellion. It seems that he aroused his father's ire because of a matter concerning his wives. He requested money from the Jews of Tetuan, but they could not go against the Sultan's command. However, the English helped him secretly because his mother was English.[48]

The man from Vienna then told me that he had news for me. On the morrow, he would travel to Cadiz.[49] Since I was a Jew, I could not come with him even in disguise because I was known to the Spanish Consul, and he would not permit me to go. "However," he told me, "I have not forgotten that you have conducted yourself loyally, and therefore, I have recommended you to the Swedish Consul. And now, accept this gift from me. It will support you until you find relief and deliverance[50] somewhere else as I sincerely wish for you."

I was shaken by what he said. However, I pulled myself together and thanked him for all he had done for me. I was sad and depressed when I left him.

He was not officially a consul. This was because the Hapsburg Emperor did not wish to hand over his consul, too, as had happened in the past there. So he was hiding under the guise of being there to study the language,[51] while at the same time, as an intelligent man, he kept an eye on his countrymen in order to rescue anyone in trouble from the hand of his oppressor by covert means. Why should he bear the title of consul in the lands of the Maghreb when his freedom to leave anytime he wishes might not be granted him? As everyone knows, the kings of Europe do not send ambassadors there, but only consuls. The reader may recall how an English consul was held hostage.[52] If one goes back even further, he will find out how they spat in the face of another English consul, how they let some lackey slap his face in order to humiliate him, and how "he went home to his native city, set his affairs in order and then hanged himself"[53] because he could not go on living after his disgrace.[54]

Having witnessed these great trials,[55] led the Viennese gentleman to anticipate events yet to come,[56] and like a wise captain who can tell the difference between the thunder and the lightning, he hastily sought shelter for himself before the storm. No sooner had he heard of the ban on Mūlāy Yazīd, than he got himself to safety before being trapped in the approaching anarchy.[57]

The following day he departed just as he said he would. There I was still in the pit of dismay. What was I to do? If I gave in to grief, I would perish with no one to help me. The gift would console me a little, but only for a short while. What I witnessed and what befell me, you will hear in the next chapter.

4

As a mirror before a face, so is human history to man. As for you, O reader, if you are still in the prime of youth, do not overexert your strength along the way for you will shorten your days. There are so many obstacles to overcome. So many snares to be moved aside! So many changes of fortune to be endured—more than one can count! Even if you should overcome these hardships, the battle will exhaust you and leave you debilitated. Do not bring yourself to these ordeals!

As long as the money I received as a gift jingled in my purse, I cast all my troubles into the depths of oblivion and turned my attention to studying the Arabic language with which I had begun to familiarize myself—insofar as I could afford to fulfill my wish—during these ten months that I had been in Morocco. This was not out of books, for they have not any.[1] Neither was it from the mouth of scribes, because the Arabs, like the Jews, will not teach their language to strangers lest it may be defiled in their mouths. It was only with the aid of the Holy Language which is cast in the same mold, and with my knowledge of its grammatical rules, that I was able to ask the pertinent questions. Sometimes, I went to a boys' school in order to know the interpretation of scriptural verses and some literary phrases. At other times, I went to groceries to see what they call the various foodstuffs. I inquired, investigated, and asked methodically until I could speak the colloquial language, not the classical language which is no longer spoken by them.[2] I formulated rules which I tested in speech. I observed, and I came to the realization that it was unwise of the Jews to speak ill of the Arabic tongue, saying that it is corrupted Hebrew—because it contains the choicest elements of the Holy Language. If you have a real grasp of this language, you will share my opinion. For each and every word, I sought its cognate in the Holy Language, or in Spanish, because the latter was also mixed with Arabic from the time that Spain was under Arab rule. I compared and contrasted all the languages I knew—in what ways were they similar, in what ways did they differ—and I deduced the following general rule:

The farther water gets from its source, the more putrid and foul it becomes. The farther people scatter from their native land, the more their language is corrupted. God decided to confound the language of mankind "and He scattered them."[3] From that time forth the languages were separated and became many groups and subgroups. But they are all branches stemming from a single trunk. The languages of each branch are entangled one with another and are intertwined. They rise holding fast to their roots. Place, time, circumstance, and necessity cause the ends of their branches to grow longer. They spread out turning ever upward, their foliage changing little by little until they become foreign, and the latter cannot be recognized when compared with the former, even though they all came into being from the same womb. They differ or resemble according to the circumstance of their origin or the time of their birth, or according to the distance or nearness of their branches from their root. The first, even though they stem from different branches, seem to resemble each other more than the last which stem from a single branch. The pronunciation and structure of a language depend upon their original environment. The anatomical organs of speech are the same in every man. Yet, in spite of this, those who have been taught and have become used to speaking according to the conventions of their native language, are unable to do so in another tongue:

The Ephraimite cannot pronounce *shibboleth*,[4] the Arab cannot pronounce *p*,[5] Ashkenazi Jews cannot pronounce ʿ*ayin*.[6] The Christian cannot say either *ḥēt* or ʿ*ayin*. The sounds *ci* and *gi* in Italian, *j* and *eu* in French, *jota* in Spanish, *th* in English, *ch* in German, and *ão* in Portuguese, are all stumbling blocks for those who study them. By the same token, so are the vowels of the Holy Language for the Jews of the Maghreb and the consonants for the Jews of Europe—as you already heard in the sermon of the Meknasi.[7]

The Spanish-speaking Jews, such as those in Tetuan, write their language in half-Rashi script, while those who speak Arabic write their language in full-Rashi.[8] They all write with a flax reed and rest the sheet of paper on their knees instead of using a writing table. As with Arabic and all eastern languages, they write from right to left. And perhaps it is the correct way, because it is our natural movement. This is proven by those who sew clothing.[9]

These studies and investigations did not take up all of my time. For a month, love too took its part. The Jews pressured me to take a wife.[10] Lord God! Oppressed, miserable creatures that they are! They have neither the mouth to answer an Arab, nor the cheek to raise their head.[11] When an Arab tells one of them to bend down so that he might strike him, the fellow bends and lets himself be hit, not even daring to look them in the face lest they should say that he cursed them in his heart. Instead of thinking of how to limit the number of the miserable, not only do they marry at the age of fifteen, twelve, and even ten,[12] but they also press others who are free to share their misfortune. Should you happen to ask them why, it is not in order to satisfy their desire and their lust which is powerful due to the heat of the Maghrebi region. They do it only to fulfill the first commandment in God's Torah[13] and to contain the inclination of man's heart which is evil from his youth.[14] They cite the example of a certain rabbi who took a wife at the age of sixteen, and had he married at fourteen, he could have said, "An arrow in Satan's eye!"[15] They also justify themselves by noting that the letters of the word *baḥur* (bachelor) stand for "virtuous by day, sinful by night"[16] because he cannot prevent himself from nocturnal emissions. Another explanation they offer is that it is to hasten the coming of our Messiah, because "the son of David will not come until all souls have been eliminated from the body."[17]

"You fools!" I said to them. "How long will you persist in foolishness? Open your eyes and see! Is this not the custom of the Arabs who are commanded in their Scripture to beget as many offspring as they physically can so that souls will not be lost in vain?"[18] But who can uproot a poison weed which has grown old in their hearts?[19] Whoever disagrees with them is considered to be denying the entire Torah. Having become so used to the weight of their yoke, they hold the bonds that tie their necks with their own hands.

As I knew that according to the Sultan's decree, no woman, whether Hebrew or Arab, may leave his realm, and that if I should marry, I would either have to remain there a slave forever, or I would have to leave my wife because she could not go out with me, I, therefore, would not listen to them, even though they tempted me ten times with dowries and beautiful maidens.[20] They wound me tightly to them like a turban with the cords of love.[21]

The gift money was slowly dwindling. I turned for help to the consuls. The English Consul questioned me concerning my passport and could not believe that I had lost it. The Swedish Consul, who had heard about me from the Viennese gentleman, brought me to his office and told me: "I shall assist you with all my heart, if you are an honest man. Tell me whom did you know in Gibraltar so that I might investigate the truth of what you are saying." I mentioned to him the name of one merchant whose son I taught French. "The man is one of my acquaintances," he said to me. "Go in peace, and I will let you hear from me at the proper time." I was not afraid of any bad report because I knew that I was innocent and had done no wrong. I looked forward to word from him.

The flame of contention between the Moroccan Emperor and the King of England over piracy was still burning. English ships were coming to Tangier every week to negotiate peace. Upon their arrival, they would buy enough supplies for their maintenance. I became friendly with their commanders and ships' captains in order to act as their dragoman. They were my salvation for some time.

During that period, I also had the leisure to discover things that I did not know before and that enlightened me so that I understood things about which I had been mistaken. While I was passing in the street, I heard a great tumult coming from a Jewish house. I approached the gate leading to the inner court, and there I beheld a crowd of women, their heads enveloped in a white shawl. I imagined they were dancing girls. I was indeed mistaken; they were mourning a dead man. The two who stood in the middle were the deceased's kin. They were beating their breasts and wailing in Arabic, while all the women around them clapped their hands together in grief. Between each verse they would scratch their faces and cry out each time: *"waw, waw"* (that is, "alas, alack").[22] It was then that I understood the biblical verse "You shall not gash yourselves,"[23] which should be compared with "And they gashed themselves . . . according to *their custom*"[24] (the latter being forbidden to us according to the prohibition against following Gentile practices[25]). This custom is mentioned four times in Jeremiah,[26] and is referred to in two verses in Amos, the first being: "Her maidens escort her with voices like doves, beating their breasts."[27] The second is: "In every street cries of 'Ah, woe!' "[28] Still another reference is the verse in the Mishna about women who wail and clap their hands.[29] All this is called in Arabic *geshdūr*.[30]

When they come to a graveyard, they say to the diggers, "May God be with you," just as Boaz said to the reapers.[31] Until all the preparations are made, they lay the bier on the ground and pull on each others dresses imploring one another to give money for charity. Women also come and sit at the graves of their relatives, calling upon them for their aid, discussing their private matters with the dead, even arguing with them, just as a person talks with his friend who is still alive. All of these things—this entire scene— are also performed on the Ninth of Av.[32]

Even wise and discerning people, all of whose ways and all of whose paths—as I have observed—are paved with justice, if they become a single community in a single place, finally after a long period of time, even among them bad laws will spring up whose origin was unknown to them. How the more so in this instance among this misguided people who do not know how to follow God's path because of their customary foolishness, but rather they "create mischief by statute."[33]

Custom, divination, and the evil eye—these are the three destructive forces under which all of the Maghreb tremble. On Saturday night, they will not take anything out of their house. Under no circumstances should one mention the word *eggs*, much less eat them, so as not to begin the week by taking anything out or with matters concerning food.[34] Now when the candle in my room went out, I not knowing any of this, took it outside to relight it and was jeered at. I lit my candle at my neighbor's house, but he would not let me take it outside. At first I thought he was jesting. Then, I almost quarreled with him. However, when I heard the reason for this, I forgave his foolishness and went out to buy another candle and to light it in a Gentile home.

The Arabs when quarreling among themselves will not take hold of each other's beard because it is sacred, and they swear by it. And it is the same with the Jews. Pious Jews will not even touch it, lest a single hair from it fall to the ground and spoil the exalted beard.[35]

One day as I was leaving the synagogue, I encountered a man at the doorway with a glass in his hand filled with spittle. He handed it to me to spit into it just as everyone else who was leaving had done. My stomach turned inside me. I pushed his hand away, causing the glass to fall, and I laid upon him all the curses and all the imprecations that are not written in the Torah. Vile scoundrel! Good-for-nothing! A mediator stepped forward to calm me down, saying that it was a medicinal potion for a sick child.[36] "A potion!" I exclaimed in shock. "A potion," he replied, "to cure the evil eye. You know that the Talmud states that the majority of children die by the evil eye."[37] "But it does not say in the Talmud," I retorted, "that he should drink spittle for medicine." "That is our custom," the man added. "A loathsome, disgusting custom," I replied.

You cannot even kiss or praise the beauty of their little sons and daughters. Should you happen to have committed this error, they will not let go of you until you spit at them.[38]

A wedding festivity is the sum of follies as the following chapter will recount for you.

5

How long will foolishness ensnare us? Let us put aside vanities and serve our Lord. Do we still not know that the earth has gone astray and has been corrupted[1] by them and that they are the source of our troubles? Where is the unalloyed Divine Word and the pure fear of God? For their gold and silver are mixed with filth and worthlessness. Woe unto those who legislate wicked laws! "Rid yourselves of the alien gods in your midst!"[2] Purge away your dross![3] These things are vanity. They avail not! God judges us by true statutes. He establishes just precepts. Let no hand tamper with them, and let us not impute things which are not right unto God.[4]

From the moment a young man who desires to marry makes a formal attestation according to the custom of Israel by the act of symbolic purchase[5] and by oath, in order that everything should be valid, he is not to go back to his fiancée's house again until the wedding celebration. He may not even pass through the street where she lives in order to be pure in Israel. As for the maiden, she is not to mention him, not even by name, and she is to avoid encountering him. (Even after having married and borne him children, she calls him "the father of my children" and not "my husband" or "my man.")[6] A widow never remarries, because there is the fear based upon the opinion of some rabbi in the Gemara and according to the Zohar that she might be a woman who is fatal to her spouses.[7]

A virgin by custom marries on Friday. On the Thursday preceding it, an ox is slaughtered for the feast in the courtyard of the bride's house. During the slaughtering, all their relatives and friends are invited and are served nuts, roasted seeds, and a glass of *eau de vie*. As they leave, each guest puts a coin on the ox's head. This is called "the good omen" (or, *pintar* in Spanish).[8] This becomes the slaughterer's fee. As each one places his coin, an old woman ululates like a swift or a wryneck.[9] Whoever hears it will have ringing in his ears. This is considered a good sign for the family and a voice of thanks to the contributor. This hoopoe may be found in every house in which a celebration is taking place. It would be utterly unthinkable for them not to have her voice heard at all on their joyous occasions. Otherwise, their festivities would turn to mourning.

In the evening, they bring the bride to the groom's house with the sound of ululating and drums. As for her, she is deaf, dumb, and blind until she arrives at her new home. And so she remains throughout Friday from the time she was dressed until she goes out from under the marriage canopy and is installed in her bridal bed—she is like a stone pillar. The attending women bind her hair with ribbons,[10] paint her eyes with kohl, and coif her tresses into two braids according to their fashion. They also paint her face with rouge, and they draw strange designs on her forehead, her nose, and on her chin with bitumen to save her from the evil eye.[11] They color her hands with a red dye called henna. They do not know anything about hair styling or fitting dresses properly. But in truth, a pretty girl is innately attractive in whatever she appears, whereas all the swarthy maiden's ornaments will do nothing to improve her homeliness.

After the ceremony under the bridal canopy, her nearest relative will lift the bride on his shoulder and seat her on a chair. And all the while she is still like a marble column, never even nodding her head. A few moments later, he carries her to her bridal bed. Virgins follow after. Her friends are brought to keep her company. They make merry and amuse themselves, enjoying games together and playing with toys until the bed curtain is drawn, after which she may not be seen any longer. Then a meal is served. When the guests finish eating, they get up to celebrate with a great deal of noise. Then the bridegroom is brought to his bride and the curtain is drawn after them. In all that I have described so far, they are

A Moroccan Jewish bride and groom in traditional costume. Gérard Silvain, *Images et traditions juives* (Editions Astrid: Milan, 1980)

not really different from us (Europeans), even taking into account difference of custom. However, upon hearing what follows, the innocent will be shocked and the modest will tear their hair. If you thought that the guests will leave and let the couple consummate their love, you thought incorrectly. On the contrary, now they start reveling while remaining there to see whether the maid was indeed a virgin. When the couple have finished, the bed sheet is spread out for all to see, just as the Catholics do with the holy shroud.[12] Who ever heard of such an abomination? Who ever saw such paganism? In the midst of this tumult, the bride is led to the ritual bath, and all the time the old woman is ululating, the drums are making a deafening din and the singers chant *piyyūṭīm*.[13]

Throughout the entire seven days of festivities, a man comes to play the lute. As he plays a song in either the Holy Language or in Arabic, all of the guests place a coin on his lute as a gift. This perhaps explains the scriptural verse "Those who strum on the harp" as meaning that they put a coin on the instrument.[14]

The art of music is totally unknown to them. Even the various types of musical instruments which are played in our theaters are merely exotic names for them. Their only musical instruments are as follow: the drums that I have mentioned; the pipe that is shaped something like an oboe and sounds as shrill as shepherds' pipes; the flute, which as played among them, has a furious sound like "he who beats with a hammer encouraging him who pounds the anvil."[15] It is with these last two instruments that the *al-Ḥujjāj* celebrate the pilgrimage. These are the people who return from the holy pilgrimage to Mecca, like the Jews who go to Jerusalem and the Christians to Rome. They are like saints. They only pay the Sultan half the regular taxes on their income. The trumpets are in appearance and sound similar to those used by the postmen in Mecklenburg.[16] They are sounded during the month of Ramadan (whose name is from the same root as Hebrew *remeṣ*, "hot ashes")[17] during which they fast for the entire thirty days from sunrise to sunset. They sound the trumpets from the minarets three times during the night to wake the people to eat, saying, "Arise, eat and drink from that which God has given you." The castanets they use are shaped like four iron cups. Two are held in each hand,

and they clap them together. This instrument is particular to the blacks. They play them while dancing like satyrs.[18]

The Jews use only the lute. In singing, they are all the same, each nation according to its own language. They do not sing precisely according to the notes, but between each syllable they add *na na aa aa* according to the tempo many times.[19] One day a singer was praising his song to me. I asked him what it was about. He told me that it was a love letter a lover had composed for his beloved, the gist of which was: "My blood is the ink, my skin the parchment, and the pen is myself."[20]

Once I came to be known to all the townspeople, they would inform me whenever ships arrived at the shore. One day, I heard that a ship had come from Gibraltar bringing the Swedish Consul the gift that his King customarily sent to the Moroccan Emperor every three years. I went down to the shore to speak with the captain. How delighted and surprised I was to see that he was the very man who had obtained the exit permit on my behalf.[21] I immediately ran to the consul's residence. "Sir," I told him, "I have done as you had instructed me in order to keep your word, not out of any worry, since no misconduct can be attributed to me. You have had enough time to receive your answer. The captain who is coming directly to you is the same one who requested the passport for me. He is Genoese and a Christian. He would not lie to you in order to aid a Jew. Now keep your word, and I shall ever hold you in esteem." He replied that even though he had till now not received any answer, he believed what I had said because the gentleman from Vienna had spoken well of me. "Here is a gift for you," he said. "Whenever you wish to return to Gibraltar or go to another place, all your needs will be provided by me. Furthermore, I shall give you another travel document. Go in peace." Then I left him.

Since I did not wish to close myself up in Gibraltar again, I thought it best to wait until my fortune turned and would send me its greetings from somewhere else. With this hope, my agitated heart was calmed. I saw that there were ships continually coming and going at the port, and I made no move. Some days later at dawn, I was standing on the roof enjoying the morning breeze—

it being the hottest period of the summer. Rays of sunlight were sparkling in the east reviving the joy of the entire countryside. As I gazed at the radiance of their beams, another ship was coming. A stiff breeze filled its sails as it skimmed over the water. I congratulated myself saying, "This is the one that will take me out of this trap." The coast guards went out toward her to examine her documents. But alas they returned and reported that it had been blown off course by the east wind and did not have any permit or certification. They would not allow her to drop anchor, but directed her to New Tangier, a small town 2000 cubits beyond the city limits. Then due to the fear of plague, no further ships approached the shore afterwards. The prophet cried out: "No King, no minister, no sacrifice, no cultic pillar, no ephod and no teraphim."[22] My answer to him was: No merchant, no trade, no Viennese gentleman, no consul, and no English ships. I regretted not having returned to Gibraltar while I still could, and I became melancholy. I realized that I had no one to help me in Tangier. So I decided to go to Tetuan. It is a bigger and better city than Tangier. It also has a port at Martil. The Jews living there are not acquainted with foreigners, neither do they know their brethren in Europe. Perhaps they would be glad to see me. I stayed another month until my beard grew in and then set out. Before arriving in the city, I put on a native outer garment which the Jew who owned the mule I was riding had lent me, and then I entered town.

6

In order for you to understand my being in Tetuan, I should let
you know that while in Gibraltar, all my dealings were with the
military and I had nothing to do with the Jews. For this reason, I
was unable to go regularly to the synagogue, albeit I went two or
three times, and I even spent one night studying at the home of
the headmaster of their yeshiva, Rabbi Judah Halevi, who happened
to be from Tetuan. Sometime later, I was told that this rabbi had
the power to "slay the wicked with the breath of his lips."[1] "Did
this ever happen?" I asked. "No," I was told, "because he feared
being brought to trial." "Then how do you know that he has such
power?" I inquired. The answer came back that while he was still
in his native land, a Jew who used to attend synagogue every morning and enter the Jewish school every day, morning and evening,
apostatized to the Arab religion. The rabbi purchased all the meri-
torious deeds that the latter had performed while still a Jew at full
price. "Tell Rabbi Judah," I replied, "that there is a man from Italy
who has come and will sell him all his blessings from 'Blessed be
he who has come' to 'Praised be the True Judge' (that is, from
circumcision to burial)."

They did not realize that I was jesting and thought I was either
a Christian or an atheist. Word of all these things spread through
Tetuan. These people considered an atheist to be a queer creature,
and they were curious to see me—so I was told. This fancy of
theirs induced me to go to Tetuan. Perhaps their silliness could
be turned to my favor. However, when I came to the Jewish quarter,

57

the whole city was in an uproar about me, saying: "This is the atheist." That very day was the Sabbath eve, and like the Ephraimite in Gibeah, no one took me home.[2] Their appearance bespoke their poverty, so I cried out in a loud voice: "who will give me a place to lodge? His fee will be doubled—only do not let me sleep in the street."[3] Poverty overcomes fear. One of them said, "Why should you have to stand outside? I shall look for quarters to your liking." He brought me to one man's home, and I lodged with him.

I went with the landlord's son to buy myself shoes. On the way, an Arab came by and struck me on the head. That is their way of humiliating.[4] My heart flared within me, and I looked daggers at him. The voice of my vengeance's blood cried out to me from shame.[5] Nevertheless, I remained silent and controlled myself, because my Jewish clothes were my bit and bridle restraining me. Whoever speaks up is taking his life in his hands. "Can iron break iron"[6] in a company of wise men? Should a sword be raised by one man against another? Is it not so that foolishness has felled victims? Indeed, the number of its victims is enormous. She incites man against man and nation against nation. O Sword of religious fanaticism, how long will it be until you are laid to rest? May you be gathered into your sheath, and may you be calmed and silent!

I asked to be taken to the house of the chief rabbi who was a pupil of the aforementioned Rabbi Judah Halevi. I approached him confidently and cheerfully and said: "Blessed be the Omnipresent Who has granted me the privilege of reciting the Mishnaic blessing 'Who has kept me alive' to see the face of a great man, the like of whom I have not seen till now and 'Who has endowed from His wisdom those who fear Him.' "[7] Then I stripped off my African outer garment and revealed my European attire beneath. I then went on: "Even if you do not believe my words, you will believe that which your own eyes behold. Without wearing native dress, upon whom can I rely? Since God has set you upon the throne of teaching and wisdom, whom do we have that is greater than yourself?

The man's face lit up like the sun, and he answered me in a voice sweeter than honey: "Go in peace to your lodging, and I shall send you a change of clothes before sunset." And so he did. While I was still conversing with him, a man came to call me on

behalf of the Vice Consul of Venice. So I took leave of the rabbi
to go to the Vice Consul. He too was a handsome man. I observed
afterwards that for the most part the Jews are fair complexioned
and attractive. Very few of them are suntanned. The opposite is
the case with the Arabs. When I came to him, he introduced himself
to me as the Vice Consul of Venice and said that not many people
in this city know how to write in Spanish, and those who do, take
great pride in it and are fearful of spoiling their glory by teaching
it to others. Their jealousy decreases wisdom.[8] He was, therefore,
happy that I had come, because God had now provided him with
a man after his own heart who could write for him until he could
teach his brethren writing.[9] I would be fully paid for my work. I
bowed and told him that I would do as he asked.

That evening, I broke bread with my landlord. I looked for some
way to sound out the man and learn his thoughts about me. He
also had been in Gibraltar, where he learned to speak broken
English which gave him pretensions to being educated. I praised
him over and over on his having attained so much in such a short
while. Then, feigning innocence, I let him know about my mastery
in many areas, and I got the upper hand on him. From then on,
he was in awe of my knowledge. On the Sabbath day, as we were
leaving the synagogue, he was asked behind my back about what
I did and what I said. Still imbued with my words of wisdom from
the previous evening, he praised me to the sky. On Saturday night,
the rabbi and the cantor of the synagogue held me back just as I
was about to leave and said, "Please stay with us, Sir. Do not be
in a hurry to go. Let us take sweet counsel together in the house
of God."[10] So I stayed. The people who were standing in the courtyard to leave came back, and everyone's mouth was agape at what
I had to say.

They examined my faith. They tested my wisdom. And how did
I reply? By bringing counsels of old.[11] By expounding at length
on the fundamental sciences. By confirming each biblical verse I
cited on the basis of a philosophical theory and each philosophical
theory on the basis of a scriptural verse. In one instance, I cited
Plato to elucidate Moses. In another, I showed that Moses's teachings were found in Socrates. I cited as proof for everything "the
words of the wise and their riddles"[12] in correct and elegant He-

brew. These people who had never in their lives seen such illumination, who had never conceived of such innovations, and who never knew such ideas, were amazed and awed. They quickly responded in unison that now they knew that those who had spoken ill of me had been misled by their own stupidity, and that they themselves had completely changed their opinion, putting an end to any complaints the Jewish community had against me. They invited me to come to their yeshiva the following day. Then they went to their homes brimming with satisfaction and joy.

The next morning I went to the rabbi's yeshiva, and the same people were also there. They showed me great deference. They were studying the talmudic tractate Bava Qama. I joined with them in their method of study. Afterwards, I showed them that knowing the Talmud also depends upon knowing the fundamentals of the language. I offered proof from the selfsame legal text before them concerning the ox, the pit and the crop-consuming beast,[13] where Rav states that "crop-consuming beast" (Heb. *may'e*) recalls the scriptural verse "his hoards are laid bare" (*niv'ū*),[14] whereas Samuel argues that it is to be connected with the active verb "to seek out" as it is written "if you seek, seek!"[15] This controversy is based upon an understanding of the importance of the building blocks of the linguistic structure.

For fourteen days I attended the yeshiva, and each day I let them hear something new, until I was asked—as I had secretly been wishing—to give a sermon. Pretending to be hesitant, I answered that the task was too much for me. They repeated this daily to the point of their begging me, imploring me with flattery, and all the while, I was kindling their passion to hear me on the Sabbath. Thus that villain Fate had its capricious way with me "poured from vessel to vessel."[16] One moment he flung me into the pit of terrors, while the next, he pulled me out with the lifeline of hope and his hands shaped and fashioned me.[17]

Regarding the sermons and the details connected with them, you will hear in the following chapter.

7

Before discussing the sermons, let me say a word about the synagogues as I remember them, for here too new things may be observed. The Torah reader's platform is only a table set on the ground near the entranceway[1] in order to have light, because inside the building one can almost feel the darkness. Therefore, whenever the rain or snow does not prevent them, they place the table outside the sanctuary, and half the congregants are inside and the other half outside. The women's section is merely the courtyard itself[2] which also serves as the yeshiva. There are chairs placed around it for whoever comes to study. The rabbis sit on the ground at the doorway of the synagogue on the outside. You may have noticed that their ways resemble those found in the Scripture. Take, for example, the passage in Malachi—"If only there was among you someone to shut the doors and not light my altar in vain."[3] He did not merely say: "Shut the doors and do not come in," or "shut the windows and do not light."[4] Furthermore, you will observe that their pulpit is shaped like the biblical altar almost down to its last detail, and which in fact is called a table in Ezekiel.[5] If you look still further in the Bible, you will find a parallel in the words of Isaiah—"in the courts of My sanctuary";[6] and in Zechariah—"you will guard My courts";[7] and in Nehemiah—"in the courts of God's house";[8] and in the words of David—"For a day in Thy courts is better than a thousand."[9] They referred to God's house by these names. Just as the elders used to sit holding court at the gates where all the people came for judgment, so too these people sit on the threshold of the synagogue's entrance, which is the place of study. Perhaps it was to this that David was referring when he said, "I would rather stand at the threshold of my God's house than dwell in the tents of wickedness."[10] Our sages in statements similar in form to this last question would say "sitting" in the permanent sense to express "dwelling."[11] However, the manner of sitting in Morocco is not in accordance with that found in the Talmud, because the students of old sat on the ground, while the scholars sat on cushions. For when a case would be brought to them for adjudication, in most instances, the necessity of taking an oath would put an end to strife, and the threat of excommunication would separate those locked in dispute.[12] Excommunication! The weapon and shield of foolishness and falsehood. It is the torrent that destroys the vineyard of the Lord of Hosts. It is an obstacle that has been removed from amongst the community of nations that follow reason and truth.

But what really stirred me up inside and embittered me was the following incident that I witnessed. On the Sabbath day, a company of Arabs from the Sultan's guards came to the synagogue like a devastating horde carrying off all the craftsmen and all the porters. They took them posthaste to serve the Sultan, each according to his occupation. They also took all the women who work as seamstresses and dressmakers to do their work without pay. The taskmasters prodded them with batons, with stones, and with their fists. They grabbed them mercilessly at the chest by the lapel of their garment. Woe to any who tried to escape! These beastly ruffians are called *sukhāra* (which means "men on a commission").[13] Jews who were in the midst of reciting the Torah benedictions, or whose feet were still planted in prayer,[14] left the Torah and the obligatory prayer and like domesticated sheep being led to slaughter, they went out to their task, at which they would be vigorously worked until evening. O you who came out of Egypt, was there ever such a thing in your days? O God, how can You restrain Yourself at these things? How can you remain silent and allow us to suffer?[15] Incidents of this sort take place in every single city and province in this wicked kingdom. And you, man of Anathoth,[16] come to our kings and officials, for they are merciful rulers, and cry out, "Seek the welfare of the city to which I have exiled you and pray to the Lord on its behalf."[17] However, in the Maghreb rise and cry out, "Up, get out of this place!"[18]

Prior to the Sabbath on which I was intending to preach, I went to the rabbi and told him that many well-educated people who love innovative interpretations desire to hear me preach not to learn from me, since I would be like one who brings straw to the Apharaim,[19] but only for a discussion of something new. "Now in order to satisfy them, I am asking you, if you consider it proper, to accede to my request and grant me a favor. When your honor comes with the others, let him as their leader come at their head. Then all my detractors will be put to shame, because you are giving me aid and comfort." He replied that my wish would be granted and they would do as I saw best. Moreover, in order that it would be known that he was defending me, he asked me to come to his synagogue first, and all his congregants would hear me. People would see his example, and the other synagogues would follow suit. I kissed him on his forehead and went out.

All of this pointed to the fact that it was from his affection for me that he did me such honor. Albeit I was unable to fathom the inner depths of his thoughts. Did he truly like me, or was he testing me with flattery? I mentioned this concern to my landlord. He related to me that the rabbi had written regarding me to his teacher in Gibraltar. The latter wrote back to him that it was true that there was a streak of heresy in me, but that I was well versed in Jewish learning and that there may be a hope that the light of the Torah would guide me along the even path,[20] blessed would be the man who through patience succeeded in showing me the light.

I was glad to hear this, and the next day at the yeshiva, I turned my discussion onto a tangent and told them a story that had taken place in Rome. A certain Caesar instead of punishing a man deserving death for his crime, elevated him and honored him to the point where the latter was too embarrassed by the honor for which he was unworthy, that he reformed his conduct and became a good and honest man. As I spoke, I knew from the expression on their faces that my words had worked their way into their hearts. After

I had won them over, I could scarcely believe that I had changed
their stone hearts to flesh, and I could only keep hinking how to
prepare the sermons properly.

On the Sabbath, there was a wedding group at the synagogue
in which I was praying. The rabbi and all the scholars came. I
realized that the moment was ripe for me even though it had
spoiled what I had prepared and forced me to change it suddenly.[21]
When the Torah scroll was brought out of the ark, I asked leave
of the rabbi and the cantor to go up to the pulpit. I pulled up my
prayer shawl and the sleeves of my tunic up toward my shoulders
and I delivered my sermon forcefully and with confidence. I do
not know who understood, who did not understand, and who
thought they understood, but all of them praised me for having
performed a miracle. They contributed as was their custom, and
indeed much more. That day my heart swelled with pride. When
I returned home, my landlord ran to greet me. He hugged and
kissed me. All the neighbors, both men and women, were rejoicing
and celebrating before me. The women had not danced like this
since David returned from smiting the Philistines.[22]

I could have settled in that country, for it was wide open for
me. I taught modern Spanish and the Latin script, and I had many
students. I could have lived there were it not for the wicked natives
and all the times I had to take off my shoes which I found burden-
some. That is why I would not consider living there for the rest
of my life. Every Jew when passing in front of an Arab mosque has
to take off his shoes from his feet.[23] Woe to him who forgets or
disobeys! In order to spare myself somewhat from the cruelty of
those Gentiles, I wore clothing in the style of the Renegadoes, so
that I would be recognized as being from Europe and treated
better.

The Renegadoes are military men who fled Spain and changed
their faith. According to the decree of the Moroccan Emperor,
every fugitive from Spain who flees to his country must either
change his religion or be returned to his native land for execution.
Many chose apostasy rather than being under the yoke of Spain
where their services had been difficult. And since the Arabs are
good-for-nothing, as I have already informed you, when these people come there, they are appointed as generals and field com-

manders. Thus, they are still in charge of artillery and defending the fortifications.[24] And since, like myself, they are not accustomed to wearing Maghrebi clothing, they wear them in a modified fashion.

At this point let me describe to you the way the Gentiles and the Jews—men and women—dress in the Maghreb. I shall begin with the Gentiles. I would say as a general observation that any hut is fit for their housing, any rag fit for wearing, and any food no matter how vile is good for eating. I do not know whether they should be considered philosophers,[25] or whether they simply resemble animals.

The wardrobe of the nobility consists of a fine linen tunic,[26] a red or green undergarment,[27] and a white cloak in which they wrap themselves.[28] On their head is a turban with a red cap under it,[29] and on their feet green slippers.[30] Only a few wear pants. Some wear a cloth cape over their shoulders in winter.[31] The poor masses have nothing but a cloak. They turn their faces to the wall when they wrap themselves so that their genitals will not be exposed to view. There are many who have neither headcovering nor footwear. Among this latter group there are those who instead of a cloak wear a tunic of sackcloth or coarse material which is open under the arms, and when they need to, they extend their arms through these openings. They all shave their head, with the exception of the mountebanks. Blacks, as well as many whites, leave a little topknot on their head, because when they go to heaven, Muhammad will pull them by the hair of their head. Some young Jewish men also grow a lock of this kind as a mark of beauty.

The Jews all wear a fine linen tunic, a white undergarment, pants,[32] an overgarment, and a wide full-length black cloak over their shoulders which is fastened at the neck, with its ends thrown over the right shoulder.[33] During the week, most young men wear a cloak similar to that of the Gentiles instead of a robe, but made of thin white cloth.[34] I dressed like them throughout my entire stay in Tetuan. The Renegadoes and I wore the cloak in the European fashion. The headcovering and footwear of the Jews are black.[35] Should anyone dare to wear either one of these in red, even in jest, he is compelled to convert. This is because black over white is for Jews, while white over black is for Arabs. The color red is the Arabs' mark of distinction, and they are identified by it as the faithful followers of Muḥammad, which they righteously affirm. They say that when Muḥammad ascended to heaven, he was wearing a red turban on his head. He found Moses wearing a black cap. When Moses saw him, he quickly took off his cap, threw it on the ground, and put on a red one in its stead. This is why every Jew who converts to the Arabs' religion (all Arabs being direct descendants of Muḥammad's seed), has to throw off his cap.

The women's indoor attire—both Hebrew and Arab—consists of a tunic. From the waist down, it is similar to the kind we have. From the waist up, it has a breastpiece in front embroidered with gold or silk thread.[36] It looks like two garments joined together. The outer garment is very ornate, consisting of a cummerbund and a very wide festive dress.[37] The skirt is a velvet[38] wraparound bordered with silk and belted at the waist.[39] In the Tetuan district, the married women cover their head with a red silk veil[40] which falls behind as far down as the hem of the dress covering their two braids. It is fastened to the back of the dress. They wear a silk headdress which is wrapped around the head seven times and resembles a Turkish turban.[41] Their earrings resemble large rings as thick as one's little finger. It is perhaps for this reason that they are called ear*rings*.[42] They put kohl on their eyes and henna on their hands, as has already been mentioned in the section dealing with the bride. Most of the virgins wear the blouse and shirt alone and cover their head with a silk scarf, as do the married women from the borders of El Qsar almost to the limits of Marrakesh. Their breasts remind one of the passage in the tractate Yoma— "they are seen, but not seen."[43] You do not actually see them, but you can make out their size and contour. (We do not have to imagine a woman in a chemise only in order to understand the talmudic metaphor, for that would not be seemly.)

When the Hebrew women go out of doors, they cover themselves with a shawl, pulling the edge of it across their face so as to cover all but their eyes.[44] These are the "veiled women" mentioned in the tractate Shabbat.[45] This Moroccan fashion helps clarify for us the veils mentioned by Isaiah,[46] as well as the verse "they stripped me of my mantle."[47]

The Arab women wrap themselves in a sackcloth. Their feet are swathed in rags.[48] They carry their infants on their back or a bundle of filthy rags.[49] Their faces are hidden by a white garment. Nothing can be seen from beneath it except a single eye.[50] The Arab country folk go about in summer as naked as the day they were born. Only the women gird a sackcloth to protect their honor.

The jealousy of Arab men regarding their wives is as fierce as Hell.[51] A man's jealousy of his son, his brother, even his own father, burns like a fire. Men are not allowed to be where women are. Take for example the incident involving the Moroccan Emperor and his son which was related to me by the Viennese gentleman.[52]

Were it not for the following experience that I had in Tangier, I would not have been able to describe the female costume: One day, a chicken wandered out of my house and ran into the bedroom of an Arab home. In my eagerness to recapture it, I ran in there after it, dressed in my European clothes. The man of the house was not home, so I stood there a few minutes to chat with the woman, because Arab women are not unwilling to talk to Christians. Only the fear of their husbands keeps them in their home. But by the same token, it only increases their passion. Any deprivation creates desire and leads them to adultery behind their husbands' backs and under their very noses. Whenever anyone, Muslim or Jew, male or female, visits someone's home, they take off their shoes and leave them at the entrance. When an Arab comes home and finds a woman's slippers at the door, he will wait outside even though he is the master of the house. For it does happen that some women, married or unmarried, would set eyes upon a man and arrange a rendezvous between them. In such cases, the male lover dresses up in feminine costume, covering his face, and leaves female shoes at the entrance so he can come in to make love. When the husband comes home, he waits outside till the lover leaves. And as he passes by him, the husband would not dare to ask him, "Who are you? And where are you going?"

The Maghrebi Jews grow their beard, but shave their head like the Arabs. Most European Jews allow the hair of the head to grow, but shave their beard like the Christians. The Polish Jews (and following them many Jews in the cities of Germany) leave both hair and beard in order to be different from the Gentiles. Perhaps it is proper for one group to exchange customs with the other, as we find mentioned a number of times in the Talmud, "one man follows the custom of his locale, and the other that of his,"[53] as in the case of Eliezer Ze'era's black shoes in the tractate Bava Qama.[54]

Because I became endeared and respected among the Jews, I made a great effort to maintain and increase their good graces in future sermons as well. I preached every Sabbath over a three-month period in twelve synagogues. There was only one more. For all these successes, may God Who grants wisdom and causes men to find favor be Blessed. My sermons were wonderful for the educated and awesome for the ignorant. During these calm moments of respite,[55] I naïvely thought that I could never fail. But my cruel Fate thought otherwise and stirred up storms on the quiet sea. Listen attentively to what I have to say in the next chapter, and you will see what lay in store for me.

8

I have always believed that only a philosopher or a dumb beast could avoid knowing new things, because the passion for knowledge is implanted in the heart of man from the moment he bursts forth from the womb. All our wisdom is required to guide it on the right path. If someone dares to fancy that this passion has been severed from his soul and extinguished from his heart, do not believe it! It burns within him even as he ignores it. Our heart is bound to our desires. They may be estranged or weakened, but they will only die when the man expires. If I have observed correctly, such are the hearts of all mankind. If I have not, so it is then with you, O my heart.

I met a Renegado in the market, who accompanied me to the outskirts of the city during the breeze of the day. At the city gate, I saw a crowd of naked blacks washing their clothing at the spring. They were stamping on them with their feet. I thought to myself that this is why the Hebrew word *rōgēl* is "laundryman."[1] I asked my companion if he was circumcised, and if so how? He replied that he was, and that it was done with a pair of pincers similar to those used to cut the wick of a candle. He told me that he still eats pork, drinks wine, and does not fast during Ramadan—all of which are great sins for the Arabs.[2]

There was a Negro with him. I asked him about the palms of his hands and the soles of his feet which were white. He informed me that the blacks are the descendants of Ham. When Noah, Ham's father, cursed him, his skin turned black. He wept and pleaded with him, and his father out of compassion, took pity on him so that his palms and soles became white again. On account of this, however, they were subjugated and sold into slavery, thus fulfilling their forefather's curse—"Cursed be Canaan, the lowest of slaves shall he be to his brothers."[3] When I heard this, I understood.

Twice a week there is an auction called *delāl*.[4] (It is related to the root *s-l-l* in Hebrew, because the Arabs have a *sādī* which is pronounced like Hebrew *dalet*.[5] Thus, for example, "my lips quivered."[6] *Dellāl*[7] is the herald as mentioned in Daniel;[8] that is, the voice that calls out. Here it is the voice of the man who periodically walks around selling as at an auction.) In this type of *delāl*, they also sell black men and women. Slaves and maidservants follow behind the slave driver. The buyer will examine a maidservant as he would examine a sheep. She then becomes his permanent possession. He may either keep her as his slave or be harsh to her and resell her to another. In olden times, even whites and Jews were sold, as we know from the story of Joseph and from the Mosaic ordinances.[9]

Just as the slaves are considered to be the descendants of Ham, so the villagers who are called *el-ghārib* (that is, the people of the Maghreb) are descendants of the Philistines.[10] So they are called by the Jews. These are the Sons of Kedar who are mentioned in the verse of Isaiah—"All the flocks of Kedar,"[11] which in the Targum of Jonathan is translated "Arabs," because their faces are black like a clay cooking pot (Heb. *qedēra*).[12] The sharīfs vaunt themselves as being the seed of Aaron. (The word *sharīf* means "priest," as in the verse—"One of the Seraphs flew over to me with a burning coal in his hand," which reminds one of the incense ceremony.[13] Our sages have said that the angel Michael sacrifices souls, and thus we say in the liturgy "the offerings of Israel."[14]) These men are also considered to be holy. Once, when I was at the yeshiva, one of these sharifs came in. Everyone got up to kiss him on the shoulders. I asked why, and he said that a sharīf is like Aaron (he knew that Aaron was a priest). I asked him who was the first sharīf, and he told me Sidi (my Master) So-and-So. I then inquired, "Who ordained him to be a priest? For Aaron was ordained by God Himself." He could not answer me, because he was afraid of being put to shame and made to look foolish. The Jews who were present were all signaling me to keep quiet—some by blinking their eyes, others by shuffling their feet, and still others by indicating with their fingers that I should keep still.[15] They made light of my naïveté, saying that I was a visitor who did not know the ways of the country. Each of them, according to his means, gave him a gift of money to mollify him. So he left us, defeated in spirit, but with silver in his purse. The wickedness of the Gentiles and the conditions of exile were a double bridle for my impulsiveness. God's loving-kindness protected me, for I was not stoned or tortured on account of my questions and what I had said.

Here is something else I saw in Tetuan: One of my students took me to see the local mint.[16] The gold and silver comes from the regions of Guinea which is close to Morocco and where there is trade in gold dust. However, when they cannot purify the gold or assay its fineness, they melt down Spanish bullion and convert it into their coins. From the quality and form of their coins, you can appreciate how poor they are. The most valuable Moroccan coin is the *mithqāl* (it is a cognate of Hebrew *mishqāl*, or "weight"). It comes in both a silver and a gold version.[17] It is worth approximately one and a half Thaler. It is divided into ten *ūqiyas* or dirhams of low-grade silver.[18] Each *ūqiya* is divided into four *mūzūnas* (the word is a cognate of Hebrew *mōznayīm*, or "scale," similar to *mishqāl* above), also called *ujūh*, or *blanquillos* in Spanish. The *mūzūna* is divided into twenty-five *fils* (cognate to Hebrew *peles*, or "balance"). They distinguish between the *mithqāl*, the *mūzūna*, and the *fils* by having each smaller in size than the next. This caused me to notice that the verb used in the biblical verse "weigh the path of your feet,"[19] is not *sheqōl*, but rather *pallēs*, and thus the message is "guide your footsteps in righteousness even in small things."[20] Each fils is 3 *zalīḥ*.[21] Two thousand *zalīḥ* equals a Thaler. They will argue and even come to blows with each other over a single *zalīḥ*. *Perūta* in Jewish usage designates a small coin or a petty sum.[22] Thus they say: *mā ʿandī ḥettā prūṭ* (which means, "I haven't a penny").

During the time I was attending the yeshiva, there appeared one day some new faces. One of the newcomers who had the reputation of being a great man was sitting with the elders next to the rabbi.

His name was Rabbi Solomon d'Avila.[23] He was a native of Tetuan, but now lived in Rabat. The rabbi bid him to look after me if I should go to his city, and he replied that he wished I would come. The others with him were secretaries in the royal office of estate taxes. I was astounded to see that they are able to perform the most difficult computation by heart with speed and accuracy. They are forced to learn to do this for two reasons—because of the shortage of books and because they are spurred on by their superiors who do not allow them a moment's rest to think.

One day, I found the members of the yeshiva terribly perplexed over having to find the square area of the field requiring two seahs of seed which is mentioned in the tractate Shabbat.[24] They kept digging, but were unable to come up with the answer. I apprised them of the solution. From that day forth, they brought every difficult matter to me. Shortly afterwards, they asked me whether I could understand Ibn Ezra's Commentary to the Torah. I answered that although he is venerated for his commentary and is considered a marvel for his words of wisdom, and although one needs a commentary to his commentary and to his commentators, nevertheless, in many instances, he is not so lofty that we cannot comprehend him.[25] I suggested that we should look for ourselves, and neither let our fear inflate minor points, nor our pride minimize major ones. They showed me Ibn Ezra's remark on the verse in the portion Va-Ethannan which begins "These words the Lord spoke unto all your assembly."[26] Ibn Ezra comments "The intent is the Ten Commandments and not the speech." What he means to say is that the passage is telling us to remember the essence and not merely the words themselves. For the Ten Commandments are already stated in the portion Yitro where, however, the text differs in a few words.[27] When I pointed this out to them, they looked at each other in amazement.

In addition to these three instances, another preacher came to show me a passage concerning the harvest season in the book *Understanding the Seasons*.[28] He told me that he had shown it to all the scholars, but none could explain it to him. The author was trying to show the relationship between the Four Species and the concepts of measurement.[29] It was so simple that even a child just beginning his studies could have pointed it out to them. I told the man what the author meant. "When he heard the dream told and interpreted,"[30] he was in awe and went to tell all the scholars all the marvels he had experienced. These incidents will give you some idea of these people's level of understanding. After these three incidents, could I rightly congratulate myself for having fortified any wavering hearts in their opinion of me? However, you shall see, that even with these people, I had "made an error in judgment."[31] For after all, who is above jealousy?

When I was to give my last sermon, there was a great uproar in the synagogue on account of a group of men from Gibraltar, whose rabbi was Rabbi Judah Halevi's son-in-law. He is highly regarded among the pietist circle known as the Abstainers. They are so called because they fast six days a week, night and day.[32] The English Vice Consul, who was one of their leaders, spoke up and swore, "Only the God-fearing should preach!" Another of them called out, "This is not the time for a sermon!" Some rose to leave. Some stood up in opposition to them. In the end, I did not preach. I left and went to the Chief Rabbi. I told him that he should avenge himself for this, not for my sake, but for his own. For the murmuring was not about me, but concerned him. The man was reproaching him by this and was pointing out to him that he had done wrong by supporting me. I spoke in a burning rage, and the rabbi and his entourage quaked at what I had to say. The rabbi made an effort to hide how upset he was and asked me to calm down, be quiet, and not to worry. He promised to restore my honor to what it had been originally. But he told me, "We are still grieving because, to our sorrow, our father-in-law the rabbi has died, and our term of mourning is not yet over. All the scholars have been eulogizing him in their sermons, each on the Sabbath assigned him." He went on to tell me that I would be included among them, and that he would designate a place for me. I was to receive the sermon on the last and most important Sabbath. "We shall all come together as a group to hear you," he said "and all the people around you will see my conduct. For I am showing you great deference. Now go in peace." I bowed low and left.

I carefully divided my sermon into its separate components and based it upon the theme of life and death. After the introductory remarks and some rhetorical flourishes in honor of the rabbi and the congregation, I pointed out that all that is dear and strong is called life, whereas all want and deficiency is death. "To furnish us with a livelihood," said Ezra about Cyrus' edict of permission.[33] "Bringing back to life the spirit of the lowly," said Isaiah about consolation.[34] "You restored me to health and brought me back to life," says King Hezekiah about his recovery.[35] "Life and grace," said Job about the good. In referring to all creation, Nehemiah said, "You give life to them all."[36]

On the opposite theme, I cited such passages as—"Do not let her be like the dead," which refers to the leper;[37] and "Give me children, or else I die," which refers to the lack of offspring.[38] I also mentioned that the blind and the poor are considered as dead,[39] and so too, the person in terror, as it is written "and his heart died within him."[40]

Indeed every man on earth is a part of the whole, like a limb of the body. Thus the intensity of suffering at its loss will be in proportion to the value of limb or part. Abraham's reward greatly increased when he offered up his beloved only son for sacrifice.[41] David would not mourn over the death of his infant son. Why? Because he had already done so for the seven days preceding his death.[42] He cried out and wept and was distressed for his son Absalom even though he was disloyal and rebellious.[43] I went on to recount the story of the Shunamite woman[44] whose son grew and became old enough to walk (as it is written, "he went out to his father") and to speak ("and he cried to his father, 'Oh my head, my head!' "). She did not respond the way David had done in the case of his infant son's death, when he said, "I shall go to him, but he will never come back to me."[45] On the contrary, she ran to the man of God, threw her arms around his feet, and implored him, saying, "As God lives, and as you live, I shall not leave you."

In the next part of my sermon, I observed that the pain at the loss of a father is greater than the pain at the loss of a son. For the latter can be replaced, but not the former. Did not Jeremiah cry out when God intensified our troubles—"We have become orphans without a father."[46] When David arrived in Ziklag, having learned on the way that the Amalekites had razed it, he and the men who accompanied him burst into tears.[47] Why did they weep? After all, we are told that the Amalekites had not killed anyone.

They were crying over the women who were taken captive, although they could be ransomed. How did they weep? "Until they had no strength left to cry." What then should the people of Tetuan do for the sake of the rabbi who has been gathered to his people? For he was not just a father to his family alone, but to all the community. How great is the pain at his loss. His sons have lost in him their father, students their master, orphans their helper, widows their support, the poor their savior, and all men their splendor, their shining light, and their glory!

These words were delivered vigorously in a booming voice to those people whose ways are crooked and whose casuistry is devious.[48] When they heard these original interpretations, it was like a rolling thunder in their hearts. They appeared to tremble and were as if in a dream.

In the second half of the sermon, I multiplied my signs and my wonders with sayings of the sages. For a righteous man, blameless[49] in this world, is a divine Torah scroll interpreted. The tablets of his heart are the work of God, and the writing is God's writing, incised upon the tablets.[50] From there the Torah goes forth and the word of the Lord.[51] If such a man dies or becomes weak, the tablets are broken. In accordance with his strength in life and in death, the tablets and the fragments of the former tablets[52] are placed in his coffin of honor with him. For he left a blessing after him. Then I brought the dictum from the tractate Menaḥot—"Be careful with regard to the scholar because of the tablets and the fragments of the tablets."[53] I connected this to the statement in the tractate Pesaḥim: "From whence do we derive that the tablets and the fragments of the former tablets were placed in the ark?"[54] I caused a stir by raising the question: which is dependent upon which? Then I justified them together by examining them. With this sermon, I redeemed my honor, added to my advantage, and I put to shame all those who had sneered at me. This was how all my sermons ended. I realized, however, that "he who is muddled by them will not become wise."[55] For if they got the point, it would arouse jealousy, and if they remained ignorant, they would think I was taunting them. Well, you get a thorn with every rose.[56]

Three days before Rosh ha-Shana, the French Vice Consul came to say in the name of the English Vice Consul who was in Meknes, that he had been ordered to conduct me there to be secretary to Eliahu Levi, a counselor of the Sultan.[57] Several days later he returned to say that I should not go and that when the other vice consul comes back, he would tell me why. During Sukkot, the English Vice Consul returned from Meknes and said that he did not want to involve me in Eliahu's troubles because he had fallen from royal favor.

In Tangier, I had been careful to escape the snares of love. In Tetuan, I was almost caught like a bird in a trap with my landlord's daughter. Her beauty[58] and innocence captured my heart without my even realizing it. Jealousy flowed through my bones. Passion afflicted me. Fear held me back, and honor chided me. Love! Mistress of desires. Where is your safe refuge? Your honey is mixed with poison. "Your wine is cut with water."[59] We find you in our heart, but we do not know how. You afflict our souls, and we do not know why. If you are God's daughter, why do you torture us? And if you are the Serpent's daughter, why do you do good?

This land made desolate by the evil of its inhabitants, the Jew oppressed and ground under, wearing the garb of slavery, his beard like a bird's beak—all these things disappeared before my eyes at that time. I would say as in the words of Pope on vice: We first endure, then pity, then embrace.[60] But before I reached the brink, there was a turn of events that carried me off.

On the morning of the first of Shevat,[61] I heard that a Tunisian named Jacob Attal[62] had come to the city and with him Eliahu. I knew of this Tunisian and his brother back in Gibraltar. These two scoundrels, who were full of deceit and intrigue, had had to flee from there because they had delivered gunpowder to the Emperor of Morocco without the permission of the British governor in Gibraltar. I asked innocently what was the disposition of this Eliahu's case. I was informed that he had been an imperial official. However, the Emperor became angry with him. (No one knew why.) He ordered that his beard be cut off and that he be led to prison, where he spent many days. Now he had been released to serve the Tunisian. The following morning before the eastern sky lit up, someone knocked on my door. I quickly got dressed and went out. He said that he was Eliahu Levi's son-in-law, and that his father-in-law had written him to have me sent to him without a moment's delay. "A horse has been prepared for your journey," he told me, "as well as food for the way and a man to accompany you." I asked, "But wasn't he given to the Tunisian as a servant?" "His enemies lied about him," he replied. "The Emperor has restored him to his position and has raised him above all his courtiers." I was trying to go over my thoughts, but the man was pressing me. I cast my soul into the arms of Fortune, gathered up my clothes, said farewell, and rode off.

9

So many changes of fortune! Time is true only in its vicissitudes. I had once set out on this path to become a secretary, and after two years I was still walking upon it. Who could know what might befall me? I could do nothing but wait. This time there was no one with me except the Arab who owned the horse. At night the sky was my blanket and the earth my bed. The moment I arrived at the city the following day,[1] I removed my filthy attire, put on fine clothes, shaved my beard, and went to meet my new master.

The man was well on in years, his face spotted with pock marks. He was sitting on a pillow in preparation for lunch. He greeted me in a low voice. His residence was a large building which had formerly been the royal offices for estate taxes. I took this to be a good sign, for only those who are close to the king receive such an honor.

During the meal, he told me his personal history in pure Spanish.[2] He recounted that the King had instructed him to import cannons and gunpowder from England. He took care to do as he was commanded. However, because of piracy on the high seas, the ships which were already on their way were afraid to continue. The Sultan, presuming that he had made them turn back, imprisoned him and fined him three thousand piastres.[3] (He never mentioned to me the matter of his beard which had already grown back over his face.) And now that the King had regretted the unfortunate incident, he hastily released him from prison, restored

his title, and instructed him to send for a merchant from Gibraltar
with whom he could carry on trade. He added—to further boast
of his honored status—that long ago he had even been an envoy
in Spain on the King's commission.[4]

From his actions as well as his reputation, it was known that this
was a man of crooked ways. However, I never realized that he
would be craftier than any serpent or than all the beasts of the
field. He was secretive in everything he did; not a thought would
pass from his lips.[5] He would reward profusely all who publicized
his glory, while depriving any who darkened his good name or
brought disgrace upon him. He was king of the arrogant and would
walk proudly erect,[6] speaking as though his words were a mighty
wind. He would even dare to pass an Arab mosque without re-
moving his shoes in a display of his power at court so that all
would come to fear him.[7]

Do not hesitate to believe these things after hearing that the
Jews are downtrodden and oppressed, for this was someone who
was close to the throne. Such people, whether Gentile or Jew, are
merely instruments of the King. As long as the King needs their
services they are valuable instruments. No one dares to harm them
lest he be devoured. But if they lose the King's favor for even a
moment, they are lost forever like their own excrement, and those
who knew them will ask, "Where are they?"[8] They are feared, not
loved. Capable only of evildoing, they know nothing of benevo-
lence. They thrive only on the destruction of others. They would
disown their fathers and mothers, seeing nothing of them. They
would not recognize their brothers, nor would they even know
their own children. Such a man would befriend another in word
and win his heart, present him with a gift, and then return to plot
his murder. They draw the mighty with false hopes and drag the
young in their terror. But as they stand upon their heights of great-
ness, the abyss widens under their feet.[9] One word from the King's
mouth and they vanish. A nation will groan under their rule; a
town will rejoice at their death. The majority of them will not die
as most men do, nor will they meet the fate of other men—
"whether by sentence of death, or corporal punishment, by con-
fiscation of property, or imprisonment."[10] Their bodies might be
cut up, and their homes turned into dunghills.[11]

I have found only one in a thousand who graced others with his goodness. Not a single one of them has come to a natural end. They are called *saḥāb al-sulṭān*, which means "the ruler's friends." Hence, when someone tells you that so-and-so has been raised to exalted heights by the King, pity him and pray on his behalf—or pray on your own behalf, for he has put his soul in the stocks and is preparing for destruction. Should you hear it said that a certain individual is one of the nobles of the land, belongs to the nation's elite, and is of aristocratic stock, do not believe it. As the Lord lives, these are lies which are said to flatter him, for he is feared. He is nothing more than a stone from the dust heap, remaining the chief cornerstone only until the King's desires are satisfied. Among the King's retainers there is no order of prominence. The will of the King grants life or death, impoverishes or enriches, exalts or brings low. Thus, in one moment they might be raised to the heavens, and in the next, cast down into the abyss, and their soul will experience its everlasting torment or bliss.

If only I had known all of this before setting foot in the land of Morocco, such things would not happen to me today. But who will read the omens for us?

I went to my room and stayed there, waiting for him to summon me and prepared to obey his orders. Two days passed, but there was no sign of him. On the third day, Eliahu came with a document waving[12] in his hand.

"Read it," he said to me, and left.

It contained the accounts of his merchandise that was in the hands of others. He wanted me to see from this that his hope for financial recovery was not lost. That night he told me to bring his account records to be read before him. The following day, he called me to his office and ordered me to write him a letter in English to a certain merchant in Gibraltar. I could not let this opportunity pass. I asked Eliahu's steward to give me some money to make some purchases, which he did.

A few days later, the Tunisian and his brother arrived in Tangier.[13] May the curse of God be on them both! They were created only to oppress people and to plague the human race. The younger worked for the elder, and together they would go wherever the King ordered them. I was very sorry that they came to lodge at our house. However, the King's servants were quick to persuade him to continue with his itinerary, and, parting with his brother, he left our house to lodge wherever he might find himself.

While waiting for a reply from the merchant, I toured the country throughout its length and breadth. When I was still in London,[14] I had heard that a Jew from Gibraltar by the name of Cardozo had been executed by order of the Emperor of Morocco, and during my first stay in Tangier, I was told that his brother remained there in prison. This time, I went with my friend[15] to visit him in prison. Upon entering I was struck by the horrible stench of the dungeon. Through a hole in the door, I perceived through the darkness all the prisoners, their legs bound in iron shackles, with collars on their necks, tied one to another so that they had to sit, stand, or lie down in unison. They pointed the man out to me, and I approached him. He was sitting on the ground by himself, chained only with leg irons. He was dressed like those of his country. The gauntness of his face confirmed his suffering. His beard was unshaven and his moustache unkempt. Seeing a man in Christian clothes, and learning that I was a Jew, he threw his face to the ground and wept. "Ha," he shouted in Spanish. "Why did you come, my friend, to remind me of my wrongdoings and make a spectacle of my misery? For two years I have been sitting here rotting away. Earth! Will you not cover my blood? I would much rather die than continue to live as I am. And as for you, Eliahu,[16] what is my crime or my sin that you have persecuted me this way?"

I attempted to calm him for he was bitter and to console him that his troubles would not last forever and that for the God-fearing such suffering is the beginning of hope. He became calm and quietly said to me, "Forgive me, my friend. I was carried away by my sorrows."

I went on to say, "Tell me about yourself, if you please, so I might know you. I have heard about you from afar. Perhaps you will find some relief in discussing your woes. And what is this matter of Eliahu that you just now recalled?"

He replied, "I shall do as you ask, for it was kind of you to come into this darkness and comfort me. But, in God's name, bury my words in the depths of your heart!" He then composed himself, sat up and related the following story:

"The land of my birth is Gibraltar, land of the free, land of delight. We were three brothers. One took up residence in London, while my younger brother and I, induced by a desire to make money and by our knowledge of Arabic,[17] came to Morocco, where for several years we were engaged in commerce on behalf of the Emperor.

What kind of man was this brother of mine? He was handsome, charming, intelligent, and sharp witted. The King never made a move without him. Through his word those close to the throne lost the King's favor, and through his word they gained it.

After some time, we were ordered by the King to go to Mazagan and to join Eliahu Levi, also a deputy of the King. (That seed of wickedness and ruin—may he be struck dead, and his name heard no more!) We were to deal with the province's wheat and other produce of the land. God granted us success in all that we did. We wanted to bring our other brother over from London so that he might enjoy our wealth and good fortune as well. I wrote him a letter to which he replied:

> The desire for property and wealth will not tempt me to leave my home of security. The Maghrebi countries would be fine were they not ruined by the evil ways of their inhabitants. Both the King and the people are deceitful. Their hearts plot evil. In his wicked foolishness he will err, and the innocent will bear the burden of his mistakes. He is quick to anger—and who can stand before a fool in his fury? If only all the people who are there could get out!
> May God be with you.

And he signed as was his custom: CARDOZO.

We filed the letter away, and, with nothing more said about the matter, forgot about it entirely. Sometime after, jealousy gave rise to quarrels between Eliahu and my brother. My brother was overbearing by nature and would boast to Eliahu of his power and prominence over him at the royal court. His haughtiness brought on his downfall. He sought an opportunity to remove Eliahu from our company, and found one. When we separated, the letters that we had thought were innocuous remained in Eliahu's possession.

At that time, the King wanted to change our positions and to transfer us to the port of Tangier. My brother, however, beseeched the King to send him to Larache. One day when my brother was boasting to and mocking Eliahu, he became very annoyed and began plotting to bring down my brother. He combed the letters, looking for some snare, and found the note that my other brother had sent from London. Why didn't we burn it in the beginning? But who would have believed that such great frauds and despicable acts could be devised? He placed the letter in his pocket. Day by day, as my brother's words angered him more and more, Eliahu would reply, 'Take care, because I have the power to do you harm.' My brother had no recollection of the letter, and continued in his ways until Eliahu could no longer contain himself. When he heard that my brother was out of favor with the King because of the matter of the Tangier port, he said to himself that the time had come to retaliate.

What did he do? My hair bristles when I remember it! He cut off the upper line of the letter. Then he came to the King in Marrakesh and acted fearful before him, as though he were tense and worried about something. The King inquired why he was there, and he replied, 'My Lord the King, you have power over my life. Draw your sword and kill me, but do not command me to speak.'

'What has happened to you?' the King asked. 'Do not conceal anything from me. Speak, and you will not die.'

'Your person and honor are dear to me,' Eliahu replied. 'Come read this and be amazed.' Then he gave him the letter which was written in Spanish.

'Is there no Christian priest here who can be ordered to explain the meaning of this writing?' He asked (for Eliahu was afraid to speak). 'Have him brought to me.' And he was summoned. Upon hearing the content of the note when it

was translated for him into Arabic, horror took hold of the
King's flesh.[18] His face was distorted, and he roared like a
young lion in his rage. Then he turned to the priest and
asked what was the sentence in Christian lands for one who
curses God and King, and he was told it was death.

The King ordered that Cardozo be brought to him. Now
my brother, knowing nothing of this, went cheerfully, as if
marching to the sound of fife and drum, to appear before the
King. As for the King, without even investigating the testimony and without even investigating the matter in order to
learn if the charge was justified, who had written the letter,
or why it was torn and in poor condition, poured out his
wrath and showed him the letter, saying, 'See the fruit of my
kindness to you! You have spilled your own blood. The King
and His throne are blameless.' Then he commanded his attendants to seize him: 'Take him and strike him down!' As the
words left the King's mouth, my brother's expression was un-
comprehending, and he was taken away still dumbfounded
from shock. Before he could say a word to justify himself or
confess, they gagged him and put a noose around his neck.
They beat him, pierced his head, and crushed his temples.
His corpse was dragged away, hacked to pieces and burned,
and the ashes scattered. His picture was exhibited on plac-
ards that were given to children to be horribly mutilated like
manure in the markets and the streets. The King had money
distributed among them because they justified his judgment.

And I, impoverished and grieved, was imprisoned. May the
Lord judge between Eliahu and me. If there is a God in
heaven, I shall see myself avenged. The voice of my brother's
blood cries out against him from the earth.[19] Complete destruction will come to the person who has caused me so
much pain. I kept quiet out of fear of Eliahu's power. There
is no one who would take the trouble on my account to
speak up for me with the King so that he might release me
from this prison, knowing 'that they have distorted my cause
with falsehood,'[20] and that I have been dealt with unjustly.
Eliahu's evil has already come back to him, and he has taken
his deed upon his own head, even though he is still in the

service of the Sultan, while I am like a lost thing. I am forgotten as if I were dead. Now you know my suffering. Nothing
has been concealed from you."

When he finished talking, he fell into my arms and wept over
his cruel fate. Tears flowed from my eyes as he spoke. I told him,
"I am sorry for you, my brother. Turn your path toward God and
put your trust in Him. He will judge you justly. Your days of weeping will pass, and He will bring you out to a life of plenty. I shall
never reveal what you have told me. And you, as an intelligent
person, will keep my visit to you a secret, for I also am in his
service. We must not arouse sleeping vipers, lest they might sting
us."

"May God be gracious to you, my son," he said, "so that the end
will not be bitter."

I went on to ask him about an incident involving a certain Arab
in London. Arabs can be found both in London and its suburbs.
They go to the homes of officials with credentials that they themselves have forged, claiming that they have come from afar, that
they are the scions of noble families, that their ship had been
wrecked in some faraway place[21] and all their possessions lost.
One of these individuals knocked on the door of Lord Sydney[22]
one day, and when the latter refused to give him what he wanted,
he took some stones and smashed the windows. Lord Sydney ordered him seized and imprisoned. He wisely decided not to punish
him himself, but had him brought instead to Tangier to have a
taste of the Sultan's wrath. I asked Cardozo what had been done
to this Arab. He told me that he had been with him in prison and
related everything that happened to him. When he was brought
before the Sultan, he responded to the charges indignantly: "My
lord, King, I wish that I had not had to return before all the Christians were finished off. I was zealous for your good name and for
the glory of our faith. For who may speak against our Prophet and
go unpunished." He was released and given a gift by the Sultan.
Thus, they are haughty in their religion, and their zeal is false.

I bade him farewell, saying that we would see one another again,
and went out. All that night my thoughts terrified me as I lay in
bed. From that time on, I could see Eliahu only as the terror of

God and the Lord's abomination, though I never revealed my hidden thoughts to him.

The following Sabbath, Eliahu went to the synagogue expecting a *piyyūt* to be sung in his honor when he would be called up to the Torah. Thus he would renew his glory in the eyes of the Jews, for he had regained his power and honor. The Jews in the Maghreb go wild over their *piyyūtīm*. They compose them on behalf of all who are called up to read a portion of the Torah during the festivals. Their *piyyūtīm* display only rhyme, but neither meter, nor prosodic measure. They place the shewa wherever they please, as in *The Songs of Glory*.[23] The subject matter of these poems is without value[24]—like most of the books of interpretation and commentary by Polish authors. They are many, but worthless. All of man's wisdom is in vain when applied to the art of poetry. For it is a gift of God and a mark of favor to special people who have been graced and blessed by Nature before they have even emerged from the womb.[25]

As I left the synagogue, I could hear shouting in the city. A flute was playing, a whistle shrieking, and guns firing. An Arab maiden was being taken to the house of her bridegroom. She was seated on a mule. A basket had been placed over her so that no eye might behold her. Those who were shooting fired at each of the mule's footsteps one by one. Mind you, all of this was done in the midst of general confusion.[26]

Sometime later I went to visit Cardozo in prison, but he was no longer to be found there. I was led to a spacious upper apartment which he had to himself. He was pacing to and fro. "What is this, Cardozo?" To which he replied that he was to go to Meknes by order of the Sultan with the brother of the city governor. The brother of the Tunisian was also to accompany him. I prayed that the God of Salvation would grant him deliverance, and warned him to be on his guard and keep his eyes open on account of this cunning man.

The governor's brother had just returned from crushing rebels and had brought with him six hundred heads to be displayed upon the ramparts of the tower as is customary, so that people will know the power of the King and fear him.

It was the Passover season. At the Seder,[27] each person follows his own ancestors' custom. No one is quite like the other. The mountains may depart and the hills be removed, but a man will not depart from his tradition.[28] "After a time, times, and a half,"[29] all these differences will come to an end, and we will know what the outcome of these things will be.[30] I cannot resist, however, telling what I observed on the first night of the Counting of the Omer.[31] For reasons that no one could explain to me, they bring salt to the synagogue, place it on the reader's platform, and as they leave, each one takes a pinch to bring home. I must confess that I stood there wondering like a pillar of salt.[32]

On the evening of the conclusion of Passover, the Moroccan Jews arrange tables with all sorts of sweets and pay visits to each other. The guests eat what they wish and bless the master of the house.[33] What can the explanation for this be? Could it be comparable to "those who prepare a table for Fortune"?[34] Should we receive the Lord Who is Exalted in His hidden place of splendor with these offerings? Is His Glory to be pleased as a mortal is pleased by our iniquitous devices? What does the Lord require of us? Only to do justly and love mercy![35]

10

I have heard the slander of the many (but then, the ignorant are many). They are vipers who spit their venom upon philosophers who delve into the source of truth. They speak without any knowledge. Let us understand the definition of words and not become divided over the issue. What is the meaning of the word *philosophy*?—The love of Wisdom. And what is Wisdom?—The knowledge of Truth. How is one to know the truth, if he does not search after it? If only we could indeed find it! Whenever people speak ill of philosophers, are they not themselves philosophizing? How can they support their arguments without it? Did not God's own prophets philosophize when they addressed the people? Did not even God Almighty philosophize with Job?[1] Furthermore, are not the laws we have received from our tradition derived from reason? Indeed they are.[2] You who ponder the Talmud! I am calling to you. When you make casuistic distinctions concerning the laws, are you not philosophizing? Did it not occur to you then to love wisdom? What is the difference between casuistry and dialectics? What is the difference between examination and investigation? Observe, that whoever speaks philosophizes according to his own powers of reason.

Sometime later, the merchant in Gibraltar[3] sent the manager of his business house to Tangier. He was Genoese and a friend of mine. Indeed, we had a marvelous friendship, like that of brothers. Eliahu was delighted he had come, because he saw that his former disgrace was not an obstacle to him and had not stained his honor.

Eliahu gave orders for provisions and a tent to be prepared, for in three days we were to set out for Meknes where the Sultan was then in residence.[4] We could delay no longer because the King's officers had come to hurry us on. We set out. At sunset, before it became dark, we halted out of fear of night bandits. We pitched our tent on a plain where there was a *duwwār*, or circular encampment. The name recalls the Hebrew cognate *dūr* in the biblical verse "and level the round hills,"[5] or "circular rows" in the tractate Megilla.[6]

The *duwwārs* consist of huts arranged in a semi- or full circle.[7] These are their villages. That is why they are called "tent dwellers."[8] Or, as it is said in the Vision of Babylon—"no Arab will pitch a tent there."[9] We decided to pitch our tent near this place. When the local inhabitants saw men with close cropped beards,[10] they surrounded us to stare at our faces. Even the women came out of their dwellings, their faces hidden by their cloaks. Every rarity creates wonder, and wonder is born of ignorance, which in turn begets wisdom. However, in the Maghreb only wonder is born, whereas in Europe it also begets.

We went into our tent. Eliahu was the first to break the silence in his gruff fashion and asked the Gentile after the welfare of his master. He replied that his master was well and had given him orders to remind Eliahu to pay his debts, because many days had passed since the date the payment fell due, and he was angry. Eliahu's face sank, and he replied, "Did I not write to my associate instructing him to pay back my debt in cash out of our joint holdings!" "Your colleague," he rejoined, "has deceived you regarding this sum and your joint holdings. You are still in debt to my master."

I had heard the sound of this trumpet before and was not careful to open my eyes to my own situation thinking that Fortune would smile upon him. In my imagination I had exaggerated his importance before Kings and ministers. This misjudgment of mine stayed with me until my predicament dawned upon me when there was no way out.

We continued on our journey when it became light. While riding across a great plain, we suddenly saw what looked like a large army arranged in bands.[11] It was market day on that very same field. As we approached them, Eliahu wished to buy some fodder for our animals, and he rode among them on his mule. The Berbers fell upon him and would have killed him. They did not know that he was a royal servant. He was a Jew, and that was enough for them. Eliahu did not lose his nerve in the situation. He plucked up his courage and began shouting at them. He haughtily informed them of his importance and rebuked them. When he mentioned the King, they trembled at his words and were stunned by his reproach. You should understand that Arabs—even if they are slaves—may ride on horseback. Whereas Jews—even if ministers—walk like slaves. A Jew may not ride except when he goes from one city to another. When he leaves town, he mounts up. When he approaches town, he dismounts. But under no circumstances may he ride in the city streets or in a crowd of people. Christians are considered *francos* (freemen), and so too are European Jews. You may see the like of this referred to in the lamentation for Tyre—"Dedan was your merchant of freedom clothes for riding."[12] On the third day, while there was still some distance before we reached El Qsar,[13] we came to a mosque. The Arabs turned toward it raising their hands in front of their faces and prayed.[14] We went down from the shrine toward the city. We had to cross a rushing stream. It was in this stream that Mūlāy Muhammad son of the Emperor Mahrūq drowned when he came with Don Sebastian to fight his uncle Mahlūq.[15] All the Jews dismounted from their mules, and only Eliahu crossed over with us riding into the city.

On the sixth day, the skies were darkened with clouds, and we found ourselves in a driving rain. It was Friday afternoon, the Sabbath eve, and there on the roadside was a lion's den. Terrified and in panic we stayed close to one another. We urged our beasts on with prods on their flanks. Like people fleeing from the sword, we hastened to find a safe haven. We were tired and weary, but Eliahu would not let us enter Meknes, which was just a bowshot away. He went on ahead with his attendants and the Gentile, while we spent the Sabbath there until Sunday.

In the imperial cities of Meknes, Fez, and in the capital of Marrakesh, the Jews do not live in the city itself. Their quarter is at the outskirts. They can only enter the main part of the city bare-

foot.[16] All the Christians who come, stay with the Jews or by themselves in houses outside the walls, as in the case of the monks
there.[17] The Sultan's palace which was built by Spanish craftsmen
during the reign of Mūlāy Isma'īl was still standing as when it was
built.[18] The Jewish quarter lies between the palace and the main
part of town.[19] On Sunday, Eliahu went before the Sultan to inform
him of the Christian's arrival. The Christian, however, was not
summoned to appear before His Majesty for thirty days. Either the
King had no desire to see him, or he forgot about him, or he did
not leave his private quarters, or it was raining. Or perhaps all
these excuses were merely made up by Eliahu, as is the wont of
the Emperor's servants, to stretch things to the very limit of their
credibility.

There was a wedding in the house next door, and the Gentile
and I were invited. We went to take a look. It differed in two
respects from the weddings I had seen in Tangier. Just before the
bride leaves her father's house, an egg is broken on her head.[20]
Also, she is carried to her bridegroom's house on a chair like the
one on which Astasia was carried in the opera *Axur*,[21] or like the
ones borne by Gentiles on their shoulders for the images of their
dumb deities.[22] Likewise, the bride neither opened her mouth,
listened, looked, nor even moved. Even for this, Eliahu became
angry with me. He demanded to know why I had gone and taken
part in the wedding feasts without asking his permission. "Am I
not your master?" he said. "Without me you cannot lift a finger!
Perhaps you might even reveal my secret.[23] To make matters
worse, not only did you go on your own, but you even took the
Gentile with you. Watch yourself. Never do anything on your own
again. For if you do, you will most assuredly be removed from my
household and never see my face again."

I realized that he was looking for reasons to find fault in me in
order that he might send me away and be able to justify it. Or he
may have wanted to spoil the friendship between me and the
Gentile. He had been harsh with me in Tangier and kept it up
until he reached the stage he wanted. Now that he could bear the
burden no longer, because his patience was at an end, he sought
to unburden himself. However, all his strenuous efforts were in
vain, because the Gentile stood up for me and spoke forcefully

with him, telling him that I had not been sold to him as a slave, and furthermore, that he wished me to be his friend. Eliahu sought to appease the Gentile since he was the object of his own hopes.

The following day, he changed his attitude and ordered me to go to the scholars in the yeshiva. He had three aims in staying by my side: to keep me away from the Gentile, to keep me busy all day, and to make sure that I failed when I would be arguing with them during a debate on a talmudic controversy. Feigning innocence, I went and foiled his trick with my own. The method of study is the same everywhere, and indeed, I found some of their judgments to be correct. They showed me the interpretation someone had written on the tractate Berakhot where the biblical story of the sun standing still at Gibeon is mentioned.[24] The interpretation concludes that the sun did not actually stand still. For that would have caused the destruction of the entire structure of creation. Rather, a pillar of fire appeared in the sky that created the illusion of the sun shining until the Israelites wrought vengeance upon their foe. These Meknasis were inclined to accept that interpretation, or the interpretation of Maimonides in his *Eight Chapters*, who states that from the very beginning of creation, God planned that the sun should stand still at that particular moment, so that it would neither cause that which He had intended by His Will to fail, nor bring about the breakdown of creation.[25] These manifestations of my scholarship proved that I would not be put to shame among them. Instead of accusing me of philosophizing with them on speculation alone, they declared to me that they approved of it. Scholarly investigation makes a greater impression upon the intelligent man than a hundred words of idle gossip upon a fool.[26] For the wise man will do willingly what the fool will do only under coercion. If we educated children in this way from a young age, they would not become entangled in a thousand irremediable errors in maturity. I attended the yeshiva a day or two and then stopped.

Every day at noontime, I noticed a man coming to take a bowl of pottage and a piece of bread. I asked him who it was for, and he told me for Cardozo. Then I recalled what had happened before and exclaimed, "Merciful and Compassionate God! Is he still in prison? Has he reached the point where he has to beg for a loaf

Jewish jewelers in Meknes. Gérard Silvain, *Images et traditions juives* (Editions Astrid: Milan, 1980)

of bread?[27]—And from his enemies no less?" I knew that his day of darkness was at hand.[28] The man answered me that if he did not do this, his enemies would surely take his life.

The man went and told Cardozo what had happened. He later returned and called me out of the house to tell me that Cardozo wished to speak with me. I consulted with the Gentile who advised me to take care and not even let the name of Cardozo pass my lips for my blood would be upon my own head. I then told the servant to go tell Cardozo that I was deeply sympathetic to him, but it was not in my power to help him in his distress. I would only lose my own life and not save his. Being an intelligent man, he would understand at what I was hinting. I asked the servant to tell me how all of this had come about. He told me that the Tunisian had deceived him. Cardozo had left all he possessed with the Tunisian, who then absconded.[29] When the senior brother passed through here, he promised to repay what had been swindled in weekly installments.[30] He only made the first of the installments he promised, and that was all. "Aha!" I thought to myself, "I am lost in my misery because I did not listen to his advice, and he is lost because he did not listen to mine."[31]

In Meknes, I saw a *delāl* (auction) among the Jews.[32] It was an auction they were holding against their will. A portion of all merchandise brought to Morocco goes as customs duty to the King. When his storehouses are full he sells back to the Jews whatever he does not want at a price that he sets for them; and the Jews cannot refuse.

The Gentile became heartsick at his hopes deferred.[33] One day after eating, he suggested we take a walk outdoors to sightsee. He took along two men to guard us because the people of this city were not used to seeing Christians. When I arrived in Tangier, the first sight I encountered was the Arab blacksmiths. Here it was the silversmiths who are Hebrews. These silversmiths are craftsmen only. They themselves do not own any gold or silver. A hammer, some chisels, a file, a crucible, and a hearth—and there you have their shop and its equipment.[34] That is about all most of them have. The bracelets, earrings, and beads are negligible because they are so few. I remarked that their craftsmanship was not gorgeous, but it was appropriate to their means at hand, as one of them pointed out to me saying, "Our skill is greater than yours. For your improved tools show you how to work things, whereas we here are like an artisan without any tools at all." This same idea has been expressed by a poet who said:

> Necessity schools man in things that were too hard for him
>   before.
> Because of it, the warrior is able to sleep despite the din
>   of battle.
> Because of it, the sailor can hold a steady course amidst
>   the roar of crashing waves.

And because of it, even Death holds no fear.
When necessity requires, even the faint-hearted creatures
    will dare to be brave and pluck up courage.[35]

The city of Meknes has many dark covered streets resembling
caves in rocks. These are the streets of the merchants and vendors
of all sorts of goods. We toured the entire city and on our way
back we made the rounds of all the Jewish houses. No Jew gave
us even so much as a threatening look. The boys and girls ran
away from us (for the fear of Gentiles is engraved in their hearts).
Some brave souls greeted us. Who would dare open his mouth to
freemen? In one of the houses we stopped, we found the bride
who had been our neighbor in her new husband's home. She was
surrounded by girls who were feeding her slices of bread soaked
in water to fatten her up, for she was slender. This is their custom
and their notion of beauty.[36] They set before us olives in brine
and plenty of *eau de vie*. With each glass we placed a gift of money
in the bride's scarf or on her forehead to the accompaniment of
the crier's ululation for good luck as when the ox is slaughtered.[37]
The strength of the brandy combined with the salty olives made
us lightheaded and took its effect without our realizing. It did not
take much to overwhelm us. When we left, the trick the brandy
and olives had played upon us was plain for all to see but us. Our
heads wobbled and rolled and our legs gave out from under us.
We were speaking incoherently and acting without discretion.
Eliahu and his servants became sufficiently alarmed to search for
us in the markets and streets. They found us and brought us home.
They spread out our bedding, and we lay there all night until
morning. In the morning, we had to answer to Eliahu. "What will
you say and how will you justify yourself[38] before the Sultan when
he hears of this terrible thing?" he said to the Christian. "You have
become worthless. What excuse can you offer him?" "As for you,
Italiano," he said in a low voice as he turned to me, "get ready to
go your way—whether back to Tangier or anywhere else." We
apologized as much as we could—for the incident was inexcus-
able. We explained that the *eau de vie* was too potent for us and
that we were unaccustomed to it. He refused, however, to be rec-
onciled with us.

At this, the Gentile became bold and said to him that he had come to deal with the Sultan and not to serve Eliahu. If he was no longer wanted, he would return to his country. Eliahu was stunned by this and left our presence. On the one hand he was afraid to bring the Sultan's wrath upon himself, while on the other he feared losing the goodwill of the Gentile. As for me, he had another trick in store. He brought some good-for-nothing scoundrel to my room to berate me with false accusations and sully my honor. The Gentile could contain himself no longer. Enraged, he got out of bed, grabbed his cane and chased him away. He then turned to Eliahu and said, "Señor Eliahu, why are you going to all these lengths? Give him his wages and dismiss him. He can put himself under my protection." Eliahu did not answer a word. He was terrified of him. When he saw that all his schemes to separate me and the Gentile had only succeeded in reinforcing the bond between us, and that he was not able to pay me since his funds had run out, he chose to pardon my offense and to reinstate me in my office.

These were the consequences of rest[39] and relaxation that had brought me to this point. A weary man will rest and renew his strength. An easy-going person will tire and not sin. "All things toil to weariness"[40] and exist, but let them rest for a moment and they are lost. For relaxation at first tires; next it erupts, and in the end leads to destruction. Therefore, do not abandon what tires you—and it will be well with you!

11

Trouble and anger were forgotten. The Sultan finally remembered the Gentile, and he knew nothing of what had happened to us. He commanded Eliahu to inform the Gentile and to bring him to him the following day with full honors. The Gentile brought with him the model of a cannon which he had transported by ship to sell the King. The carriage on which the cannon was mounted was made of iron. It was ingeniously designed so that it took only a finger to aim it wherever one wished. The gift was prepared, decorated with fringes, flowers, and covered with silk scarves.

Ever since Antiquity, a gift has been the token of submission to the receiver whether from fear or respect. Abel brought an offering to the Lord out of respect;[1] Jacob to Esau out of fear;[2] the sons of Jacob to their brother Joseph,[3] and Joseph served them portions from his own table.[4] Ehud presented a gift to Eglon,[5] Saul to Samuel,[6] Moab and Aram to David,[7] all the kingdoms to Solomon,[8] Naaman and Hazael to Elisha,[9] Hoshea to Shalmaneser,[10] Judah and Philistia to Jehosephat,[11] the Ammonites to Uzziah,[12] Merodach to Hezekiah.[13] Still other examples in a general sense are: "Let the kings of Tarshish and the islands pay tribute, the kings of Sheba and Seba offer gifts,"[14] and "O daughter of Tyre, the wealthiest people will court your favor with gifts,[15] and kings shall bring You presents."[16] Whoever does not give a gift is considered to be rebellious or contemptuous. An example of this is what certain scoundrels did to Saul—"and they scorned him and brought him no gift."[17] Another is the conspiracy in which Hoshea the son of Elah was discovered "for he had not paid the tribute to the King of Assyria."[18] And so it is done even today in Persia, in the Moghul Empire, in Turkey, and in olden times also in Poland. Some aggrandized themselves while sullying their honor by receiving such gifts, while others like the King of Morocco extricate themselves from their poverty in this way. The offering is a sign between God and Israel that we are his servants. Thus it is written—"they shall not appear before me empty-handed."[19] To this day, the kings of Europe continue this practice with the Emperor of Morocco. Whoever comes to have an audience with him may not appear before him empty-handed—be it the rich man with his ox or the poor man with his lamb. The consul's gift is presented to the accompaniment of musicians whom they bring with them to dazzle his eyes and lull his heart.

I dressed up in Jewish attire once again in order to be among the bearers of the gift. I donned this disguise so that the Sultan would not take any notice of me and ask for more detail about me than about the other people. One ought not to adorn oneself too much when going before the Emperor of Morocco; neither ought one to dress too simply, lest the first result in a trap and the second in contempt. We sat in the outer court until he came out. All his servants and his men, as well as anyone who had brought a dispute to the King for arbitration were there. The King emerged riding on his white horse.[20] All the people responded by shouting in Arabic, "May God bless our Master the King's judgment!" The Sultan was of a ripe old age, but with a robust, strong physique. His eyes are like burning torches, and his voice is powerful. When he speaks people tremble. His dread look inspires fear. "When he rears up the mighty are afraid."[21] If he should become irritated, anything can end up ashes at his feet in an instant. When he passes in review between his troops who are posted a bow's length apart, anyone who comes too close will be put to death. No hand may touch him. Even if he falls or is thrown by his horse, no one supports his arm so as not to encounter the misfortune of Uzzah.[22] During the summer the royal servants chase flies away from a distance with silk scarves. His troops carry a firearm on their shoulders and a sword at their side. Their clothing is no different from that of others. They are not marked by insignia or ranks. There is a regiment of blacks who dance before him with their castanets to amuse him. In addition, the Renegadoes bring cages of wild animals for his entertainment.

Whoever comes forward to the King without being summoned, there is but one law for him—that he be put to death,[23] unless the King shows him favor, and then he is called by name. All who wait upon him try to judge his thoughts by the glint in his eyes. If his glance darkens, they become terrified and quake with fear until it is known upon whom his wrath will fall. There is no specially designated person who acts as executioner. No sooner does the King utter the order, then the object of his wrath falls at the hand of whoever is nearest him, and there is no one to intercede. If a man is to be punished by scourging, then everyone will flog him with their sticks without mercy. When prisoners are brought before him in chains, he asks what each has done, and the charges are enumerated. Concerning this one he might say, "Throw him down!"—and he is hurled down. Concerning another, "Cut off his hands and feet!"—and they are amputated.

Consider if you will the example of Mūlāy ʿAbd Allāh, the successor of Mūlāy Ismāʿīl, and what he did to one of his own people in the presence of an Englishman. On that day, a man was brought before him for judgment. He commanded that one of his hands be cut off, and so it was done. He then asked whether they had cut off the right or the left hand and was told the left. "I said the right!" So they cut off the right hand as well.[24]

The men who have been executed are not buried unless the King has forgiven them. The corpses of those who are not so pardoned are thrown to the dogs. He has a barbarian's sense of justice, and thus he is all the more fearsome. His throne is founded upon terror and abject fear, for any show of kindness might cause it to totter and threaten his life. Thus, he maintains a tight, harsh reign over his people, and in so doing keeps in check any outpouring of popular sentiment.[25]

We had all taken up positions in the front row in order to be seen. Whoever brings the most, comes first. He called Eliahu, who answered, "*Naʿam a Sīdī*" ("What does my Lord wish." This expression is used to indicate both "I am at your service" or "Yes," as the case may be. Even when the King punishes someone, the person who is being punished must answer yes in order to accept the sentence.) The Sultan inquired where was the Englishman.[26] "Here he is," answered Eliahu, "bowing down at your footstool." The Gentile bent over to remove his shoes (for Eliahu had prepared him to do so). The King told him he could stop, but he declined.[27] We had his attendants present the gift. As the King passed, Eliahu and the Gentile walked toward him to show the model of the cannon. Eliahu, acting as interpreter, explained its construction. The King saw that it was good, and it was covered up again. Nothing concerning these matters was discussed that day, because the King did not mention them himself. He sent the Gentile to see his gardens and to stroll in his orchards. He gave him as a gift a horse and also a leopard whose legs had been broken while trying to flee. We left the King's presence joyful and brimming with hope. The Renegadoes skinned the leopard, taking the carcass for themselves, while the Gentile made a bed cover from its skin. Hiram sent Solomon ivory, apes, and peacocks.[28] The Portuguese send the King of Morocco wildcats, hyenas, and ferocious beasts.[29] The Emperor also makes gifts of his country's animals. Do not covet his gifts because from beneath the flower a snake will bite!

For seven days from morning till evening we knew no rest and were never still. The Sultan's servants, and his servants' servants, and the foreigners attached to them, all came to celebrate with the Gentile and to receive gifts. One cannot refuse, because otherwise they would conspire to sabotage one's efforts. All Arabs, great and small, are after bribes, and the King is a prime example of this. They have no self-respect in this regard. When important people come to visit you, if they happen to find something valuable, they will lay their hands on it and take it either by hook or by crook. Lesser individuals will simply do it by asking for charity. Just try living among them with all your wisdom and without chicanery!

Forty days went by, but the Gentile was not summoned to reappear before the King. Eliahu's money was running out. One Saturday after sunrise, a royal officer arrived to announce that the King had gone to Rabat and that we were to follow after him. Before noon Eliahu, his servants, and the Gentile were on their way. Those who remained prepared to leave in the evening.[30] I also hurried to prepare my bags. However, one of Eliahu's household came to tell me not to bother because Eliahu had given orders to the guards at the city gates not to let me pass. "O you deceitful, unjust man!" I shouted shocked and angry. "Is this the way you abandon me? Where is my salary and the compensation for my work? Who asked you to take me out of Tetuan with all haste? Was it to entangle me in your net? Of what help or use is a Spanish secretary here among people who neither understand the language nor have any use for it? Now I know your deceitfulness and what evil schemes you devised for me! Why did I not listen to Cardozo or pay attention to the Gentile's words to you in the field?" Eliahu's brother came and tried to hearten me, for he saw how intense was my pain, and he was concerned for his brother's honor. He said that since today was the Sabbath when one should not travel, Eliahu's wife, children, and retainers were still here. They would join him that night. He promised to give me a letter so that upon their departure I could leave.

In the afternoon, Eliahu returned to the city riding his mule to hurry his household. His brother spoke to him about me. He then returned to me and told me to make ready to leave with them. Just before I was given a mule, Eliahu said in a loud voice in Arabic for everyone to hear: "Watch out, Italiano, I am only taking you to Rabat, and there I am leaving you." Some of the retainers whispered in my ear, "Cover your mouth and do not answer a thing, for tomorrow all will be forgotten."

We departed. I had no greater wish than to stick closely to the Gentile, for I had no savior but him. I guessed correctly that on account of his wife, Eliahu had brought two tents. When we reached the campsite, the Gentile ran to me and brought me into his tent where he swore that he had quarreled with Eliahu on my behalf. He held back nothing from me of the bread he ate.[31] And so Eliahu in spite of himself fed me his choicest food and best wine. However, in order to make me unhappy, he incited his servants against me so that they would maliciously annoy me. For five days I was tortured in this way. As we approached the city, their hearts grew weaker as mine grew stronger. But the burden of suffering and pain burned within me and engendered a fever.[32]

The moment I arrived in Rabat, I spread out my bedding and lay down until the next day. That morning, I wrote the following letter:

Señor Eliahu!

If you are still not satisfied with me, let me go my way. You will find a better secretary than I. As for me, I will look for someone whom I can please. Give me my wages for the service I have rendered you and for the suffering you have caused me, and tomorrow I shall go live wherever I can. Peace.

I begged the Gentile to hand him the letter and to fill in my words orally. When Eliahu read the letter and heard the Gentile's eloquence, his attitude changed and he decided to let me be.[33] He came downstairs to bring me up to his office. He let me do his accounting and restored me to my former position. How the lack or abundance of money can alter us!

In Rabat, the Lord removed the constrictions I felt in Meknes. This city was a better one. It was situated on a harbor. The city called Salé is the ancient provincial capital which is situated opposite it across the river. Rabat designates the city on the other side. Only the river separates them,[34] just like Tarascon and Beaucaire in France. They are no farther apart than the sister cities of Hamburg and Altona. The river comes to an end in the town harbor where it spills into the sea. The opening at the mouth of the harbor is narrow. Its water churns and flows with foam like a boiling cauldron preventing any ship from entering the river until the sea is calm and the wind dies down. It is rare to find it quiet more than once a month. Even then, it does not remain that for even a quarter of a day, and this short interval is not worth the damage to the King and the merchants.

Rabat is more beautiful and better fortified than Salé. An impregnable fortress and a mighty tower in which was once the royal treasury stands on the right bank of the river.[35] Likewise, the minaret of their mosque is one of the tallest and most beautiful in the Maghreb.[36] The Arabs of Salé are harder on the Jews than are the people of Rabat. This is because the Jews in Salé have to walk barefoot all the time because they have no special quarter of their own as in Meknes.

The stones cried out from the wall of Eliahu's house in Meknes broadcasting his decline. However, the remnants of his elegant house in Rabat told of his former glory. But who would give him even half of its actual worth to extricate him from his tight straits? There was no buyer, and Eliahu bemoaned his money which he had thrown away. All three of his wives were assembled together there. The one who surpassed them[37] all in beauty, wisdom, and youthfulness was the one from Tangier, which is why she could speak Spanish. She even knew how to pray, which is a marvel! She had borne him a son. The eldest had also given him sons and daughters. But the one from Meknes (who was as fat as a cow) was barren. Perhaps her superabundance of fat had blocked her womb, and the blubber on her loins[38] had denied her the fruit of the womb. There were no mandrakes to be found[39] that could quiet the feuds between them as to who would sleep with their husband. Many a time Eliahu slept alone rather than make a choice. The feuding between the Tangerino wife and the fat one intensified, and likewise their jealousy and hatred, until finally the Tangerino came to me asking if I could perform some magic spells that would get rid of the fat one. I replied that Jezebel's magic was to paint her eyes with kohl and dress her hair[40] in order to arouse love in the eyes of those who beheld her. I also told her that even if all the magicians of Egypt together with their spells were to be placed on one side of the scale and the endowment of charm and romance placed on the other, the latter could outweigh all of the former.

The Tunisian also came there to spy on our doings and to flaunt his rank. He too brought a merchant from Gibraltar. He was lodged in the home of a Jew from his homeland who had married a local woman and settled in Rabat. His name was Jacob Pacifico. He acted on behalf of the English consul. We also encountered a Dane, who each year brings a cage full of rare birds as a gift in the name of his King to the Emperor of Morocco.[41] All of us Europeans formed a single company: One day we would be invited to a feast at one person's home, the next day at another's. Everyone took great pains to prepare everything as we were accustomed with elegant table settings. We made the rounds of all the Jewish homes. However, we stayed on our guard against the pitfall of drunkenness and its consequences.

When the Sultan arrived at Rabat, he pitched his tent outside of the military encampment, some distance from the city. During this time, the ship carrying cannons came. The captain attempted to bring her to shore, but could not because the sea was becoming increasingly stormy. The King gave orders that it should be directed to Mogador.[42] A few days later the ruler set out for Marrakesh, saying that from there he would let us know what to do.

It was summer. The steely sky gave no rain to the land. The Arabs raised their voices in prayer for a late rainfall. They sent their children into the marketplaces and streets to cry *Yā Rabbī arḥamnā* (that is, "Lord God, have mercy upon us!").[43] However, their prayers were not answered. When this failed, they sent grownups (because their voices are stronger, and perhaps Muḥammad was sleeping and needed awakening).[44] They too were not answered. Then they sent the Jews, but they got no response. It is customary for them to send the Jews last. If their supplication is answered, they consider it a sign that Muḥammad wants them and is entertained by their pleasant voices. The Jews raise their stench to the sky and when he can no longer stand smelling it, he says: "Let them have it and let me not hear their voices!"[45]

The Gentiles of Spain, in contrast to these fools, are even more foolish. In periods of drought, they drag the image of their most venerated saint through the streets so that, in order not to see his honor desecrated and his statue overthrown, he will intercede on their behalf with God and will bring them thunder and rain.[46] The Jews—in spite of their abundant goodness—were not heard, while the Spaniards—in spite of their abundant wickedness—were granted their petition. Wanton men! Do not be wanton![47]

The Arabs, who would rather fall victim to the sword than to famine, cried out to the King to look out for the future. So he issued a royal decree throughout all his provinces stating that anyone who tried to export grain during the next three months would forfeit his life. He wrote another letter to the governor of Rabat saying that the license which he had given to a Jew residing in Mogador to export wool should be revoked and given to the

Gentile. If, however, there would be rain, then he would renew
his decrees.

All this spelled disaster for the Gentile because he had not completed his mission. It was a double calamity[48] for Eliahu whose
daily bread was now gone. The Gentile quickly wrote to Gibraltar
to dispatch a ship to him for transporting the wool he was going
to buy. Eliahu, in order to shore up his position, cast his eye upon
the horse the Sultan had presented as a gift. He kept pressing the
Gentile to exchange it for another, and afterwards to sell it once
and for all at full price. Thus he was able to survive a little longer.
One day, the Gentile received a letter from Gibraltar informing
him that the ship had set sail. The next day, a letter from the Sultan
arrived revoking his license and returning it to the Jew. When the
Gentile heard this news, he was stunned and fell over backwards
from his chair. He sighed as though his heart were broken[49] and
said, "The King treats me cruelly! He has changed my wages ten
times. He has tried me beyond the limit of my patience. Señor
Eliahu, tomorrow let me go to Marrakesh. Please come with me,
otherwise I shall go myself." No one said a word to him.[50] Eliahu
was in mourning. His wives wore desolate expressions. His servants' hands were trembling. They kept whispering to each other
all night. At daylight they got up to prepare all their provisions for
the journey. My heart could not bring me to say to myself, "Get
up and go with them." For I saw that both of them were in a bad
temper. "Well, if I perish, I perish,"[51] I thought. I decided to speak
my mind[52] to the Gentile and ask him to speak with Eliahu to patch
up my grievances as best he could before he leaves never to return.
Eliahu—who was jealous about leaving me in his house with his
wives—increased his oppressiveness, sticking in the hilt after the
blade.[53] He sent the Gentile to me to say that he would give me
a document sealed with his own signet and addressed to the steward of his house in Tangier, allocating for me some amount from
money of Eliahu's still in his possession.

"Who can believe his word?" I answered the Gentile. "Who
would trust a man who has set falsehood as his strength and protection?"—"What other choice do you have?" countered the Gentile. "If you are going to take it, go ahead and take it. For there is
nothing else beside it."—"Nothing else? Then give it to me." I

took the letter and my clothes and left his house. I never went back to him again.

Here I was once again "a wayfarer who stops only for the night."[54] The situation was not as difficult as in Tetuan. I went to Pacifico's home—perhaps he would take me in. However, Eliahu's name struck fear even from afar. "God forbid I should do this!" Pacifico told me. "I would ruin myself with Eliahu and never recover. Go find yourself some place to lodge, and then you can come to my house and we can have the pleasure of an intimate talk together."[55] Just as a sparrow finds a home, so did I. Then I returned to his house to hear what he had to say. He told me that Eliahu had given up on me and that the Gentile who came with the Tunisian had settled in Larache[56] or Mamora[57] (a seaside spot a quarter day's journey from Rabat). He proposed we make a solemn agreement, he and I, and he enjoined me to be on my guard. Just a few days later, all of the Europeans separated from one another. Everyone going his own way. The Gentile who came with the Tunisian went to Marrakesh. During his stay there, he wrote a letter to Pacifico that the Sultan had not agreed to let him settle in Larache. Therefore, he was returning to his homeland. He went on to write about the following event:

"Three leading European merchants in Mogador, two of them French—M. Secard and M. Barré, and one of them English—Mr. Layton, went out hunting accompanied by their Arab servants. Some Shleuh[58] came by, and the hunters' dogs set upon them. The servants saved them, but a quarrel ensued. The villagers were infuriated over the incident and made the false accusation that Mr. Layton had hit an old woman in the face with his fist and had broken one of her teeth. The merchant did not agree to buy them off arguing, "Would you murder and also take possession?"[59] The villagers then denounced them to the King. Immediately couriers were sent with all possible speed on the King's commission to bring them to him. The trial was to be held in Marrakesh.[60] M. Barré was ill, and so he was dismissed and left. They pleaded in vain that their hand had not broken that

tooth, nor had they even set eyes upon that woman. To no
avail they pointed out that the tooth was old, its roots in the
old woman's mouth were dried up. The entire town roared
that they were guilty. Those administering the beating gathered around the Frenchmen with sticks.[61] By the King's order, they were to receive two hundred blows. They smashed
two of Mr. Layton's teeth with a hammer as retribution for
the woman's tooth. Their monetary fine, the expense of their
journey, the loss of their belongings, their affliction and pain,
the cost of their medical attention—all this was like nothing
to the Arabs. Their shame crushed them, and they refused to
be consoled. The Frenchmen, depressed and shamed, returned to Mogador, while Mr. Layton is being kept in my
house. Perhaps it would have been possible for our consul to
inquire as to what really happened, but as of late he has had
enemies, and therefore remained silent. I have no idea how
their fate will turn and how the matter will end."[62]

If gentlemen such as these who are the elite of the merchants
can be treated as such, you can imagine what they do to the Jews
whom they consider to be like thorns or dung on the ground!
Now where is Pacifico's house? Where is the pavilion of the merchant in Mamora or Larache? What is man on this earth? His life is
a multitude of changes, and his host of days is a chain of terrors
stretching from the womb to the grave. His days are vanity, his
nights travail, his life but a breath. Men are distinguished from
one another only by their different calamities. But no one escapes
their turbulence and commotion.

12

Where was I to go now? Pacifico did not have the power to do as he wished. There was no demand for my sermons since I did not speak Arabic as I do Spanish. I turned to the French Consul who was there.[1] I had visited his house regularly while I was in Eliahu's service. He saw how I was mistreated, and he had heard about me from the Gentile. I did not have to wait in vain. He offered me two choices—either to go with him to Tangier, if I so wished, or to take a sum of money due me on the day I departed. I decided to save the money for a time of need, and went instead to Rabbi Solomon D'Avila's house. As you may recall, this was the man whom I had met at the Yeshiva in Tetuan.[2] He was one of the leaders of the community. His wealth was in the past greater than now, but he still was well endowed. For seven years, he had a partnership with a merchant from London in Mamora. He had had close ties with the royal house. However, he discontinued them in order to distance himself from the King's attempt to swindle him in the case of a ship laden with flax which the King contested and seized. He also had ceased his royal connection on account of lies that had been spread about him in order to put him out of favor with the King. After the Englishman left him, his affairs became entangled and his accounts confused. He instructed me to put them in order and check them to ascertain what was due to each individual creditor. Thus, I found another source of aid.

I observed two things during that period which I shall not hold back from you. The town of Rabat used to be a pirates' haven; and even today corsairs still circle her walls as they contemplate acts of piracy against the islands of Terceira and Madeira. Would you believe it if I told you that an Arab sea captain I met there did not know the compass coordinates for Rabat's location? He happened to have at hand a book of charts in English. He asked me to explain the charts to him. The very first thing he asked me was about Salé.

The second incident involved an Arab who went insane. He cut off his penis. He was still living as a hermaphrodite when I spoke with him. If he were an ox or a sheep for sacrificial offering, he would not be accepted whether his member was "torn or cut."[3] Indeed his member was entirely cut off!

Even though Salé and Rabat are almost one city, I did not spend as much time in the former as in the latter. Once when I was there, some Arab—a quarrelsome fellow—attempted to accuse me falsely of hitting one of his sons. He did this so that I might mollify him with money. I defended myself because no such thing had taken place. "If that is so, then my son is lying," he snapped back with bitterness dripping from his lips. "If this is what you are claiming, you have trapped yourself with your own words, for an Arab never lies." I said to him that perhaps it was someone else. But nothing did me any good until I gave him some money. After that, I stopped going there.

Should you be wondering how Jews can possibly win a case in court in their disputes with Arabs, know that "money answers everything."[4] If you go to an official sitting in judgment and present him with a gift, he will be the first to take your side, and you will be considered in the right. When your opponent appears, he will cross-examine him and declare him to be false. But if you happen to be poor, you will remain miserable and oppressed forever.

Eliahu's letter was still in my pouch. The French Consul no longer went to Tangier. I learned that Pacifico had another brother in Mazagan named Jesse. He was secretary in the house of a communal leader named R. Mordechai al-Baḥḥār, or de la Mar in Spanish.[5] He was a wise, honest, God-fearing man. He harbored an intense dislike of Eliahu on account of the Cardozo affair. I had already dispatched a letter to him telling him about myself because I thought he might help me just to vex Eliahu. I handed over the letter from Eliahu to someone trustworthy and instructed him to bring me the money at Mazagan. Then I took the letter from Pacifico to his brother and the money from the consul and set out on the road with an Arab. I passed Mamora that same night. We slept on a hill inside the Manṣūr fortress (its name means the watchman's tower).[6] A Makhazniyya, or troop of scouts, passed by (the word is related to Hebrew hōze).[7] The following day I came to Dār al-Baydā' whose name in Arabic means white house, a dwelling the color of an egg.[8] It is located directly on the shore. It was the Sabbath eve. Some rural Jews were living there, and I spent the Sabbath with them. Two Spanish traders did business in the region. They had a fortified house built on foundations with cannons all around for protection.

On Sunday evening, I arrived at a *duwwār*[9] and made camp there. Monday noon, I crossed the stream in the vicinity of Azemmour in a rickety boat. Azemmour is an open, unwalled town by the seashore.[10] Its citizens are wicked, sinful folk. There are Jews living there too.

Two thousand cubits away from the town, Mazagan begins to appear before your eyes. The place is called by the Arabs both Mdūma and Brijiyya (the first from the word for red and the second from the word for rib). This is because it seems red from a distance and because it sticks into the sea like a rib.[11] The Portuguese gave it the name Mazagan when it was under their rule.[12]

Before I entered the town, the Arab stopped, washed his feet on the beach and prayed. Seeing no one else around, I stood by to observe. He took off his pants, spread them on the ground, and then stood on them facing the sea. While whispering some inaudible words, he fell to his knees and bowed three times to the ground, exclaiming each time—*Allāhu Akbar* (God is most great). After that he said: *Allāh yin'al-Naṣāra wal-Yahūd* (God curse the Christians and the Jews). Finally, he turned his face to the right and to the left saying, *Salām 'alīkum 'alīkum salām* (Peace be upon you, upon you be peace). I thought to myself, "You Christians must be considered greater because he curses you first!" The blessing "Peace be upon you" is addressed to the guardian angels who stand about them to receive their prayer in accordance with their thoughts.[13]

I was now in Mazagan. I went to R. Mordechai's home and handed over the letter to Jesse. R. Mordechai had four more brothers. One lives in Amsterdam in wealth, honor, and security. Another is in Mogador. He is the youngest and the bravest of the brothers. The others were with R. Mordechai in Mazagan. Jesse had been appointed by the French consul to take care of his affairs there. It was true what I had heard in Rabat about R. Mordechai's deeds and his learning. Jesse's home was a breadwinning house[14] for me as well as for some Frenchmen who worked for R. Mordechai. It was a counting house. I had spent four days there, but R. Mordechai had not said a word to me about my affairs even though I urged Jesse to intervene on my behalf.

In order to chase away my malaise, I took a walk in the countryside in search of new sights. The beach comes up to the flank of the entranceway to the town. Behind it there is a hidden opening onto the ocean so that seawater collects between the two walls. The Portuguese used that as a shelter in wartime to hide their operations. The foundations of the walls are still firm, but on their upper edge the building has collapsed and fallen into rubble. In a chamber beneath it which speaks only of desolation and ruin there is a cistern.[15] However, due to neglect its water has become stagnant and putrid and its former splendor has become foul. I was seized by a dark fear while inside it. There was an echo that reverberated loudly. It was as if Lilith resided there amidst her tumultuous horde of demons.[16]

The mosque was formerly a church. The Muslims had removed the images and sanctified the place for their own worship. This is the opposite of what the Muslim ruler Sulayman did when he fought the Christians. He installed a picture of an idol which a magician had spirited away by trickery from a church to his home.[17] Because this mosque was originally a church, the Jews maintain the custom to this day of not taking off their shoes when passing it.

Outside of town, I found a company of infantry riflemen doing military exercises. A Jew's cap was the target for their bullets.

On Wednesday, R. Mordechai hurried off to Marrakesh to see the Sultan. Everyone in his household, his friends and his associates, rented a mule or a horse in order to accompany him out of town. I did as they did and went with them. As we were taking leave, I said to Jesse, "Go take him aside and speak to him on my behalf. For this is the right moment." He did so and was successful. He then returned to me and told me that my words had been heard and that I should accompany him to Marrakesh. He was on his way to catch up with the Pasha (the city governor) who had passed us in his hurry to leave. We were to find him accompanied by four hundred men when we reached the province of Dukkala.[18]

The people who had come to see him off now went home.

Night spread its cover of shadows over the sky. The twilight stars cast their glow to brighten the land, as we went by their light through the darkness until they had reached half their course.

What a difference between R. Mordechai and Eliahu. It was the superiority of light over darkness. He gave me shelter in his own tent. He let me lie down on his own bedding. He would not eat his bread alone, but only if I ate also. He spoke kindly and gave orders as if requesting a favor.

When Dawn lifted its wings to take its place beyond the sea, each man rose from his place to set out. It was market day in Dukkala. There were countless camels, asses, and mules laden with figs, dates, raisins, and big juicy watermelons which were brought to us as a gift. Dukkala is a rich and fertile land, a land of wheat and barley and the choicest produce. If it were located along the coast, a measure of fine flour and two measures of barley would cost only a shekel[19] even in the nearby ports of Europe. It lacks nothing except drinking water. I said jestingly to R. Mordechai that if only it had streams of water, it would take the place of the Chosen Land from me. This is why Mazagan and Dār al-Baydā (Casablanca) which are adjacent to it are so good for their merchants.

In order to be able to observe the village girls, I said that I was a physician. Anyone who wears a hat on his head is a doctor for them. The desire for life is instinctive in every person's heart. And what is their faith when their heart speaks up! But on this they all agree, whether a man lives or dies, it is from God, and the physician cannot be judged guilty of a capital offense. They open their homes only to doctors. This is true even for the King's harem.[20] I went from tent to tent dispensing medicine and working more cures than Hippocrates or Galen. The Arabs have a strong physique.

Their strength lasts a lifetime. Lameness, blindness, and serious handicaps are not common among them.[21] I thought to myself, "Is there no balm in Europe, or any physician there?"[22] Why is everyone there sick and every heart depressed?

We were sitting down in our tent to eat, when we were informed that the Pasha had just left. With the meat still between our teeth we left the tent and the equipment as is for the servants to bring later, and ran hastily after the Pasha. Such was the behavior of the Pasha, for he was a Berber, and the mores of the land were indeed barbaric.

Three days later we reached Marrakesh. Before entering the city, we had a meal in a wooded area filled with cedars from end to end. Who would come to us in the Maghreb to take these trees for the Sukkot festival? God's perfect wisdom is apparent in all His deeds, whether He causes abundance or scarcity. He has endowed every creature with deficiencies so that the creature will seek what he lacks from another. Each person thereby helps his fellow man, and in so doing they unite to form a political order. Their deficiency is their wholeness and testifies to the Almighty's perfect ways. For this reason, we recite blessings for the creation of many souls and their deficiencies.[23]

We passed by the royal tower on our right and bore left into the Jewish quarter. All the women came out to greet us with dancing and timbrels.[24] Even the rabbinical council and the leaders of the community came to inquire of our welfare. We arrived late in the day on the eve of the Sabbath, and already on Sunday, R. Mordechai was summoned to the King. From this I realized that he favored him over Eliahu.

No amount of wealth can satisfy this ruler. His eye and his mind are directed only toward his own gain. He gives a sum of money for commercial use to his favorites (a favoritism that is only a step away from death). Once a year they bring him a portion of his investment. If it pleases the Sultan, he allows the favorite to retain his position. If it does not, he confiscates all his property. R. Mordechai was one of these favorites. On the day, therefore, that he went to the King, the Jews prayed and fasted on his behalf so that he would be treated mercifully. In Meknes the King would go out riding his mule, but here he was in his carriage with a parasol

Street scene in the Mellah of Marrakesh. Gérard Silvain, *Images et traditions juives* (Editions Astrid: Milan, 1980)

shielding his head. These are things that distinguish the Sultan from others, and no one else should be seen having them.

The God of Heaven granted R. Mordechai success and caused him to find favor with the King. And so R. Mordechai went forth on that day in high spirits and the city of Marrakesh rejoiced.[25] If only I were given all the money that he gave on that day to the Sultan's retainers and countless portions to those in need and to the Jews for their songs and prayers, my house would almost be filled with gold and silver! You cannot be stingy with your money if you wish to trade in Morocco. "Sow in charity and you will reap in kindness,"[26] while "the mouth of all wrongdoers will be stopped."[27]

When God let things calm down around us, I took with me one of his mounted guards and went into the Muslim part of town. Marrakesh is like Meknes—dark with most of its streets covered. Here too, the townspeople thronged about me in order to get a look at the *Rūmī* or *Nasrānī* (the terms for Christian). There is nothing in the town to attract a European even if he only happens to be a villager.

I found the Tunisian there too. Like a dog following his master or a plague that appears in every house, everywhere he spat, he left muck and mire. He had returned there from Gibraltar, where he had been sent by the Sultan on royal business. Were it not for the English's respect for the Sultan, he would not have been able to set foot there after having fled.[28] I asked him why he did not stay in the secure haven of Europe. Perhaps he wanted to do so but could not? He replied that he would wait until he was sent as ambassador to London, as he trusted he would be. His hope, however, deceived him as you shall hear.

I cannot resist telling you about still another person I encountered. Take care lest you forget anyone of all those whom I have mentioned or will mention because they will reappear in the concluding section and you should recognize them. This was R. Mordechai of Meknes who was known popularly as el-Ḥazzān Bekka, that is R. Mordechai the Master. Thus one should understand the mishnaic text "A *ḥazzān* (schoolmaster) may look where the children are reading, but he himself may not read (on the Sabbath)."[29] He was a scholarly and honest gentleman. He was also very wealthy. He was a giant among the Jews, who looked after his people's interests. In addition, he was respected by the Sultan and his ministers. He also had two wives. He occupied the foremost position at the royal court after Cardozo's death. But he too went beyond the bounds of his high rank with his pride and self-aggrandizement.[30] He alone among the Jews would ride through the marketplace and the streets while smoking. He became the target for all the arrows of jealousy even though he seemed to be respected, feared, and loved. He was among the people who came to celebrate R. Mordechai's good fortune with him.

Word of the Freemasons Association traveled all the way to Marrakesh. Without even knowing what it is, they despised these people and considered them beyond the pale of God's community, saying that whoever goes astray after them is serving other gods.[31] They directed satiric barbs against them in a song that concludes with the verse: "May my person not enter their council."[32] It was said that Ezekiel was speaking of them when he stated, "There is nothing from them, nor from their mob, nor from their wealth, and there will be no wailing for them."[33] Only malice tempts us to judge what is hidden from us. The blind cannot distinguish colors. If the Masons' secret has been revealed or will be revealed, we would not know, nor will we. This much, however, we do know from their own testimony and their symbols (if they are not lying), namely that their secret tenets are honest, and there is nothing against the Almighty and his followers, irrespective of whatever religion they belong to. Why then should anyone become enraged and reveal his own foolishness?[34]

We stayed in Marrakesh several weeks, and we might have stayed even longer had not the Tunisian caused us to make haste with his villainy and deceit. He saw a valuable clock more costly than pearls in R. Mordechai's house. He praised it to the Sultan in order to incite him to take it from him. Shortly after midnight on Sunday while it was still dark, everyone got out of bed to leave the city quickly. Thank Heaven, the King had dismissed R. Mordechai on the day before, and the Pasha, R. Mordechai's friend, secretly revealed to him the Tunisian's treachery. The city gates were opened for us, and we left as if we were fleeing. The Pasha and his men followed after us, and in Dukkala we met up together. We stayed three days in order to see trained warriors on maneuvers.

Cavalrymen, troop by troop, dash out like lightning with their weapons cocked and yell as they gallop, "*Hā il-Qā'id*" ("Here you have the person who is fit to lead").[35] When they reach the boundary they had set up, they would fire their weapons. They would do this back and forth in a great hurly-burly, not in unison like a firm wall as you would in European battle lines. This is not their style of gallantry.[36]

At sunset sentries were placed around the Pasha's tent and ours. The army's commander made the rounds from one guard to another and shouted: *Hā el-'Assās* ("You there, Guard!"), to which the sentry replies: *Rā balāk* ("Here I stand at my post").[37] For the entire night until morning they would not keep still.

The infantry staged a mock battle. They were arranged in two crooked, twisted lines. A man who stands at the sidelines is the commander. He has a white cloth on his headdress and a staff in his hand. He gives the order to someone standing near him: "*A'igwā*" ("All right, fire!").[38] That man fires, and after him all the riflemen fire one after the other to the last man.

Conducting maneuvers, changing stratagems, and arranging battlelines—all these are burdens which are too heavy for their brains which have become thick from their laziness and dogmatism. Throughout the entire period that they were training in camp, no Jew would so much as dare to be seen. For who could discern in the midst of this thick human tumult anyone who might wantonly fire upon him? And then who would there be to hold that man responsible for shooting him?

Three days later, the cry went through the camp calling upon everyone to assemble and to break camp. We too began to make all the necessary preparations for our journey and then set out. On the way, I got into a debate with one of their commanders on their method of warfare. He firmly asserted that even without strategy an army will be saved and that victory would come without planning.[39] For victory belongs to God, whereas diligent plans are superfluous.[40]

I replied to him: "If one plays a chess game knowledgeably while his partner plays according to chance, even if he knows the rules, which of them will win? Is it not man who does the planning and God the execution? A wise general will plan his course of action, and God will grant the victory. Why did Joshua send spies to Jericho? Why did God order him to blow trumpets while marching around the city? Why did he set an ambush behind Ai? Did he not believe in God who had promised him that wherever the sole of his foot would step, that place would be his?[41] Why did Gideon take the empty jars and torches after God's angel had told him that he would be with him and would deliver Israel and after he himself had tested him with the fleece and dew and knew that this was the Lord's angel?[42] Does this not teach us that God's salvation comes after man's preparation? Is not this what is alluded to in the mysteries of the Zohar, *viz.*—'When earth awakes, then Heaven will too,'[43] and in what the Sages have related in the tractate Berakhot, *viz.*—'No blessing rests upon an empty vessel'?[44] If it was so for such great men as these whose hearts were firm and true, what more can we do, therefore, who have not stood in God's council? Was not Gideon, for example, who was commanded by God to destroy the altar of Baal, afraid of doing it during the daytime on account of his family and the citizens of his town, and so he did it by night?[45] Or consider the case of Samuel who took a heifer with him to conceal from Saul that he was going to annoint David as God had commanded him.[46] Still another example is when God said to Solomon at Gibeon, 'I will establish your throne of kingship over Israel forever.'[47] And yet, Solomon arose early in the morning to build the citadel, the wall of Jerusalem, and cities for storage, chariots, and stables.[48] God spoke of peace, but Solomon prepared for war. Take note that God was pleased with these individuals. Then may His grace be upon us and may He establish the work of our hands.[49] God confounds human plans,[50] even if there are plots to frustrate the intentions of clever men and to cause a setback for the wise. However, the devices of man are in God's hands, and He acts upon His creatures in His wisdom." But Arab ears are deaf to any argument.

I asked the Arab what his name was. He told me ʿAbd al-Rahīm. As it was my habit to seek out the root of Arabic words and names, I turned my attention to tracing this name. Jews add onto their names the suffixes *-iah* or *-el*, as in Isaiah, Jeremiah, Samuel, and Israel. The Chaldeans added the prefixes *Bel-* or *Nebu-*, as in Belshazzar, Belteshazzar, Nebuzaradan,[51] Nebuchadnezzar, Nebushazban.[52] The Persians use the prefix *Ahash-*, as in Ahashuerus and Ahashdarpanim.[53] The Phoenicians used the suffix *-bal* in such names as Esdrubal and Hannibal in the writings of Rollin.[54] The Greeks used the suffix *-cles* as in Themistocles, Empedocles, and Sophocles. The Arabs use the prefix ʿAbd- as in ʿAbd al-Malik, which means "the King's slave" ("King" being an epithet for God, as for example in the case of Ebed Melekh the Ethiopian who is mentioned in Jeremiah. For according to Kimhi, this was his name).[55] Other names in this category include: ʿAbd Allāh, which means God's servant (like Obadiah in Hebrew), ʿAbd al-Salām, which means the servant of peace, like Absalom (in this name too is an epithet for God),[56] ʿAbd al-Qādir, which means servant of the Almighty (*qadir* means ability and is referred to by the author of the Thirteen Articles of Faith),[57] and ʿAbd al-Rahīm, which means "the servant of the Allmerciful." Perhaps this is also the meaning of the name Abraham with the *h* transformed from ḥ, even if it is indeed Aramaic. For all the ancient languages are built upon a single foundation as Ibn Ezra has noted in his commentary to Ecclesiastes.[58]

An Arab schoolteacher complemented my observation, saying that ʿAbd in Arabic with ʿayin really means a slave, while with *alef* it means someone who has submitted to another authority.[59] We, therefore, have to distinguish between the two usages in Hebrew, even though there is no difference in their orthography and pronunciation. Take a look, for example, at Goliath's challenge: "If he bests me in combat and kills me, we will become your slaves" (using the word alone, he means it figuratively with regard to deference), "but if I best him and kill him, you shall be our slaves," to which he adds "and you shall serve us" (here he is using the term "slave" literally).[60] We observe from this that he was so insistent in order to entrap Israel by any means.

As we traveled on, God let loose a great downpour. R. Mordechai was delighted by this "early rain of kindness," because his granaries were piled high with grain,[61] and now he was able to bring it out for sale. When we reached town, we heard that the merchant who had gone with Eliahu received en route a message from the Sultan telling him to return to Mogador and to export only one shipload of grain. If the rainfall ending the drought had caused happiness to sprout in R. Mordechai's heart, the reply to the letter I had sent to Tangier,[62] gave birth to joy in my own.

I had given up on it, like some wretched broken object, and now I was like Saul who went looking for the asses and found a crown.[63] I felt a sense of pride and exultation,[64] and I indulged in thoughts that were too great for me. I remained silent for a few days to allow R. Mordechai, who was tired from the journey to repose and to give myself some respite. I heard that Jesse wanted to leave his post in R. Mordechai's household, and I wishfully thought that I might fill his position. However, R. Mordechai thought otherwise. He had in mind sending me to Mogador to stay with his brothers and to divide his business affairs among them. Hurrah! Hurrah! My wish had been answered. I was going to exchange Mazagan, an isolated Godforsaken place, for Mogador, the choicest of all the cities of the Maghreb. And so it was. After several weeks, R. Mordechai paid me in full, provided me with a mule and his Arab servant, and sent me on my way.

13

This time I cannot complain about my Fate. Perhaps He wearied of tiring me and took pity on me. But His grace is not bought only with hardship or as a result of toil and travail. The path leading to Him is full of thorns and overgrown with nettles.[1] Our hearts pluck up courage to pass over all of these barefoot in order to reach the treasure He has prepared.[2] If you will be His servant today, then He will be yours forever. Let us search out His paths and examine all the ways in which He does good after we have come to know how He can do harm.

I had not gone two thousand cubits from the city when the mule collapsed from under me. It was thoroughly diseased and could not stand, and when it stood up, it could not walk.

It happened to be the time of the *'īd*, or festival. (The word is cognate to Hebrew *gīd*, or "sinew," just as the Hebrew festive season is called *ḥag*, as in "the festivals come in their cycles."[3] Or, perhaps it is cognate to Hebrew *mō'ēd*, "appointed season.")[4] At holiday time, the Arabs go from one *duwwār* to the next to wish each other well.

Some children saw me and began making fun of me and throwing pebbles.[5] I did not wish to pick a quarrel with them, for the incident involving the merchants in Mogador was engraved in my mind.[6] And so not to be like Don Quixote on Rosinante, I hopped off and chose to walk on foot for two days.

The Arabs have two holidays which are called 'Īd al-Kabīr and 'Īd al-Saghīr. 'Īd al-Kabīr means the Great Festival and comes at the end of Ramadan, like Easter after Lent among the Christians. ʿĪd al-Saghīr, or the Minor Festival is Muhammad's birthday.[7]

The masses calculate the months according to these holidays. Thus, for example, they say: *qbil el-ʿayād* (before the holidays), *bayin el-ʿayād* (between the holidays), and so on. They also reckon time on the basis of plowing, harvesting, sowing, etc. However, they do have other specific names such as Shaʿbān, Ramadan,[8] and so forth. There is no difference between the holidays and the other days of the year except that there is more praying—as with the Musaf prayers.[9] But they do engage in work.[10] The days of the week are reckoned by number as in Hebrew up to Thursday. Then comes Nahār el-Jumʿa, or "Day of Assembly" (cognate to Hebrew *va-yeshammaʿSha'ūl*, "and Saul summoned"),[11] and Nahar el-Sibt, or Sabbath Day. Their house of worship is called *el-jāmiʿ*, meaning "place of assembly."[12]

The following day, I reached Safi[13] close to evening. The leading citizen of the Jewish community—either out of respect for, or fear of R. Mordechai—brought me to his house and treated me graciously with a festive banquet. Early the next morning, I set out for Mogador with another mule and another Arab. With the foot of the mountains on one side and the seashore on the other, I traveled for three hours. Then I began ascending steep, jagged mountains which rolled upward and were enveloped in a thick cloud,[14] until I reached the Zbel el-Yahūdī, or the Jewish Mountain, so called because of a Jew who had fallen from it. Thus, for example, Gibraltar, which was formerly under Arab rule, retained its name of *Jbel*, meaning "mountain," and *tār*, meaning "flying."[15] I read allusions to it in the biblical verses "Flee to your mountain, ye birds!"[16] and "Lord of the Gebalites" mentioned in Joshua.[17]

I had to dismount from my mule because the place was so narrow that there was no real path even for walking. I, therefore, had to climb crawling on all fours. How many "saints"[18] were invoked by the muleteers and camel drivers as they pass through there! The descent from the mountain is via a great hollow, full of obstacles, below which is a valley where the sun's rays do not penetrate.

The sun was setting in the west, while we (for other travelers[19] had joined us) were in a Vale of Tears, deep in the thick forest—

Mogodor as depicted in an early nineteenth-century engraving. James Grey Jackson, *An Account of the Empire of Morocco* (London, 1814)

a haunt for bandits. We removed the horseshoes from the mules, lest their footsteps be heard. We walked silently under the shadow of the trees[20] for three more hours until we emerged from this terrible wood just as the shadows of evening fell, and there we made camp. I could scarcely believe that I was still alive that day.

On the second day of the journey, we had sand dunes on our left and the rising sea on our right. I was afraid to ride because of the crashing of waves, but at the same time, I was afraid to walk on foot lest I would sink into the mud and sand. I kept on riding. Every wave that came near chased the mule with its spray into the sand, where it sank in. We went on like this for a quarter of the day, until we reached the gate of the city. I was conducted to R. Mordechai's brother. I gave him the letter and enjoyed some rest from my exhaustion.

Mogador is a new municipality built upon a site where the coast juts out into the sea. It is called in Arabic *Swīra*, or "little rampart,"[21] as in the biblical phrase *adallēg shūr*—"I will scale the rampart."[22] The word Mogador has its cognate in Hebrew *li-mevō' Gedōr* in the verse from Chronicles—"They went to the entrance of Gedor."[23]

From time immemorial, merchant ships used to go to Agadir,

the city called Santa Cruz by the Portuguese, which lies two days
journey from Mogador.[24] Agadir was formerly under Portuguese
rule. The Moroccan Emperor diverted its commerce to Mogador
after its inhabitants rose up in revolt against him. By order of the
Sultan, every consul and merchant who had been based in Agadir
had to build himself a house in Mogador. It is, therefore, the finest
city in all the Maghreb, because it was built by Europeans.[25] The
city is divided into two parts: the lots of the government citadel[26]
which form the commons of the city and is also where the royal
palace, the governor's residence and the homes of the great merchants are located; and the other part is the medina where the
rest of the people live.[27] The city is entirely surrounded by walls
and has two fortresses: one on the seaside to guard the port, and
the other to protect the outskirts of the city. Two hundred Renegadoes garrison the city. The following are the products exported
from Mogador and all the Maghreb: sandarac, gum arabic, lau-
danum, walnuts and almonds,[28] dates, wheat, wool, copper, olive
oil, argan oil (argan is a species of fruit found in Morocco),[29]
moroccan leather, oxen, calves, fowls, and oranges. In exchange
for these they import: linens, coffee, tea, knives, mirrors, cloth,
iron, as well as tools for craftsmen and household implements.[30]

R. Mordechai's brother, out of respect for his older sibling, seated me with him in the room reserved for himself. However, he behaved strangely in all his actions from beginning to end.

It was the day prior to Rosh ha-Shana eve, and there was a circumcision celebration being held in the home of Abraham de Lara.[31] He was from Amsterdam and had come to Morocco, where he became successful and settled down. He married the daughter of R. Gedalya,[32] the richest man in all Morocco. I was among those invited, so I went. I must confess that I was indeed astounded when I saw a group of men there actually seated on chairs and dressed in our fashion. They included the master of the house and his brother, the four sons of Gedalya, a member of the Abudarham family[33] from Gibraltar with his two sons, three members of the Akrish family from Livorno,[34] and a man named Pinto, who though a Moroccan, was also splendidly dressed in our style. The rest of the people were local inhabitants. The faces of most of them revealed that which their dress concealed, for their suntanned faces testified that they were Maghrebis.

Abudarham, who was proficient in many languages, examined my words, tested my ability in languages, and cited many proverbs to test my knowledge.[35] I began to catch on to his scheme the moment he switched languages for no reason. But when he changed his speech a third time, I did not hesitate in my mind.[36] I carefully worded my sentences, put myself on my guard and outwitted his cunning with my own.

That night I made friends and enemies. Wherever there is honor, jealousy follows behind, and it shall never die.

The next morning before dawn, the sound of the shofar awakened me with a start. Lo and behold, I saw a group of yeshiva students that R. Mordechai's brother Joseph had assembled in his house to pray the Taḥanun prayers.[37] I complained to him, saying that such a thing would not be done in our country nor in any other self-respecting place. For I had enough lack of sleep for the last three nights and needed rest. But I spoke in vain. For the entire Ten Days of Repentance,[38] I slept to the sound of the shofar and to the screaming voices of the men at prayer. It was this to which I was referring when I indicated that Joseph was of a difficult temperament and was the harshest of his brothers. He made his temperament even worse with excessive drinking, and when he lost control of his senses, he went beyond all bounds of decency. For two months, I served him diligently and did all his work faithfully, but to no avail. One day when he insulted my name and sullied my honor, even the members of his household took my side. I wrote to his brother, but he did not answer. So I made up my mind to seek a refuge that would be better for me.

I found there a man from Tetuan named Rabbi Abraham b. Sa'dūn. He was an intelligent fellow, cantor of the synagogue, and head of the Yeshiva in the Gedalya house. I begged him to speak to these people on my behalf, for their business dealings were great and varied. Perhaps they might have need of an assistant. The man did not delay doing this as he wished to see me installed in the household of Jacob Gedalya, the most distinguished scion of the family.

He succeeded in his mission. He brought me from Joseph's house and presented me to the Gedalya family. All of the Gedalya brothers know how to speak and write Spanish—some less, some more. R. Jacob, the eldest, does the writing. Jacob Zevi oversees the work, R. Judah was in charge of religious instruction and of the office records, while David, the youngest, was idle. They were called by the Arabs *Ulād el-ḥazzān,* "the Sons of the Rabbi" (*ulād* being cognate to Hebrew *velad*).[39] They were so called after their ancestors, two brothers who were both rabbis. When the two of them were in Amsterdam and saw the differences between freedom and slavery, they commanded their sons before they died as follows: "Do not get involved with the ruler and do not make yourselves known to the authorities." This goodly legacy of theirs[40] was more valuable than any precious object. This is the reason they have been able to hold on to their great wealth and even increase it.

Akrish, who lived close by our new house, rejoiced at my good fortune when he saw me, saying "Give thanks unto God, for He has redeemed you from the hands of rough masters! You have made me remember my past mistakes today.[41] Know that before Jesse came to Morocco, I was a secretary in R. Mordechai's house, who at that time was here [in Mogador]. I also engaged in commerce for myself and settled down here. He became very angry

at this and out of jealousy wanted to take me with him to Mazagan.
He went to the Sultan and obtained a letter from him to compel
me. This was a terrible complication because it allowed me no
time to look after my affairs. Dispairing of any help, I fled and
sought refuge in the royal citadel. Everyone who seeks security
from his pursuers runs there[42] and sacrifices a bull. I made the
customary sacrifice to the spirits, took the offering, and brought
it as a gift together with a letter of petition to the King.[43] Jesse
arrived at just the right time. He stood up on my behalf and was
my salvation.[44] If he had not come quickly, I would have been
destroyed.[45] I am still mourning the loss of my money which has
gone never to return."

In interpersonal disputes, a sacrifice performed at the royal palace will enable the party who makes it to find a way out. For this
is a great honor for him and on account of this the King's face will
seem like the divine Countenance as described by Abravanel in
his commentary to the pericope *Va-Yishlaḥ*.[46] Or they have preserved here an ancient custom, seeing in it the rationale that the
Kuzari saw in sacrifice.[47]

As my trustworthiness and ability became evident, greater re-
sponsibility was placed upon my shoulders; first, I was to oversee
the work; after that, I was set to copying correspondence, and from
there to keeping the accounts. Finally, I was promoted to auditing
the books.

Because the Arabs are confused in all their conduct and practices, they are not prepared to set up their business according to
a single plan. Therefore, the consuls and merchants—both Jewish
and Christian—appointed someone especially for the purpose of
carrying letters on a monthly basis from Mogador to Tangier and
back. He is called the Commercio courier, because all the merchants as a group are called simply Commercio.[48] They gather
together each night in a different man's home either to celebrate
or to discuss their affairs.

There are many prostitutes among the daughters of Israel everywhere in Morocco. In Mogador, however, they are beyond number.[49] The heavy hand of the Arabs provokes their fear. Christian
money is a temptation in their poverty. The prison that is their
country thwarts their desire. Once, a Jew in the service of the King

set his eyes on one of them. But when he spoke to her daily, and she would not listen to him, he became enraged. He went and brought a gift to the Sultan and informed on all of them. The Sultan sent a decree to Mogador ordering that forty prostitutes whom he had specified by name be taken to Tarudant.[50] They were arrested and imprisoned in one house. Forty women huddled together in terror! You can imagine the tumult they made and all their chattering. Ten were taken away, and two died en route. For a single gift, the King issued his decree, and for another one, he revoked it. Thus they were brought back to Mogador. Do not ask me how these people who are strict in their faith can countenance prostitution among the daughters of Israel! How it is that they enclose themselves under the protection of their Arab paramours and are not afraid.

Not just on one or two occasions I happened to be at the shore attending to the exporting or importing of our merchandise, when Sīdī ʿUmar, the governor of the city, came to collect the tariff. Even so, I still did not know who he was. I thought he was only a royal secretary when I saw him. One day he sent for me and asked if I knew English. I told him that I did and turned to go. He ordered me to halt, took out a letter from his bosom, placed it on his forehead, then kissed it and said: "This letter came to me from Mūlāy ʿAbd al-Salām, the Sultan's son residing in Tarudant. I am ordered to bring him someone to act as translator between him and an English physician who was captured together with sailors and officers of a ship which was wrecked off the coast of Guinea.[51] The prince's eyes are diseased and he can barely see." He went on to say that he would send me to him and that my recompense and prestige in serving the Sultan's son would be immense.

If God had ordained something like this for me in one of our lands, I would have been delighted, but in Morocco, this would be a trap for me. Who knows when I would get out? Who can question what the prince does? Who would guarantee my wages and my freedom? Now I realized that this man was the governor. My heart prompted me to say[52] that I really did not know English. "So why did you say that you did know?" he bellowed. "Either you lied then, or you are lying now, and in either case you have committed an offense."

"I was lying," I answered stubbornly. "It was no crime, for I did not know you, and so I was only jesting."

"You have been trapped by your own words," he said, "and you cannot get away with it."

I made no further reply and walked out of his presence. R. Jacob Gedalya did not appear in public because he was afraid of being ensnared in the traps of the wicked. But he hid himself in vain. The governor asked his attendants for whom was I working, and they told him Gedalya. He commanded them to summon him to him in order to hear what he had to say, and so he was brought before him.

The governor demanded of him, "Did your secretary tell me the truth, or was he lying to me?"

R. Jacob replied, "My lord, your knowledge of the language is the same as mine. However, there is among us someone who can verify the matter—the Genoese Consul.[53] Let him examine him."

The consul was brought to test me. I gave him to understand that I could not. At this, the governor suggested to the consul to take me to his home and there examine me at leisure. That afternoon, I found all the Commercio had gathered to dine at the consul's house. He told me to speak to him in English. I answered in Spanish. He asked me why I was trying to run away from this? He suggested that this opportunity might even be for my good. "Sir," I answered, "you are an intelligent person. We are in Morocco. The word of the King's son is all-powerful.[54] I do not know the names of medicines, and if I err, it is the Angel of Death for me! Go tell the governor that I am incapable of carrying out his orders."

"Watch yourself," replied the Genoese Counsul, "You are afterall a foreigner in this land, and you cannot leave without someone to help you."

"The point is not missed on me," I told him. "It will not be too difficult for me to obtain a helper when I leave." They persisted with their questions and schemes until I screamed: "What extraordinary blows my Fate has dealt me! When I say that I am wise, I am treated as a fool, and when I say I am a fool, I am treated like a wise man." They were amused by what I had to say, and their seriousness turned to laughter. How fine indeed is a well-timed reply.

The consul promised to say to the governor what I asked, but he said that he did not know if this would satisfy him. I bowed and went out, happy to have been triumphant in my ordeal.

The following day, the governor's servant returned to bring me before his master. He angrily told me that he was giving me a mule and a guide and that I was to leave without a moment's delay and without any protest. He was trying to frighten me with this confrontation so that R. Jacob would appease him with a gratuity. R. Jacob, however, refrained from going against his wishes. When I realized that there was no one to help me, I said: "Please listen, my Lord, I shall go as you have commanded, but know that you are taking your life in your hands. Where will you flee from the prince when you send him someone who is incapable of fulfilling his wish?"

Everyone present was astonished that I had answered the governor so harshly. An Arab who had been sent by R. Jacob and just happened to be there, incidentally, looked at me contemptuously and said, "Who is this anyway that he should go to the prince as a translator? *Amar Allah* (By God!), I know more English than he does."

The governor turned to him and asked whom then should he send and was told that someone had arrived from Gibraltar, who could successfully undertake the mission. In the end, he sent this person as the English translator together with a Jew for Arabic and a Renegado for Spanish. As for me, he fined me twenty piasters to be rid of me.

Now just go and try with all your intelligence to combat all of the Arabs' tricks and snares. If you can come out of it clean, then your wisdom and courage deserve to be praised!

Before I conclude this chapter, I must tell you one more thing that I cannot omit. You have heard mention many a time of conversion to Islam and have seen how the Arabs use coercion in this matter. Till now, however, you did not know precisely how it is done, which is as follows: Clothing and a horse or a mule are brought by royal servants who dress the apostate, put him on the horse, and lead him through the city streets crying aloud, *"Lā ilāh in Allāh, Sīdī Muḥammad Rasūl Allāh."*[55] The bystanders repeat these words after him. After he had gone around the entire city, they make him a feast and send him on his way. The apostate, be he Christian or Jew, great or small, may not change his mind. There is no wisdom or cunning that can deliver him from their hands. There was, however, a Jew who made the profession of faith in a moment of anger. After having been led around on the mule, he regretted what he had done and looked for some pretext by which to save himself. Whether from cunning, by accident, or out of fear, he urinated on the saddle. When the stench reached their noses, they beat him and and drove him off, thinking he was mad. He is still living in Mogador. His folly was his salvation.

You have heard and seen, dear reader, strange things up till now. If they have given you cause to wonder, I cannot blame you for it, because I too find it amazing. But all this is nothing compared with that which you are about to read in the next chapter. Be prepared to hear such terrible things, that whoever hears them will be shocked and horrified.

14

Deceit, injustice, oppression, licentiousness, greed, folly, jealousy, faithlessness, and shamelessness—these are but a bare outline of the Arabs' ways.[1] These characterize all their intentions and acts as I saw them and as I have shown you in the preceding chapters. What about the Jews? Their intellects are muddied, but their hearts are pure. Though wretched, they suffer with hearts humbly open before God. Though their foolishness is deplorable, the object of their hope is commendable. Their sinning is not directed against God, and their righteousness is turned toward their fellow men. Their homes are not full of wealth and riches, but they are happy with their lot. They are not overly clever, but neither are they very mischievous. There is no better than the best of them in their land of bondage; however, you cannot find worse than the worst of them when they go out of it, because when they find themselves free of their oppressors and can cast off their yoke, you can no longer tell them apart.

In short, here you have the qualities of all the people of Morocco.

The rich will not leave because they will not abandon their possessions. Very few wish to leave a city, and when anyone does, he must leave behind his family and property as a pawn, as in the case of R. Mordechai's brothers or of Gedalya's ancestors.[2] The poor will not leave their wives and children. However, when pressed by necessity, a few members of a family will go to find shelter in Gibraltar or elsewhere. One person in ten thousand gets out by the Sultan's kindness and by the power of much silver and gold, as in the case of the Ben Sason family who reside in Gibraltar. However, the King's kindness is not granted to everyone. As for the women of poor families, you may find one in a thousand who goes overland to Algiers and thence to Jerusalem to pray for their brethren who are in the Diaspora. They are, however, taking their lives in their hands since they may be recognized while attempting to leave the country.

After all the upheavals and the hostility that beset me,[3] I contrived a scheme to establish my own business and to save up some money while "the Lord grants me respite all around, with no adversary or misfortune."[4]

In Gedalya's house there was no secretary other than me, and neither was there any other house than his that was suitable for me. I thought to myself, "Here I will dwell, for I desire it."[5] However, I put off laying the cornerstone until after Passover would be over. But can a person rule over his spirit and his desires so that he can rely on the outcome? Can he control his own affairs? Every outcome is from God, and from Him are the results of all actions. He will make them turn the way He wishes, and He will pull each man's heart in their direction as a horse is steered by its rider or an ox by a farmer on a furrowed field.[6]

When I came home the day after the holiday. . . . Why was this day different from other days?[7] The doors of the house were locked. I knocked. They let me in and closed the doors after me. So they did for all who came. The Ben Gedalyas were in their office, while the women of the household were closed in their rooms, and the yeshiva students were huddled in fear whispering to one another. Astonished at this sight, I asked R. Abraham[8] for some clarification as to what was all this panic about. He did not wish, however, to say. That afternoon, I went to R. Judah's room and to David's,[9] but could not find either of them. They had gone, their shoes without buckles on their feet, staff in hand, aboard a Dutch ship. These were men who never set foot on the road[10] except to go to synagogue on the Sabbath or to the port on business. This clearly testified to the fact that they had not gone on some minor matter.

At night, all the gates on all sides of the house were closed. No one went out or came in. R. Jacob[11] gave me some letters to copy

in my room in order to thwart my desire to ask questions or to
go outside, and he sent an armed guard to protect me. I tried to
learn something from the guard, but to no avail. Jacob Zevi[12] gathered some people to sleep in his room with him, and I among
them. He gave each of us weapons and warned us to be ready to
defend ourselves in any event that might arise. He also armed
himself.

In the morning, I pressed R. Abraham to explain to me what
was going on. Fear of a mysterious calamity is worse than its dis-
closure. "Had a ship sunk on the high seas? Had relatives of theirs
been killed? Had they gone bankrupt? What had happened?"

R. Abraham told me that something even worse than all of these
had befallen them. "And what was this calamity that could so terrify
them?"

—"The King had died. That is what Pinto, the secretary, had
written from Mazagan."

—"What was so terrible about this for them—or for us for that
matter? After all, monarchs die in our countries without anyone
knowing or caring."

—"It is not like that in our land," he retorted. "For when word
spreads that the King is dead, the entire country is open for looting
and pillaging. They are all lurking for blood. Every man hunts his
brother with a net.[13] Each man does what is right in his own eyes.[14]
They rape the women and the maidens. The violent element of
the population stand at all the crossroads to cut down any pass-
erby.[15] The caravans cease to operate. Hunger spreads throughout
the country. How long does this go on, you may ask? Until cities
are laid waste by sword and famine,[16] and one of the king's sons
will be strong enough to seize his father's throne and rule by
oppression and force. This Sultan, however, had ten sons. Who
knows which one of them will prevail and what will be the extent
of the destruction that he will wreak to achieve his goal? God
protect us and have mercy upon us! Watch out for yourself. Do
not let a word of this pass your lips."

My flesh crept with fear when he said this. Then I really knew
I was in the Maghreb. Then I forgot everything that had befallen
me up to that moment. Perish the day I joined the merchant[17] and
the night his servant said to me "come to Morocco."[18] My Fate has

indeed been cruel; the Constellation under which I was born has been harsh. For it has bent its bow and made me the target of its arrows.[19]

The news that followed terrified me even more. The local governor tried to conceal what had happened from the commonfolk, and he ordered the merchants not to tell it in the city or to publish it in the streets lest the Berber towns rejoice and the villages exult,[20] and they throw up a siege against the city.[21] The Jews who rushed to stock up provisions against whatever might happen were interrogated and beaten by the police.

That evening the officers of the English vessels came to get food for R. Judah and for David. Quietly, I went upstairs to my room, put on an extra layer of clothing, and went out with them to the ship where the members of our household were staying. I thought that either they would be together with me in my hour of distress, or I would be with them in their hour of salvation. On the third day, a letter from the Dutch Consul was brought to us saying, "Go back, go back. Come out of there.[22] Return to your homes because the city is calm and peaceful, but do it unobtrusively."[23] So we returned ashore.

Friday was the most difficult time, because it is the day on which the village folk come into the city to pray, each man with his weapon of destruction in hand[24]—sword, dagger, or firearm. The first thing the governor did was to relocate the open-air market outside the city, and he placed Renagadoes as guards at its gates. Whoever came had to leave his weapons at the gate until he left. Should he refuse, orders were given to compel him with force if necessary.

When the word got out and the governor saw that he could keep the secret no longer, he put a second force of guards at the city gates and all around its ramparts. The Christians realizing that there was gunpowder in the arsenal outside the city advised the governor to bring it into town both to prevent it from falling into enemy hands and to have it ready for any emergency.

In order to maintain his authority, the governor convened a meeting of all his men on the following Friday in the Meshwar (Hall of Justice).[25] He told them: "It has been rumored that our King has been gathered to his ancestors. Perhaps it is not true. If he is still alive, may God protect and exalt him. But if it is true, may his soul be granted eternal life. And now, you and I are equal. I am no longer your governor, and you are no longer my slaves and servants. Let us, however, protect ourselves from the pack of ruffians that have surrounded us. If you want me, I shall be your protector and leader. And if not, choose someone else to defend you. You must realize that the Haha and the Siyadma tribes (the latter's name is derived from Sodom) have us under surveillance. If we sit still, they will find a way to set a trap for us."

All the people responded that he should be their commander and just as they had obeyed him till now, so they would from that time forth. And no one would contradict him. The governor then confidently bore his office upon his shoulders. He acted wisely and succeeded through this speech in finding—by some miracle—such a fickle group to be of one mind.

During this period, there was not a house among the homes of the merchants and consuls that did not have twenty or thirty men guarding it; and even so, we were still worried. The guards did not feel safe from the bandits, and we did not feel safe from the guards. They reinforced the watches and strengthened all the weak points of the city. Many people plastered up the windows and doorways to their countinghouses, or they buried their money in the floor of the house.

The face of things changed every Friday. That is the day when the Arabs appeared. For it is a tradition of theirs that the country will be delivered over to the enemy on that day. That is why they close the city gates while they are praying.

Three hundred Haha and two hundred Siyadma were among the inhabitants of the city. Their leader accompanied by twenty men approached the governor demanding the keys to the royal treasury claiming that after the death of the Sultan, they alone were in charge of it according to an appointment dating back to an earlier time. They demanded that he should hand over the keys peacefully. The governor retorted that he was not going to inquire into the justice of their demands, telling them moreover, that he was not free to take any step, for indeed it was still not confirmed that their sovereign had been taken from them. Perhaps his spirit had carried him off to some mountain or valley[26] which they did not know. He told them to go and investigate further, find out for themselves, and see the place where he had set his feet. They should find whoever saw him there dead or alive and then return to the governor. So they turned and went.

Every day the rumor spread more and more, but not in a single version. The governor cunningly spread the word in secret that the Sultan had gone to Marrakesh. The unruly and the rebellious insisted that the King had died near Rabat, which was true.

The King was a very old man. He had some internal affliction or illness. One day, either his bile hemmorhaged or his kidneys ruptured.[27] He vomited blood, but did not take it seriously thinking it was merely a chance occurrence. On the second day of Passover, while he was riding in his carriage with his attendants behind him (he was driving without any attendant) suddenly calamity struck. The tumor burst inside him, and he hemmorhaged in the carriage. The horses kept on going unaware without anyone controlling them. His servants waited a long time, but he made no sound. They hurried over to him to see what was happening, and there was their master lying dead before them in a pool of blood.[28] They kept the matter quiet, "and to this day no one knows his burialplace."[29]

The word was about and grew every day like a storm that in Tetuan, Mūlāy Yazīd had been recognized as Sultan. He is the son who had rebelled against his father. The governor suppressed the rumor in order to calm the storm.[30]

That Friday, the governor decreed that no one, armed or unarmed, be allowed to enter the city. All the gates to the city were closed. As people were coming out from the mosque, he put on a good face and waved a scroll in his hand (a document that he had cleverly forged). He acted as if he was bringing this news to the people in the name of his beloved Sovereign. And to further pull the wool over their eyes, he declared the day a holiday. The guards began shooting like madmen[31] at the feet of the rebel leader, saying, "That's to you for the keys to the royal treasury." However, every heart was in fact quaking until the matter could be verified. And if it were indeed true, could we content outselves that we would enjoy peace? Alas. It was then that the dreadful disaster began to overtake the Jews.

Mūlāy Yazīd came to Tetuan with a large force on that very same Friday moved by a deadly destructive spirit against the Jews. He was still bitter from the time they had refused to help him when he was fleeing.[32] He would hear no counsel but that of his own vengeance and no voice but that of his own wrath. The vice consuls[33] came out to greet him dressed in their finest. They were seized, stripped, and tied to the tails of his men's horses all the way back to the city. On Saturday, he gave orders that the Jews should be smitten with his fury. They slaughtered the cream among them, and they struck down the choicest of Israel.[34] This would have been completely carried out were it not that God inspired one of their Ṭālibs, or clerics, to say to the Sultan, "Heaven forbid, that my lord should put the righteous to death with the wicked! Will he who judges according to Muḥammad's law not do justly?[35] Let those who have sinned against you feel your hand, but these sheep, what have they done?[36] If you want to crush them and to inspire fear in them, put forth your hand and touch all that they have,[37] for a pauper is like a deadman.[38] Only do not lay a hand upon them."[39] Had not the Lord been with them by raising up this man as a savior, they would have been swallowed alive by the fury of the troops.

The King replied, "So be it," and ordered his men to plunder all they possessed. They swarmed over the houses, climbed through the windows to loot and pillage. They dug up the wells looking for buried treasure. They searched every home, seizing whatever caught their fancy. Everything that was of little or no value they utterly demolished.[40] They filled the houses with dirt and refuse. They trampled the synagogues and dumped the sacred objects at every street corner.[41] They tore off the gold earrings from the women's ears and the bracelets from their wrists. They stripped the men naked. They raped the virgins and defiled the married women.

The cry of the Jews echoed throughout the land as the wind roared. They had no possibility to flee this way or that.[42] Some tore their beards in their anguish, others scratched their flesh. Women stretched out their hands to plead for mercy, but there was no one to take pity on them. Infants poured out their hearts at their mother's breast, but were torn to pieces before their very eyes. They all raised their voices weeping bitterly with tears in abundance. They made their final confessions before God since they assumed that they were at the point of death. But then compassion for their parents and pity for their children stirred them to go and seek refuge at the tombs of their saints.

When the looters had finished pillaging and went off with their booty, the Jews sent their young people and children to beg for bread. The adults were enveloped by hunger for three days, because they could find nothing.

These things were described in a letter to R. Abraham Koriat in Mogador (the son of R. Judah, who died in Tetuan)[43] by his son. It was written with charcoal on both sides of a scrap of paper which he had found by the wayside, and on it were lamentations, dirges, and woes.[44] The bearer of the letter filled in the details and showed a necklace, an anklet, and a bracelet which he had snatched from a woman.

Can your heart remain steady, O Reader, can your hands keep from trembling, and you not weep like these oppressed people? What a heart of stone that would not be melted!

What amazes all who hear about this is that not a single person caught in this tragedy abandoned his religion as a way out of his distress. They saw the finger of God in their affliction. Their sins were the cause. The Sultan was only the instrument of God's Wrath. For them it was a sign and a divine omen that three of their sages had died during the preceding two months.

Wherever the King set foot, his enemies were scattered and his foes were put to flight.[45] Wherever he turned, he wrought havoc. Then things returned to their former state of chaos.[46] Rumor upon rumor and news of calamity upon calamity kept coming all day.[47]

The new ruler's father had made peace with all the nations, but harbored a grudge toward the English because of his son, who, as you have already learned, had their blood in his veins. The Sultan hates the other nations whom his father had loved, but loves the English on account of his mother and because of the help that they had given him. Only the English had correctly understood and realized that the father was already old and was not going to live forever. Therefore, they secretly supported his son. For this reason, the Sultan pardoned the Vice Consul of England, returned his clothing to him, and reinstated him in his office. For similar reasons, he made it a point to bring near all those who had been forcibly distanced from his father's throne, while at the same time driving away those who had been near. He boasted, citing one of his holy men who had prophesied that a new ruler would arise who would purify the land. His claque of sycophants abetted him by telling what suited him, namely that this prophecy referred to him. They thereby added fuel to his fury and justified his abominable and disgusting deeds as righteous acts.

All of this was done and heard before it was even known whether the people of Mogador wanted to recognize him as their sovereign or whether any of his brothers, who was nearer to them than he, would challenge him. The governor had all he could do to hold back the rebels at this time, because if war were to break out, they would join their enemies and fight against them.[48] It was not enough—all of this noise from a King who had seized power some twenty-days' journey away, in addition to that, other orders were being brought to the governor that limited his actions. The Jews, as a result, wavered between fear and hope—perhaps someone better than Yazīd would rule over them, someone who bore no past grudge against anyone and had no enemies.

The King had vanished from the land, and there was no authority over men. "Everyone did that which was right in his own eyes."[49] Anyone who had a creditor would openly snatch the promissory note from his hand. Anyone who had an enemy would simply get up and kill him. A Jewish young man locked himself in his house, and had the word spread that he was dead because during another interregnum his father had killed the father of an Arab who was now seeking his life. It was only during this period that I saw a Jew (it happened to be Akrish)[50] strike an Arab and avenge himself. During this period of flux and panic, I too tasted freedom and raised my hand against an Arab! Such is the way of the Arabs: They maliciously mistreat whoever is not of their faith because their law puts a muzzle on the unbeliever's mouth so that he cannot reply to them. If this protection is taken away from them,[51] have no fear of them! They will not persecute anyone except the cowardly, but will turn tail and run from anyone who is courageous

The Ben Gedalyas did not show bravado because they were

anxious about the future. A person they had never seen before appeared saying that he had made a loan to their late father twenty years ago and had lost the promissory note. They simply went and got the money and paid him without saying a word, and they would not allow me to save them from him.

On Shavuᶜot, while we were in the synagogue at the reading of the Torah, runner came dashing after runner and messenger to meet messenger[52] to report that one of the late Sultan's sons, by the name of Mūlāy ᶜIsān, was approaching Mogador. Worthless characters and every desperate person had gathered about him—some five hundred in all. Now five hundred men are not much, and are not sufficient to fight against a fortified town in which there are two hundred Renegadoes, all of whom are skilled in warfare, plus two hundred other Europeans. The men of the Haha and Siyadma who were in town did not dare raise their heads anymore, lest their mischief redound against them. Even if they were to join forces with the prince, they were still too few to be effective. But who wished to argue with him? Who and how could anyone say to him: "You shall have no share in your father's property."[53] Whether one turns left or right, he will be going into a trap. If he follows after one of the pretenders, and in the course of the struggle, the opponent prevails, his offense can only be expiated with his life's blood.

The lookouts on the tower and on the ramparts called to one another to be on the alert. No one was to leave his post. The entire city was abuzz.

Abraham de Lara[54] rose to his feet and said to the congregation, "For God's sake, take care of yourselves. The Muslims are rushing to arms. How can we sit here in safety celebrating the holiday before their very eyes without them stoning us?" At this, each of us got up and went to watch over his home and his children. As for me, I went up to the roof of our house which overlooked the sea, the tower, and the Meshwar. From there, I observed through a spyglass people coming over the crests of the sand dunes. I was prepared to hear nothing but the thunder of weapons and to see clouds of smoke, the clashing of swords, and the blood of the fallen. However, the governor wisely calmed all strife and won over every heart. He sent a vanguard of forty men to the prince with a letter saying that if he had come in peace, then he should come alone and he would be received honorably. But if he had come to make war, he should not even try to come up to the city, because the gate will be shut and will not be opened.[55] The messengers returned to the governor to say that the prince was on his way to Tarudant and had no intention of turning aside. The prince had thought that simply by showing himself, people would gather round him and he would be strong enough to challenge his brother. When he realized that his plan would not work, he changed course and hid his intentions. For indeed the road he was taking from town to town was untrodden.

Rumors increased from day to day. One was that the Sultan had ordered that the governor of Tetuan be executed along with three of his secretaries because he had not compelled the Jews to help him during his hour of need. Solomon Hasan, the Spanish Vice Consul (Hear this, O Reader, and be outraged!) was falsely accused[56] of revealing to the governor of Ceuta that the Sultan was intending to besiege his city. He was hanged on the Sabbath in front of the entrance to his home before his entire family (for so the King had decreed). He was left like this until his intestines came out, and he was given them to eat. He expired three days later in terrible agony although he was completely innocent.[57]

After having made his arrows drunk with the blood of poor innocents,[58] and after having finished smashing the Holy People in Tetuan, the Sultan came to Tangier. The Spanish Consul together with his entire family fled prior to his arrival. For this, the governor of the city had to pay with his own life. The Sultan fined the Jews an enormous sum which they had to bring in three days to the royal treasury. The soldiers whipped the Israelites and beat them mercilessly until they sold all their household possessions in order to quench the King's thirst, and they were left naked and penniless.

The sins of the two Tunisian brothers were requited that day. The bitter fruit of their crimes had ripened. The day of their downfall was upn them. Their fate had brought them to Tangier. (For had they been in Mogador or Marrakesh, perhaps they might have escaped.) The elder had an iron choker placed over his mouth and throat, and he was torn apart as if by a lion.[59] The younger who was fated to end like his brother, damned his soul and changed his religion to save his life. To be more precise, he really was only changing his outer cloak, because his heart had been corrupted from youth.

The few Jews living in Arzila, a small town two-days' distance from Tangier, also drank the royal cup of bitterness. They too despoiled themselves of everything they owned in order to collect the sum levied upon them. And it was the same for the people of El Qsar.[60]

Wherever the Sultan cast his eyes there was either death or impoverishment. He turned next toward Larache in order to carry out his plan to attack its inhabitants and to place a heavy yoke upon them.

From there, he sent for Eliahu to be brought to him. His agents of destruction emptied out Eliahu's house, seizing him, and beating him badly. When he realized that the King had resolved to destroy him,[61] he too shook off his faith and cried aloud the formula which they use for this. Thus, he escaped further mistreatment. When he came before the Sultan, his conversion was announced to him.

"Eliahu," the Sultan said to him, "It was out of fear that you converted. This time it will be of no avail to you." He aimed a gun at Eliahu's toes and told him, "Choose whichever you wish! Either as a Hebrew or an Arab, one way or the other, you will die and be buried. You and your friends who served my father, you advised him to treat me badly. Their day is coming too. Get on with it and choose for yourself!"

—"My lord, King," Eliahu replied, "I would rather die in the Arab religion than live in the Jewish faith."

—"Watch out," the King interjected, "there is only a step between you and death."[62]

—"I stand by what I said and will not go back," said Eliahu.

The Sultan tested him in this way ten more times, but Eliahu stood by his word. Finally, the Sultan pardoned him and commanded him to proceed to Fez to be instructed and sanctified in the teachings of their creed. However, the multitude of his tribulations and his abominable deeds that had collected in his heart haunted and tormented him, and he died a few days later bitter and depressed, tainted with Cardozo's blood and besmirched by his own detestable acts. As was his life, even so was his death.[63]

The Sultan arrived in Rabat. In the first incursion, he made R. Solomon D'Avila's[64] fortune the victim of his fury. He did not leave him so much as a thread or a shoelace.[65] R. Solomon had until now lived like a poor man so as to avoid coming to the King's attention. He had denied himself any luxury, and thought only to gather up and hoard. In the end, God did not grant him to enjoy it. He was, however, not alone in his misery. All of the Jews were dragged down after him and were made to shoulder the weight of the punishment that was meted out to them. The Sultan gives an order, the taskmasters run, and the rod is diligent.[66]

Wrath, indignation, trouble, and a band of all evil messengers cleared a path for his anger.[67] These accompanied him on his march to Meknes. They rushed to destroy at the sign of his hand. Righteousness did not save any righteous person. The netherworld and the abyss were satiated, but not the Sultan's raging eyes which were not satisfied with destroying the innocent and the just.

The first evil emanating from the breath of his fury came to roost upon the house of the Ḥazzān Bekka.[68] It consumed his trees and his stones and devoured all his property as an ox devours the grass of field. His wives and children were seized with terror and fled in haste, but the man himself was caught. The guards advised him on the way that the only chance to save his life would be to convert to their religion, otherwise he was certain to die. However, Bekka sanctified the Holy One of Israel, and would not consent. He was not like Eliahu who had corrupted his body and damned his soul so that they were both cut off. Nor was he like ʿAttal who wanted to apostasize, and was unheeded. Bekka did not pray to God to be spared. He prepared himself to suffer saying, "O Righteous God, my sins have brought these things upon me. I am condemned. Now I shall perish. For how can I live to see the evil that will befall my people and the destruction that has already overtaken my family."

When he came before the Sultan, the latter exploded with rage, "You son of perverse rebellion![69] I have found you, you who were my enemy and my chief detractor. Were you made my father's adviser just to make me a villain in his sight? How much trouble you have caused me! My wrath will trouble you this day. Take him out and burn him," he ordered.

God of Vengeance, O Lord. Awake! Why do You slumber? Your people, O Lord, is being oppressed. How can You behold those who betray them and remain silent? Give heed to the cry of one of the righteous men of his generation. Out of his dire straits he cries to you, 'Violence!' See how the folds of his flesh are shriveled in the flame. Know his pain which is not from any wrongdoing! Do You wish a death such as this for your pious ones? If so, what is the fate of those who are the objects of Your ire?

Every heart melted at the reports that came in. Panic seized the inhabitants of Mogador, because the misfortune of others perhaps heralded their own misfortune. Fear on account of their religion grew in many hearts, and there were those who converted. On Friday (a day determined for destruction), a man arrived from Meknes bearing a letter from the Sultan for the governor. When the Muslims came out from prayer, it was read aloud in the Meshwar before all assembled:

> From the river of Tetuan to the city of Meknes, throughout the Berber territory and the coastal region, the people have acknowledged Mūlāy Yazīd as King. All the peoples in the rest of Morocco should see their example and do likewise. Whoever refuses to obey will be put to death. All administration and commerce should continue normally and not stop until either the King himself comes or sends word. Furthermore, until such time, the Jews should continue as they have been and be treated as in the past.

These three things were the main points in the text of the document.

The first point was positive; namely, that the country had become peaceful. The townspeople unanimously acknowledged his sovereignty over them and cheered, "Long live the King, Mūlāy Yazīd!" They gave their allegiance to the clap of gunfire. All the Jews assembled too and cheered. They paraded around the markets and through the streets carrying banners made from their wives' sashes[70] hung from a single pole. One of them would call out,

"Allāh yebārek f-amr Mūlāy Yazīd" (God bless His Majesty's affairs), and all the rest would respond, *"Allāh yenesserhu"* (May God protect him).[71]

The second point of the letter was also entirely positive, for it allowed all the ships to sail.

The last point was the bitter one. Its implementation would mean grief and sorrow. Either the Jews did not comprehend the full meaning of the language of the letter, or they contrived to obfuscate its substance for the Gentiles. For according to the text of the letter, they were still awaiting the Sultan's reply and did not know what a storm was brewing about them. This was how they interpreted the substance of the letter. The Arabs, however, understood it to have a different meaning. Hearing the words at the end "the Jews should be treated as in the past," one of them who was falsely inspired stood up before the governor and said that in the old days the Jews did not wear shoes within the city for that was the way it is in Marrakesh, Fez, Meknes, and Salé up to the present. The audience had not considered this interpretation because Mogador was a new region and was only settled some thirty-five years earlier. This law had never been imposed upon the Jews there, and they had never observed it.

The people remained silent, and their silence indicated their consent. There was no one to be found among them who would speak on the Jews' behalf. The moment they left the Meshwar, they began shoving every Jew they found, ordering them to remove their shoes. They heaped upon them insults, curses, and a rain of blows. The governor was unable to help them because the populace rose up against him and surrounded his residence threatening to kill him, saying that he was protecting the Jews for bribes. After the incident with the shoes, there were complaints made concerning the Jews' manner of dress. The hem of their cloaks which they fashionably gathered up over their shoulder now had to trail along the ground. The length of their pantaloons which reached to their knees, now had to be raised high up on their thighs. The Muslims added insult to injury in order to vex the Jews by throwing pieces of glass and sharp stones on the streets to prick the soles of their feet. Even those who dressed in the European fashion were afraid to go out, lest they too get the same treatment. We stayed shut up indoors for many days. When we started to go out, it was only with a guard.

Prior to Mūlāy Yazīd's coming to the throne, the people of Dār al-Baydā surrounded the house of the Spanish merchants ordering them, too, to hand over the royal coffer to them. After pressing a geat deal, they moved forward to break down the door. Then the Spaniards fired their cannons and put them to flight, killing some twenty men.[72]

To this day, there has been no word of R. Mordechai.[73] May God be with him, and may he survive this cataclysm! Perhaps his righteousness will stand protection for him.

Two Frenchmen who were in Mazagan fled out of fear to Cadiz before the day of wrath.

Three other individuals saved their lives in what seems to us an amazing way. Whether these were merely coincidence or acts of Providence, let the reader be the judge. Just before Passover, Abudarham[74] had a premonition that he might fall into the hands of the police, because his creditors had set up traps all around. The premonition was in vain, because this was not the case. He acted prudently, however, and turned his misfortune to good advantage. He left two of his sons and his wife as security and went with his oldest son to London on the intermediate days of Passover, and thus he found his salvation in his debts. De Lara's brother had had a boil for a long time on his cheek which festered and putrified. Now in Morocco, there is no doctor or medical dressing. So on one of the intermediate days of Passover, he too traveled back home to recuperate. As in the case of Nahum of Gimzo, he also found his cure in his affliction.[75] R. Judah Halevi set out from Gibraltar to return to Tetuan just before the Passover holiday. When he was four hours out to sea, the Lord caused a great wind storm upon the water which carried the vessel and made it run aground in Algiers. It was unable to get back, and he found his salvation in this tempest.

R. Solomon of Tetuan was not so fortunate. Three months before he had had an urge to go to Gibraltar to see his teacher. His bad fortune prompted him to return to his homeland, and he arrived with many valuables just three days before the calamity and was swept up in the misfortune of others.

Jacob Pacifico left his wife and children and escaped (I do not know how) to Algiers, and his brother Jesse to Amsterdam. But as for me, where could I flee? My heart sank within me[76] over this. My soul was being eaten as a moth does a garment, and my heart as a worm eats wool.[77] I suffered from sleeplessness all night. In the morning I was in a sullen mood. The Ben Gedalyas did their best to cover up their anxiety and heavy heart. But a dark cloud appeared that drove away any pretense of putting on a good face.

Sīdī Aḥmad Fennīsh,[78] who had served the late King and who had been reappointed to serve the new monarch, arrived bearing letters from the Sultan concerning Mogador and its surrounding provinces. We were sitting at the Sabbath noonday meal, when Fennīsh's brother came with a message he delivered orally that the Jews of Mogador had been fined one hundred thousand piastres to be paid to the King, as well as three shiploads of gunpowder and a certain quantity of weapons. Every face turned green, and everyone was overcome with great horror and dismay. The food that was still in their mouths turned to gall. Shocked and heartsick, everyone rose from his place. "Woe!" they cried, "For the Lord has decreed the ruin of all His people in our country. Their day of doom is at hand! Where can we possibly find what the King's minister has demanded, even if we were left with nothing but our own naked bodies?"

On Sunday, all the Jews were imprisoned except for the big merchants. This was either because the latter's wealth stood security for them, or perhaps because they themselves had contrived this in order to place more of the burden on the small fry and thereby make it lighter for themselves. All of them, however, were under the threat of royal punishment, and the evil scepter would not be removed[79] from their backs until they swore that they would pay the amount levied upon them.

Seeing all these things that happened and all that was yet to happen on the day the enemies of the Jews expected to have them in their power[80] and do with them as they wished, I said to the Muse that inspires me, "Let's look for some stratagems and seek some way to get out of the snares of the evil one. In eight days a ship is scheduled to set sail for Amsterdam, and I have heard that there are two other Hebrews preparing for the journey, one from Gibraltar and one who was dressed like a Franco in residence. We must understand this to be the moment of opportunity.[81] Be of strong heart! Seize the moment, and do not weaken. If you dillydally, you are doomed. Get out now either to victory or death, either by wit or cunning. There is no other chance."

Three obstacles stood between me and salvation. I had to overcome the hurdles and clear the way. The Ben Gedalyas refused to assist me, because I was their only secretary. But who would put his life in the hands of such a vile, bitter, impetuous people who will not listen to the voice of honor and integrity and whose spirit is as adamant as death and the grave? The Genoese Consul did not want to give me a laissez-passer, nor would the governor issue me an exit permit because I had not listened to them about going to Tarudant.[82] The captain of the vessel would not allow me to go on board his ship without these documents. My only remaining hope was Abraham de Lara. It was he who was responsible for the coming and going of all Dutch subjects who came there. He detested[83] the Ben Gedalyas who were keeping him from leaving the country, and in order to spite them and to show them that he was not their inferior, he gave me a letter to the Consul of Holland. The consul instructed his Jewish steward (for there is no Gentile home that does not have a Jewish steward, servant, and cook) to accompany me to the governor and to speak on my behalf. The governor, however, replied angrily to my face that I was not going to leave. My heart melted and became like water. The terrors of the darkness engulfed me,[84] and I was seized by a spasm of trembling.[85] How many bitter disappointments can I take? Wretched and melancholy, I returned home.

"Why such a long face?" one of my friends inquired. "There must be something deeply troubling you, because this is not like you."

"Why shouldn't I look this way?" I replied, and told him what happened with the governor.

He whispered in my ear that this was the Ben Gedalyas' doing. They had set up someone to ambush me. They are the kind of people who throw the stone, but without showing their hand. "Don't lose heart, however!" he told me. "You know the Arabs have no word that is final from one minute to the next. It is all for hire. The governor behaved as he did in order to intimidate you. Take my advice and you will be saved. Would that I were in your position! Go and fawn over the governor's steward and flatter him with pieces of silver.[86] You will blind the governor's eyes with a bribe[87] and get him to do whatever you wish."

I came back to my senses and went to the governor. He exhausted me with his questions and his tricks. But in the end he asked, "How much is there in it for me if I let you go?"

I told him to set his price and I would pay it. However, I reminded him that I was terribly poor and that if he opened his mouth too wide and demanded too much,[88] I would be unable to meet it.

"Go bring me one hundred mithqals," he replied. "After that, you may depart. But you cannot take anything with you, not even a penny. You have lived in this province for a year now, and you should, therefore, be considered like the native Jews and shoulder their burden along with them."

I stripped myself naked in order to get out of this prison, throwing into the depths of the sea the fruit of my four years of toil. I put my trust in God's salvation, hoping that He would raise up relief and deliverance for me from another quarter.[89] I took the laissez-passer from the consul and the exit permit from the governor. I paid the captain of the ship prior to departure and purchased some provisions. Under my clothes I hid ten gold pieces which the Ben Gedalyas gave me as an act of kindness. They told me that since I had witnessed the terrible oppression that had overtaken them, if I could tarry awhile, maybe God would take note of their affliction and save them from their misery, and then I would receive my full pay since who knows what a new day will bring. . .

"You are all false comforters,"[90] I answered. "Better a dry crust in peace[91] than fistfuls of travail, a troubled spirit, and eating bread amidst turmoil and desolation, and drinking water in fear and anxiety."[92]

I left and ran to the shore and never looked back. The moment the soles of my feet were off the dry land, I raised my voice to sing to the Lord for He has been good to me.[93] As in the days of our exodus from Egypt, God showed me wonders—except I did not go out with great wealth,[94] since they despoiled me,[95] rather than the other way around.

From that time on, I knew nothing about events in Morocco, nor did I inquire about them.[96] Only look at what I have found out: If anyone tells you bad things about events in Morocco, multiply what you have heard, and you will not go wrong. If what you are told is good, do not believe it unless you can see it with your own eyes!

On the first day of Tammuz,[97] I came out of the upheaval, and on the eighth of Elul,[98] I was strolling peacefully and safely in the streets of Amsterdam.

Then I stopped and took a look at myself, for I was stripped bare of everything. What would be in future events, and what was in the happenings of the past? I was too overwrought to speak.[99] I was struck dumb. My heart still trembled from my ordeals in the land of darkness. My mind had been absorbed in my joy at getting out to the world of plenty, but now it raged at the thought of my present predicament and screamed, "Woe is me!" To whom could I turn now? Who could I lean upon? Upon Him Who rides the clouds![100] Upon the Lord![101]

I decided, therefore, to sing of my many hardships—even though I would place only a small portion of them on the strings of my lyre—so that they shall always be a reminder for me of that knowledge which is too wondrous for us[102]—whether God will be gracious or destroy. This will teach young and old, master and pupil to be in awe of Him.

The sea is calm, its waves roll in their gentle course
A fresh breeze fills[103] the sails
A ship glides with ease like a bird in flight
And at the stern, the pilot sleeps at rest.

But suddenly the sea is roaring like Hell below
Opening its maw, it boils like a seething cauldron.[104]
The mariner sees the abyss beneath his feet.

And through the stormy tempest, the wind is raging.

At wit's end from heavy hardships
He casts his cargo overboard
Lowers sail and takes down mast
And miraculously reaches shore.

Saved . . . But how? Like one escaped from fear,
Like a stick from the flame, like chaff from threshing wind,
Weary, stumbling, he pants and gasps together,[105]

His thoughts are sharpened—
From whence comes his help,[106] a remedy for his affliction,
A hope for his future, and an end to expectation?

Yes, I am that man—
Who now inveighs against cruel-bitter Fate,
Fleeing the devastating ruin of the Daughter of my People.[107]

Notes

Preface

1. For Benjamin of Tudela, see the edition of Marcus Nathan Adler (ed. and trans.), *The Itinerary of Benjamin of Tudela* (London, 1907); and for Petaḥya of Regensburg, see L. Gruenhut (ed.), *Sibbūv hā-Rāv Rabbī Petaḥyah mē-Regenspūrg* (Jerusalem, 1905).

2. There are numerous examples of this in J. D. Eisenstein (ed.), *Ozar Massaoth: A Collection of Itineraries by Jewish Travelers to Palestine, Syria, Egypt and Other Countries* (New York, 1926; repr. Tel Aviv, 1969, in Hebrew).

3. The other editions are those of: Vienna, 1834; Vilna, 1835; Warsaw, 1848; Warsaw, 1854; Cambridge and Vienna, 1886; Warsaw, 1926; New York, 1926; Jerusalem, 1968.

4. In German: J. Zedner, *Auswahl historischer Stücke* (Berlin, 1840), 220–40; A. Lewin, "Geschichte, Geographie und Reiselitteratur; Samuel Romanelli," in J. Winter and A. Wünsche, *Die judische Litteratur Seit Abschluss des Kanons* (Berlin, 1897), III, 463–69; N. Slousch, "Le Maroc au dix-huitième siècle. Mémoires d'un contemporain," *Revue de Monde Musulman* 9 (1909), 452–66, 643–64; Alfredo Ravenna, "Impressioni marocchine di un viaggiatore ebreo italiano del settecento," *Rassegna Mensile di Israel* 18:5 (May, 1952), 222–29, 19:6 (June, 1953), 281–86.

5. H. Z. (J. W.) Hirschberg, *A History of the Jews in North Africa* (Leiden, 1981), II, 290–91.

6. See for example, Norman A. Stillman, "Muslims and Jews in Morocco: Perceptions, Images, Stereotypes," *Proceedings of the Seminar on Muslim-Jewish Relations in North Africa* (New York, 1975), 25.

7. Samuel Romanelli, *Ketāvīm Nivhārīm* [selected writings] (Jerusalem, 1968), 21–149.

8. See Gideon Toury, *In Search of a Theory of Translation*. Meaning & Art 2: Studies on Poetics and Communication in Culture (Tel Aviv, 1980).

Introduction

1. Some later writers give his name as Samuel Aaron Romanelli. However, this middle name is never indicated in Romanelli's own writings or in contemporary sources. It first appears in F. Servi, "Samuel Romanelli," *Corriere Israelitico* 30 (1882), 87–88; and T. A. Weikert (ed.), *La Merope, Tragoedia*. Following these latter two, the *Encyclopaedia Judaica* 14, cols. 228–29, has its entry "Romanelli, Samuel Aaron."

2. The best biographies of Romanelli are Ḥayyim Jefim Shirmann, *Shemū'ēl Rōmānēllī: ha-Meshōrēr veha-Nōdēd* (Jerusalem, 1968), and Joseph Klausner, *Hīstōreya shel ha-Sifrūt hā-'Ivrīt ha-Hadāsha* I (3rd ed.; Jerusalem, 1960), 307–19. For further details on the Romanelli family, see Shlomo Simonsohn, *History of the Jews in the Duchy of Mantua* (Jerusalem, 1977), index, s.v.; and Schirmann, *Shemū'ēl Rōmānēllī*, 10–11, n. 5. Concerning the Portaleone family, see Simonsohn, *Jews in the Duchy of Mantua*, index, s.v.; and *Encyclopaedia Judaica* 13, cols. 907–909.

3. For a description of the school and its program during the eighteenth century, see Simonsohn, *Jews in the Duchy of Mantua*, 590–99; for a comparison with the preceding centuries, see 581–90.

4. Samuel Romanelli, *'Alōt ha-Minḥa ō Ḥāvēr Me'ushshār* (Vienna, 1793), 3. Concerning Marini and his translation entitled *Shīrē ha-Halīfōt le-Ōvēd*, which was never published, see Ḥayyim Jefim Schirmann, "Marini, Shabbethai Ḥayyim," *Encyclopaedia Judaica* 11, cols. 994–95, and the bibliography cited there.

5. Moritz Steinschneider, "Die italienische Literatur der Juden," *MGWJ* 44 (1900), 85; Anon., *Qin'at Adōnāy Sevā'ōt* (Jassy, 1852), 6–7. The entire passage dealing with Romanelli is reprinted in Schirmann, *Shemū'ēl Rōmānēllī*, App. C, 76–77.

6. For example, he translated Maffei's *Merope* under the title *Merav* (ed. T. A. Weikert, Rome, 1903) and Metastasio's *Temistocle* under the title *Talmōn* (Ms della Torre 267, Budapest) into Hebrew. Romanelli translated many of his Hebrew poems into Italian and also his play *'Alōt ha-Minḥa (Il Pomo Traslato ossia l'Innesto felice)*. According to Lelio della Torre, "Samuel Romanelli und seine Schriften," *Ben Chananja* 5:4 (1862), 27, he madę a prose translation of Solomon Ibn Gabirol's neoplatonic poem *Keter Malkhūt*. However the work has been lost. See Schirmann, "A Manuscript Collection of Poems by Samuel Romanelli," *Tarbiz* 35 (1966), 378 (in Hebrew). He may also have translated works of German literature into Italian. See Ludwig Geiger, "Ein italienischer

Jude als Vermittler deutscher Geisteswerke," *Allgemeine Zeitung des Judentums* 67 (1903), 9–11. Schirmann, *Shemū'ēl Rōmānēllī*, 15, n. 20, questions this.

7. The complete manuscript of the translation was extant until 1862. See della Torre, "Samuel Romanelli und seine Schriften," *Ben Chananja* 5:4 (1862), 27. A few verses of the translation are preserved in the *Massā' Ba'rāv* (see Chapter 8, below) and several other works.

8. Schirmann, *Shemū'ēl Rōmānēllī*, 47, suggests that perhaps some of the more controversial material was deliberately suppressed by the copyists.

9. See Chapters 5 and 6, below.

10. della Torre, "Samuel Romanelli." *Ben Chananja* 5:4 (1862), 26.

11. Samuel Romanelli, *Grammatica ragionata italiana ed ebraica* (Trieste, 1799), 186: "ebraico Petrarca." Concerning Ephraim Luzzatto see Meyer Waxman, *A History of Jewish Literature*, III (South Brunswick, N.Y., and London, 1960), 134–35; Klausner, *Hīstōreya shel ha-Sifrūt hā-'Ivrīt ha-Hadāsha*, I, 295–306; Eisig Silberschlag, *From Renaissance to Renaissance: Hebrew Literature from 1492–1970* (New York, 1973), 66–68.

12. Schirmann, *Shemū'ēl Rōmānēllī*, 35–36; also idem, "A Manuscript Collection," 389–90, and for a listing of some of the poems written during this period, see 380, no. 26 and 381, nos. 35–40.

13. The poem which begins with the line "Alas Menahem's son has met his end, Moses has died," was apparently first published by Romanelli in his *Grammatica ragionata*, 195. It was republished later in *Ha-Asīf* 4 (1888), 189–90; and in *Mizrah u-Ma'arav* 5 (1932), 346–47.

14. Berlin, 1792. This poetic essay was grounded firmly enough in Jewish tradition to be published with the approbation (*haskāma*) of Berlin's Chief Rabbi Zevi Hirsch Levin.

15. Berlin, 1791. For a synopsis of the play, see Waxman, *History of Jewish Literature*, III, 136–37; and Klausner, *Hīstōreya shel ha-Sifrūt hā-'Ivrīt ha-Hadāsha*, I, 310–11. The first scene of Act I has been published with annotations by Shirmann in his edition of selected writings of Romanelli—Samuel Romanelli, *Ketāvīm Nivhārīm* (Jerusalem, 1968), 183–90. The German Protestant Hebraist Franz Delitzsch considered the play one of the gems of Hebrew literature. See Franz Delitzsch, *Zur Geschichte der judischen Poesie vom Abschluss der heiligen Schriften des Alten Bundes bis auf die neueste Zeit* (Leipzig, 1836), 92: "eins der werthgeschätztesten Kleinodien der Nation ist."

16. Vienna, 1793. An annotated excerpt is published in Romanelli, *Ketāvīm Nivhārīm*, ed. Schirmann, 191–95. The play was composed for the wedding of Leopold Herz and his cousin Charlotte Arnstein.

17. Only Klausner, *Hīstōreya shel ha-Sifrūt hā-ʿIvrīt ha-Ḥadāsha*, I, 312, citing Reuben Fahn, *Teqūfat ha-Haskāla be-Vīna*, 29, mentions Romanelli's employment with Hraszansky. Cf. Schirmann, *Shemū'ēl Rōmānēllī*, 38–39; and Waxman *History of Jewish Literature*, III, 136.

18. See Schirmann, *Shemū'ēl Rōmānēllī*, 63–64. The venomous author of *Qīn'at Adōnāy Ṣevā'ōt* writes that "his name was particularly disreputable in the imperial city of Vienna" (ibid., App. C, 77).

19. See the entry "Trieste: Hebrew Printing," in *Encyclopaedia Judaica* 15, col. 1393.

20. The poem is no longer extant. See Schirmann, *Shemū'ēl Rōmānēllī*, 39, n. 53.

21. della Torre, "Samuel Romanelli," *Ben Chananja* 5:4 (1862), 27.

22. Schirmann, *Shemū'ēl Rōmānēllī*, 44. The poem is published in Romanelli, *Grammatica ragionata*, 205.

23. Schirmann, *Shemū'ēl Rōmānēllī*, 44–45; idem, "A Manuscript Collection," 377, 391.

24. Schirmann, *Shemū'ēl Rōmānēllī*, 44; idem, "A Manuscript Collection," 380, no. 30 and 392.

25. For a synopsis and analysis of *Maḥazē Shadday*, see Schirmann, *Shemū'ēl Rōmānēllī*, 50–51.

26. The full title is *Ordine Cerimoniale del sacro ministero che teneva il gran sacrificatore nel giorno di espiazione. Poema tradotto dall'originale ebraico secondo il rito degli ebrei italiani*, da Samuel Romanelli (Alessandria, 1812).

27. (Republica Italica, 1802).

28. See Schirmann, "A Manuscript Collection," 381, no. 35 and 390; also *Shemū'ēl Rōmānēllī*, 36.

29. della Torre, "Samuel Romanelli," *Ben Chananja* 5:4 (1862), 26.

30. See Schirmann, *Shemū'ēl Rōmānēllī*, 46, and the sources cited there.

31. Many of Romanelli's manuscripts passed into the possession of Lelio (Hillel) della Torre, the Italian rabbinical scholar and poet, several decades after Romanelli's death. Some of this material was lost or stolen not long before della Torre's own death in 1871. The remainder was acquired by the Budapest Rabbinical Seminary (Ms della Torre 267) and is described by Schirmann, "A Manuscript Collection," 373–394.

32. Georg Höst, *Efterretninger om Marokos og Fes* (Copenhagen, 1779; German trans., 1781); Louis Chénier, *Recherches historiques sur les Maures et histoire de l'empire du Maroc* (3 vols.; Paris, 1787; English trans., 1788); Franz von Dombay, *Geschichte der Scherifen* (Agram, 1801). Also deserving of mention here is the English physician William Lempriere's account of

his journey to Morocco during the years 1789–90 on a medical mission to the Sherifan court, entitled *A Tour from Gibraltar to Tangier, Sallee, Mogadore, Santa Cruz, Tarudant, and thence over Mount Atlas to Morocco* (London, 1791; 2nd. enlarged ed. 1793; French trans., 1801). Because Lempriere's visit overlaps that of Romanelli, there are many instances where observations of one corroborates or complements those of the other. Hence, Lempriere is frequently cited in the notes to our translation. By the way, Romanelli was nearly recruited to being Lempriere's translator. See Chapter 13, below.

33. Romanelli refers to him only as "the Viennese gentleman." See Chapters 3 and 4, below.

34. Klausner, *Hīstōreya shel ha-Sifrūt ha-ʿIvrīt ha-Ḥadāsha* I, 319.

35. Romanelli's benefactor Dombay, who was a trained Orientalist, had in fact been making just such a study of Moroccan Arabic during his years in Tangier, and it was he who published the first grammar of the dialect *Grammatica Linguae Mauro-Arabicae* (Vienna, 1800).

36. See Norman A. Stillman and Yedida K. Stillman, "The Jewish Courtier Class in Late Eighteenth-Century Morocco as seen through the Eyes of Samuel Romanelli," *The Islamic World, Classical and Medieval, Ottoman, and Modern—Essays in Honor of Bernard Lewis*, ed. by C. E. Bosworth, et al.

37. It is for this reason that we have generally cited in the notes to our translation only those scriptural references that would be clear to readers using an English Bible.

38. Leopold Dukes, "Literarische Anzeigen: Die Reisebeschreibung des R. Petachiah aus Regensburg," *Ben Chananja* 4:49 (1861), 424, n. 1. More recently, some Moroccan Jews in Israel and France who are extremely sensitive to any negative images of Moroccan Jewry have impugned Romanelli's veracity for apologetic reasons, accusing him of coloring his account out of prejudice or a desire for sensationalsim. See for example, Haim Bentov, "The Ha-Levi Ibn Yuli Family," *East and Maghreb*, II, ed. E. Bashan et al. (Ramat Gan, 1980), 141 [Hebrew], where among other things, the author charges Romanelli with seriously distorting Eliahu Levi's image! All of the evidence, however, supports Romanelli's overall accuracy.

Author's Introduction

1. Mogador (called *al-Ṣuwayra* in Arabic), on Morocco's southern Atlantic coast, was the country's chief outlet for trade with Europe. It had been built with the help of a French architect only some twenty years

before Romanelli's visit. When Romanelli states that there are only three or four Jewish traders, he is referring only to big-time merchants who are well known from the European consular correspondence of the period. See Norman A. Stillman, *The Jews of Arab Lands: A History and Source Book* (Philadelphia, 1979), 368–69; and Jean Brignon et al., *Histoire du Maroc* (Casablanca, 1967), 278.

2. At least one author in the preceding century had devoted an entire book to Maghrebi Jewry. See Lancelot Addison, *The Present State of the Jews in the Barbary States (more particularly to those in Barbary)* (London, 1675).

3. Ceuta is still under Spanish administration today.

4. The first Arabic printing press was the lithograph press of Fez which opened in 1865. There had been, however, an early Hebrew printing press in Fez between ca. 1516 and 1524 that was established by exiles from Portugal. It is known to have published fifteen books. See A. Freimann, "Typographisches: Die hebräische Druckerei in Fez im Jahre 1516–21," *ZHB* 14 (1910), 79–80 and ibid. 15 (1911), 180–81; also Hayyim Dov Friedberg, *Tōledōt ha-Defūs ha-ʿIvrī*, 2nd ed. (Tel-Aviv, 1955/56), 143–44.

Chapter 1

1. Prov. 19:21.

2. The image is from Job 8:14.

3. This town, which lies 33 miles southeast of Tangier, was populated largely by the descendants of Muslims and Jews expelled from Spain. During the seventeenth and eighteenth centuries, it was one of the principal outlets for trade with Europeans.

4. The Wad Martil. Tetuan is situated on a plateau at the foot of the Jebel Dersa. The green river valley lies below the plateau.

5. The incident referred to took place in 1770, when a Muslim woman was accidently wounded by a European while hunting. See Louis Chénier, *The Present State of the Empire of Morocco* I (London, 1788), 19; and William Lempriere, *A Tour from Gibraltar to Tangier, Sallee, Mogodore, Santa Cruz, Tarudant; and Thence, over Mount Atlas to Morocco: including a particular account of the Royal Harem, etc.* (London, 1791), 7.

6. The republic of Dubrovnik, which had commercial ties with Morocco at this time. See, for example, Besim Korkut *Arapski Dokumenti u Državnom Arkhivu u Dubrovniku: Dokumenti o Odnosima Dubrovnika i Maroka* (Sarajevo, 1960).

7. Approximately a kilometer.

8. Romanelli has the Spanish form of the place name, Martin.

9. Romanelli is referring to the famous Battle of the Three Kings (called by the Arabs the Battle of the Wād al-Makhāzin) which took place on August 4, 1578, (and not in 1577). For the circumstances surrounding this disaster in which three rulers lost their lives, see Charles-André Julien, *History of North Africa: Tunisia, Algeria, Morocco: From the Arab Conquest to 1830*, trans. J. Petrie (New York and Washington, 1970), 227–28.

10. These Jews were eminently suited to act as interpreters since, in addition to speaking Moroccan Arabic, they had continued to speak their ancestral Castilian dialect. Their distinctive form of Ladino, or Judeo-Spanish, is known as *haketia*. Concerning this language, see José Benoliel, *Dialecto judeo-hispano-marroqui o hakitia* (Madrid, 1977); and also C. Benarroch, "Ojeada sobre el judeoespañol de Marruecos," in *Actas del Primer Simposio de Estudios Sefardies*, ed. I. M. Hassan, et al. (Madrid, 1970), 263–75.

11. This was to guarantee the kashrut of the brandy.

12. See Dan. 1:3–16.

13. This is not entirely so. Muslims may eat Jewish meat, but not that of Christians. In fact, there is a Moroccan proverb that states: "Sleep in the beds of Christians, but don't eat their food, eat the food of the Jews, but don't sleep in their beds." See Edward Westermarck, *Wit and Wisdom in Morocco: A Study of Native Proverbs* (London 1930) 130, no. 467. Romanelli, who was a keen observer, certainly learned otherwise later. At this time Morocco was still totally new to him and he explained this eating apart by a false analogy with Gen. 43:32, whose language he employs here.

14. Isa. 24:2.

15. In the original edition, Romanelli has a note here: Fontenelle in the book *Plurality of Worlds*. He is referring to Bernard le Bovier de Fontenelle, *Entretiens sur la pluralités des mondes* (1687); English. trans. by Glanvill (London, 1688), repr. in Leonard M. Marsak (ed.), *The Achievement of Bernard le Bovier de Fontenelle*. The Sources of Science, No. 76 (New York and London, 1970), see especially 39–60.

16. I Sam. 21:14.

17. Romanelli is referring here to Antonio Salieri's opera, *Axur Re d'Ormus*. See A. Loewenberg, *Annals of Opera*, 2nd ed. (Geneva, 1955), I, 443–44.

18. Romanelli makes a note here: The poet Metastasio in "The Dream of Scipio." He is referring to the aria in the play *Il sogno di Scipione* which opens with the words: Voi colaggiu ridete d'un fanciullin che piange." See Metastasio, *Poésie* II (Paris, 1755), 420.

19. Portugal ceded Tangier to England as part of the dowry of Catherine of Braganca for her impending marriage to Charles II of England. The British maintained control over the city until 1682.

20. Romanelli offers here a very accurate description of the traditional Moroccan urban house. For the floor plan, cross section, and interior views of such a home, see Ernst Rackow, *Beiträge zur Kenntnis der materiellen Kultur Nordwest-Marokkos: Wohnraum, Hausrat, Kostüm* (Wiesbaden, 1958), Tafel IV.

21. The bed Romanelli is describing is set into a niche or alcove (called *ḥniyya d-l-frash* in northern Morocco). This sort of sleeping quarters is illustrated in Rackow, *Beiträge*, Tafel IV.

22. There are no special beds for children in many traditional Moroccan homes to this day. We have on numerous occasions been in Moroccan homes where the parents simply threw a coverlet over a child who had fallen asleep on the carpet, a cushion, or the divan in the room in which we sat talking and would leave them there until morning.

23. These wall hangings (called *ḥaytiyyin* in northern Morocco), which can also be of fabric, can still be found in traditional Moroccan homes. For an illustration, see Rackow, *Beiträge*, Tafel IV; and also *Ḥayyē ha-Yehūdīm be-Mārōqō*, Israel Museum Catalogue No. 103 (Jerusalem, 1973), 166–67, Pls. 332 and 333.

24. Italian Jews did not share the iconoclasm of most other traditional Jews. Paintings by Christian masters hung both in private homes and in the synagogue. Even sculpture could be found in the Jewish quarters of Italy (to the chagrin of East European Jews). See Cecil Roth, *The Jews in the Renaissance* (Philadelphia, 1977), 203–204.

25. For illustrations of traditional shops of this sort, see Roger Le Tourneau, *Fès avant le Protectorat* (Casablanca, 1949; repr. New York, 1978), Pl. LXIII; and J. Goulven, *Les mellahs de Rabat-Salé* (Paris, 1927), Pls. XXVIII and XXIX, and the illustration on p. 26 above.

26. Concerning the Chiappe brothers—Giacomo, Giuseppe, and Francesco, who were held in very high esteem by the sultan of Morocco, see Ramón Lourido Díaz, *Marruecos en la segunda mitad del siglo XVIII: El Sultanato de Sīdī Muḥammad B. ʿAbd Allāh (1757–1790)*, Cuadernos de Historia del Islam, Serie Monográfica-Islamica Occidentalia, No. 2 (Granada, 1970), 120–21. Three years before Romanelli's arrival in Morocco, Francesco Chiappe was given the extraordinary appointment by Sīdī Muḥammad of chief intermediary between the Sherifan court and all foreigners—consuls, ambassadors, or merchants. See Norman A. Stillman, "A New Source for Eighteenth-Century Moroccan History in the John Ry-

lands University Library of Manchester: The Dombay Papers," *Bulletin of the John Rylands University Library of Manchester* 57:2 (1975), 477, no. 20.

Chapter 2

1. The Hebrew expression *bnē hōrīm* is probably used here by Romanelli to translate the Ladino *francos,* which had the double meaning of "Franks" (i.e., Europeans) and freemen not subject to either the government or local Jewish authorities. See Norman A. Stillman, *The Jews of Arab Lands: A History and Source Book* (Philadelphia, 1979), 93; and also H. Z. Hirschberg, "Francos," *EJ* 7, cols. 51–52.

2. Isa. 48:6. Literally, "well-guarded secrets."

3. Paraphrasing Prov. 24:7.

4. Prov. 26:7.

5. The proverb, which is of medieval Ashkenazi origin, was probably known to the Moroccan Jews from the commentary of Tosafot to BT Menahot 20b, under the heading *"Nifsal."* Romanelli's criticism of the Moroccan Jews' adherence to custom even when it runs counter to *halakha* is nothing new in Judaism. Concerning the ancient debate as to whether "custom overrides the law" (*minhag mevattēl halākha*), see Menachem Elon, "Minhag," *EJ* 12, cols. 13–19.

6. The parallel Romanelli seems to want to make here is with Jehu b. Jehoshaphat b. Nimshi, who, although he extirpated the cult of Baal from Israel, did not move against the cult of golden calves apparently because it went back to the time of Jeroboam. Cf. II Kings 10:28–31.

7. BT 'Eruvin 21b. This is the version quoted by Romanelli and not the slight variant in BT Menahot 29b cited in Schirmann's note to the text, 32.

8. Paraphrasing Jer. 50:38 (misprinted 48 in Schirmann's note to the text, 32).

9. Ps. 104:4.

10. Combining paraphrases of Jer. 51:30 and BT Shabbat 33b.

11. Paraphrasing Job 17:4.

12. Other visitors of the period were struck by the good looks of Moroccan Jewish women. Cf. for example, Lempriere, *A Tour from Gibraltar*, 2nd ed., 205: "The Jewesses of this empire in general are very beautiful, and remarkably fair."

13. Concerning their Ladino dialect, known as *haketia*, see above, Chapter 1, n. 10.

14. Mishna Tractate Berakhot 3:3—"Women, slaves, and minors are exempt from reciting the Shema' and from putting on phylacteries. However, they are required to perform the prayer (i.e., the Eighteen Benedictions), have the mezuzah (on their doorposts), and recite the grace after meals."

15. Mishna Tractate Sota 3:4. There is a pun here, since in unvocalized Hebrew "prayer" (*tefillot*) and "wantonness" (*tiflut*) are homographs. Although this statement which is attributed to Rabbi Eliezer was not the prevailing rabbinic opinion, it did represent the popular point of view among Oriental Jewry. See Yedida K. Stillman, "Attitudes toward Women in Traditional Near Eastern Societies," in *Studies in Judaism and Islam Presented to Shelomo Dov Goitein on the Occasion of his Eightieth Birthday*, ed. S. Morag, I. Ben-Ami, and N. A. Stillman (Jerusalem, 1981), 354.

16. According to Lev. 12:4, a woman in a state of impurity is not to enter the Sanctuary, but there is no rabbinical ordinance against her praying or going into the women's gallery of the synagogue. In both Muslim and Jewish popular piety in Morocco there is considerable anxiety over ritually impure individuals, and particularly menstruating women, approaching holy places. See, for example, Edward Westermarck, *Ritual and Belief in Morocco* I (London, 1926; repr. New Hyde Park, 1968), 230–32. This anxiety is a common theme in Jewish folktales from Morocco. For examples, see Norman A. Stillman, *The Language and Culture of the Jews of Sefrou, Morocco: An Ethnolinguistic Study*, JSS Monograph Series, No. 11 (Manchester, 1988), 66, 85, 105.

17. That is the school for higher education (*yeshīva*), as opposed to the elementary (*slā*). For a thorough survey of traditional Moroccan Jewish education, see Haïm Zafrani, *Pédagogie juive en terre d'Islam: l'enseignement traditionnel de l'hebreu et du Judaïsme au Maroc* (Paris, 1969).

18. Here Romanelli has a note: R. Jacob Frances in *'Eṣ ha-Daʿat*. The quote is from the anti-Kabbalist poem "Happy is the People Whom the Lord has Chosen" by Jacob Frances (1615–67). Romanelli is citing the poem from Solomon Morpurgo's philosophical work *'Eṣ ha-Daʿat* (Venice, 1704), 35. The poem may also be found in the complete edition of Frances' poetry. See P. Naveh (ed.), *Kōl Shīrē Yaʿaqōv Frānsēsh* (Jerusalem, 1969), 405, lines 53–54.

19. Lam. 4:1.

20. Ps. 45:14. The princess here is a metaphor for the true Kabbala.

21. That is Maimonides' *Guide of the Perplexed*.

22. Paraphrasing 1 Sam. 2:29.

23. The Great Mosque of Tangier lies only a little over 100 m. from shore.

24. Romanelli has confused matters here somewhat. There are five required daily prayers in Islam. There are, however, two supererogatory prayers—one at midnight, the other before dawn. See A. J. Wensinck, "Ṣalāt," *Shorter EI*, 491–99. The Arabic names given by Romanelli reflect Moroccan dialect and not Classical Arabic. Here too there is some confusion: *el-mwodden* is the muezzin, not the dawn prayer; *dhor el-luwlī* is the first call to the noon prayer (*dhor*), concerning which see William Marçais, *Textes arabes de Tanger* (Paris, 1911), 226; *el-ʿāsar* is the afternoon prayer and is "the second noon prayer"; *el-maghrib* is the evening prayer; while *el-ʿashā'* is the night prayer. Romanelli's inaccuracies here are probably due to his Jewish informants whose knowledge of their Muslim neighbors' religious practices was superficial at best. Of course, the Muslim's knowledge of Jewish practices was equally hazy. This mutual ignorance has persisted to the present in Morocco despite the close proximity of the two groups.

25. Romanelli's attempted philological explanation is a bit off.

26. BT Yoma 20b (where it is R. Shila, not Samuel, who responds to Rav). Romanelli is poking fun here at the muezzin.

27. The simplicity of Moroccan synagogues must have appeared especially austere to a Jew from Italy, where the synagogues were very ornate.

28. The Ninth of Av is the traditional day of mourning for the destruction of both the First and Second Temples. On this day, it is customary to sit on the ground or on low stools as a sign of mourning.

29. The *sade* in the Dutch Sephardi tradition is /ts/ as in the Ashkenazi reading. Moroccan Jews pronounce it as /s/.

30. Actually, the Moroccans pronounce spirantized *gimel* as /gh/ (voiced). However, they do sometimes pronounce it as /kh/ (voiceless) like the Dutch "g."

31. Romanelli is referring to R. Jedidiah Solomon Norsa's (fl. late sixteenth and early seventeenth centuries) great work on the Masorah *Gōdēr Pereṣ*, which in its published edition was given the title *Minḥat Shay* (Mantua, 1742–44). The opinion Romanelli is referring to is in the Appendix to ibid., II, fol. 4b.

32. That is, they do not clearly distinguish between /e/ and /i/ and between /u/ and /o/. This is still true in the traditional reading of Hebrew in Morocco. See the comparative chart and notes in Shelomo Morag, "Pronunciations of Hebrew," *EJ* 13, cols. 1139–42.

33. Actually, the /t/ is pronounced as a fricative /ṭ/ (= ts as in "cents") by the Arabic-speaking Jews of most of the major cities of northern Morocco. It could easily have been mistaken by Romanelli for /ch/ amidst all

the unfamiliar consonantal clusters that result from the Moroccan habit
of swallowing vowels in rapid speech.

34. Gen. 29:19: "Better that I give her to you than that I should give
her to an outsider." In the Meknasi rabbi's pronunciation this phrase would
be rendered: *ṭob ṭiṭṭi ōṭaḥ lakḥ meṭ-ṭiṭṭi ōṭaḥ le-īs aḥīr.*

35. The simile is from BT Shabbat 30a.

36. Romanelli is describing the short Rifi jellaba which only extends
to the knees.

37. The fruit described is the prickly pear of the *Opuntia* cactus. The
Spanish name *higo chumbo* has been garbled in the text.

38. Literally, "whatever the fork turns up." See I Sam. 2:14.

39. Isa. 44:20.

40. Literally, "that splintered reed of a staff that was his protection."
For this metaphor, see II Kings 18:21.

41. Paraphrasing Jer. 2:13.

42. Hos. 9:7.

Chapter 3

1. These opening verses are from Romanelli's play *Ha-Qōlōt Yeḥdālūn* (The Thundering Voices Shall Cease), Act I, Scene 7, ll. 1–6 (Berlin,
1791), 32. For a synopsis of the play, see Meyer Waxman, *A History of
Jewish Literature*, III (New York and London, 1960), 136–37. Excerpts from
the play are included in Schirmann's edition of Romanelli's selected writings, 183–190.

2. That is, Christian Europe.

3. Paraphrasing Isa. 22:16.

4. The cantor recited the blessing *Mī she-bĕrakh* ("May He who
blessed our fathers . . . ") on each of the well-to-do members of the congregation in return for which, they would pledge a sum toward the preacher's emolument.

5. The Jew who had guided Romanelli and his party from Tetuan. See
Chapter 1 above.

6. Paraphrasing Ezra 7:10.

7. The Aramaic doxology recited at the conclusion of various parts
of the service and at the end of a lesson.

8. Isa. 50:4.

9. As a native of Mantua, Romanelli was a Habsburg subject. The
Austrians had taken over rule in various parts of Italy earlier in the century.

10. The man—though never mentioned by name here—is obviously Franz Laurenz von Dombay (1758–1810), a career civil servant and pioneer orientalist, who among his numerous works, wrote a history of the Sherifan dynasty and a grammar of colloquial Moroccan Arabic. For a biographical sketch and survey of his works, see N. A. Stillman, "The Dombay Papers," *Bulletin of the John Rylands Library* 57:2 (1975), 466–69.

11. Paraphrasing Job 16:5.

12. Such amulets were used by European Jews at this time as well. For illustrated examples, see *Ḥayyē ha-Yehūdīm be-Mārōqō*, Israel Museum Cat. 103, pp. 96–97, Pls. 156, 159, and 160. For an eighteenth-century German example with David's Shield, see *EJ* 11, col. 691, fig. 4. It is clear from Romanelli's words that the *māgēn Dāvid* was still not a specifically Jewish symbol. See Gershom Scholem, "Magen David," *EJ* 11, cols. 687–97.

13. There are numerous ethnographic descriptions of the rites and practices commonly used by both Muslims and Jews in Morocco to ward off or propitiate the *jnūn* (spirits). The most comprehensive survey is Edward Westermarck, *Ritual and Belief in Morocco*, 2 vols. (London, 1926; repr. New Hyde Park, 1968). For a description of the traditional Moroccan Jewish birth practices, see Elie Malka, *Essai d'ethnographie traditionnelle des Mellahs, ou Croyances, rites de passage et vieilles pratiques des Israélites marocains* (Rabat, 1946), 18–30.

14. Ps. 49:14.

15. Literally, "because this is the portion and the lot for Azazel." See Lev. 16:5–29 and Mishna Tractate Yoma 3:9–7:4.

16. Once again, Romanelli mentions the ubiquitous *eau de vie*, known as *maḥya* (the Arabic name is the literal equivalent of the French). It is usually made from figs, but also from raisins or dates. It was not that the Jews of Morocco did not know how to make wine. They did, even in Romanelli's time. Simply, *maḥya* was the favorite alcoholic beverage. Indeed, it was much more than that, having a special place in Moroccan Jewish social life. As one French writer has charmingly described it: "Mahia, an unctuous *eau de vie*, has no parallel in animating a conversation. It accompanies all joyous family occasions. It is used at all festivities: Sabbath, religious holidays, circumcision, marriage. People drink it when they have colic, or take a shot when they are tired or frightened. If they are hurt, they mix a little with cumin and spread it on the sore." Pascale Saisset, *Heures juives au Maroc* (Paris, 1930), quoted in J. Mathieu, R. Baron, and J. Lummau, "Etude de l'alimentation au Mellah de Rabat," *Bulletin de l'Institut d'Hygiène du Maroc*, 3–4 (1938), 118.

17. This line could also be interpreted: "People send portions of couscous as Purim gifts to friends."

18. *Mémoires du Maréchal Duc de Richelieu* I (London, 1790), 186: "Mehemet Rizabeg, the ambassador of Persia, had to come to Paris. . . . When the Baron de Breteuil came into his room, he found him lying near the fire on Persian carpets and a sort of cushion, with his legs folded in the manner of Orientals. 'I swear,' says Bretueil in his memoires, 'that at first glance, it seemed to me that there was a fat ape lying by the fire.' When the Baron de Breteuil was seated, the Persian, who was lying by the fire, sat up on the little cushion, without raising himself on his legs."

19. Turning fresh meat into *khlī ʿ* was the standard way of preserving it in Morocco prior to the advent of refrigeration. It is commonly mentioned in both Arabic and European travel literature. For the numerous sources, see Reinhart Dozy, *Supplément aux dictionnaires arabes* I, 3rd ed. (Leiden and Paris, 1967), 395a–b. (Although it is no longer necessary to prepare meat this way for preservation, it is still a very popular dish among Moroccan Jews.)

20. In the Hebrew text *skhīna* is misprinted *skhāna* (Ar. for "fever"). *Skhīna* like Mishnaic Hebrew *ḥammīn* (Mishna Tractate Shabbat 2:7) means "hot food." This savory dish is cooked in a single pot over a slow-burning fire from Friday afternoon until Saturday noon in order to comply with the biblical prohibition against lighting fires on the Sabbath. However, it is not the normal holiday and festival dish, unless the holiday happens to fall on the Sabbath. Concerning *skhīna*, also called *dafīna* in Tangier, and other coastal towns of Morocco, see Mathieu-Baron-Lummau, "L'alimentation au Mellah de Rabat," *BIHM* 3–4 (1938), 120–21 (and the photographs between the last two pages); also Yedida K. Stillman, *From Southern Morocco to Northern Israel: A Study in the Material Culture of Shelomi* (Haifa, 1982) 51, 57 [Heb.].

21. These words are in the new JPS translation: "(He who splits wood) will be harmed by it." Many medieval commentators understood the meaning to be "will be heated by it." Ibn Ezra, however, dismisses this interpretation.

22. Paraphrasing Num. 33:55.

23. Jer. 5:28.

24. Prov. 31:26.

25. Romanelli quotes in a footnote here: "And be as long-lived as the phoenix" (Job 29:18).

26. Felix Lope de Vega Carpio (1562–1635) was a prolific Spanish poet

and playwright whose work was tremendously popular both during and after his lifetime.

27. The Jews of Meknes, both in Romanelli's day and in modern times, have been noted for their learning. The present Chief Sephardi Rabbis of Jerusalem and of Haifa are both Meknasis. For a general sketch of Meknasi Jewry, see Gabi Levi, *The Jewish Community of Meknes* (Tel Aviv, 1982) [Heb.].

28. Gen. 30:1.

29. See Gen. 16; Gen. 29:16–30:16; I Sam. 1:1–9, for each of the three examples cited by Romanelli.

30. Romanelli is referring to the prohibition against polygamy among Ashkenazi Jews, known as the Ban of R. Gershom (*ḥerem de-Rabbēnū Gērshōm*), concerning which see Benzion Schereschewsky, *Family Law in Israel*, 2nd ed. (Jerusalem, 1967), 67–80 [Heb.]. Although permissible, polygamy was never very common among Moroccan Jews. The descendants of the Spanish exiles had a number of ordinances to limit the practice. See Haïm Zafrani, *Mille ans de vie juive au Maroc: Histoire et culture, religion et magie* (Paris, 1983), 81–83.

31. The practice of magic and divination was widespread in North Africa into modern times. For a broad survey, see Edmond Doutté, *Magie et religion dans l'Afrique du Nord* (Algiers, 1909). The practice described here seems to be a form of the divining technique known as *zā'iraja*, concerning which see the detailed description in Ibn Khaldūn, *The Muqaddimah* III, trans. Franz Rosenthal (New York, 1958), 182–227; also N. A. Stillman and Y. K. Stillman, "Magic and Folklore, Islamic," *Dictionary of the Middle Ages*, VIII (New York, 1987), 21.

32. These were a device used by the priests in ancient Israel to obtain oracles. See Ex. 28:15–30; also Moshe Greenberg, "Urim and Thummim," *EJ* 16, cols. 8–9.

33. This, of course, is not true. Although there were no printers there were Muslim writers in Morocco. Furthermore, many religious texts were studied in addition to the Koran in schools for advanced study (*madrasa*). In the Muslim elementary school (*msīd*), which Romanelli goes on to describe accurately in the following sentences, the Koran was the sole text in use.

34. There is no Koranic dictum exactly like this. The closest one seems to be: "Woe unto those who write the scripture with their hands and then say, 'This is from Allah' " (Sura 2:79). Perhaps he had also heard the verse: "Who does greater wrong than he who invents a lie concerning Allah" (Sura 10:18).

35. Ancient Egyptian cities mentioned in the Bible (e.g., Jer. 2:16).

36. Storks are still considered to be charmed creatures in Morocco. For some of the many superstitions connected with them, see Wester-marck, *Ritual and Belief* II, 329–31.

37. A scene such as this can still be seen daily in places like the great square of Marrakesh known as the Jama' el-Fna.

38. Pope, *Essay on Man*, Epistle II, ll. 27–28.

39. The 'Isāwiyya is a Sufi brotherhood that was founded in the early sixteenth century by Sīdī Muḥammad b. 'Isā, after whom it is named. The devotees of the order are mainly blacks and members of the lower classes. They have long shocked onlookers with their ecstatic rites that include dancing, inflicting wounds upon themselves, tearing apart animal carcasses and smearing themselves with the blood, handling snakes, and imitating certain wild beasts. The long braid of hair, known as a *gaṭṭāya*, is the 'Isāwī's badge. It grows from a matted patch at the top of the skull, while the rest of the head is shaven. The 'Isāwiyya have been considered unsavory by the scholarly Muslim establishment. See R. Brunel, *Essai sur la Confrérie religieuse des Aissaoua au Maroc* (Paris, 1926), and J.-L. Michon, "'Isāwā," *EI*^{2} IV, 93–95.

40. The Būjlūd is a grotesque character in Moroccan folk plays whose costume consists of animal skins (sometimes freshly flayed). The character is usually played by a poor man who is often paid with something to eat. In some places, it was customary for the actor assuming the role to have a loathsome skin disease. See Westermarck, *Ritual and Belief* II, 134–43, 154; also Edmond Doutté, *Magie et religion dans l'Afrique du Nord* (Algiers, 1909), 496–540.

41. Romanelli is referring to the Muslim profession of faith (*shahāda*) which states: "There is no deity, but *Allāh*; Muhammad is the messenger of Allāh." The recitation of the formula by a non-Muslim is considered an act of conversion to Islam. Some forty years after Romanelli's stay in Morocco, a young Jewish girl, Sol Hatchuel, was accused by Muslim neighbors in Tangier with having recited the profession of faith. When she stubbornly denied the allegation, she was executed for apostasy from Islam. See Norman A. Stillman, *The Jews of Arab Lands: A History and Source Book* (Philadelphia, 1979), 103–104.

42. Literally, "No one can save him."

43. Isa. 59:19.

44. All of these ethnographic details reported by Romanelli are quite accurate and may still be observed among traditional Moroccans.

45. Paraphrasing Job 20:5.

46. There are copies and translations of numerous *dahirs* or decrees sent by Dombay back to Vienna in the Haus-, Hof- und Staatsarchiv (Vi-

enna), Marokko Karton 3, as well as in the collection of Dombay's personal papers and correspondence in the John Rylands University Library, Manchester. See n. 10 above.

47. In 1778, Mūlāy Yazid, who until that time had been one of Sīdī Muhammad's favorite sons, allowed himself to receive the loyalty of the rebellious Black Slave Corps (the *ʿAbīd al-Bukhārī*) after his older brother Mūlāy ʿAlī had refused to be their candidate. Although he was later pardoned, he was thereafter kept under surveillance until he was sent off to Mecca in 1784. His disreputable conduct abroad caused him again to fall into disfavor. He returned to Morocco in 1789, hoping to lead an uprising against his aged father, but was forced to take refuge in the tomb of Mūlāy ʿAbd al-Salām b. Mashīsh near Tetuan. See Ramón Lourido Díaz, *Marruecos en la segunda mitad del siglo XVIII: El sultanato de Sīdī Muhammad b. ʿAbd Allāh (1757–1790)* (Granada, 1970), 60–67.

48. Actually, his mother was the daughter of an English renegade in Morocco. See William Lempriere, *A Tour from Gibraltar*, 2nd ed., 435. Franz von Dombay, however, refers to her as the daughter of an English woman. See his *Geschichte der Scherifen* (Agram, 1801), 220.

49. Between 1787 and 1790, Dombay was attached to the Austrian embassy in Madrid. He kept a close watch of Moroccan affairs, usually from his listening post in Cadiz.

50. Esth. 4:14.

51. In addition to being the unofficial consul and an intelligence agent, Dombay was indeed a student of Maghrebi Arabic. His book *Grammatica Linguae Mauro-Arabicae* (Vienna, 1800), was a pioneer study and is still useful for students of Maghrebi dialectology.

52. The reference is probably to the English Consul Logie, who served in Tangier until 1780. See Pierre Grillon (ed.), *Un chargé d'affaires au Maroc: La correspondance du consul Louis Chénier, 1767–1782*, II (Paris, 1970), 1000.

53. Romanelli is quoting verbatim from the story of Ahithophel in II Samuel 17:23.

54. Romanelli is referring to an English merchant in Rabat who was humiliated for having sold gunpowder to the Sultan's rebellious uncle Mulay Mustadī. See Louis Chénier, *The Present State of the Empire of Morocco*, II (London, 1788), 284.

55. Paraphrasing Deut. 7:19.

56. Isa. 41:23.

57. The prescience Romanelli is attributing to Dombay is in the light of Romanelli's hindsight. The "approaching anarchy" was still more than two years away.

Chapter 4

1. What Romanelli means is that there were no grammar books for colloquial Arabic. See the following note.

2. Throughout the Middle Ages and unto the present day, the linguistic situation in the Arab world is characterized by the phenomenon known as diglossia, whereby people speak one language, but read and write (and on some formal occasions speak) another. The situation is not altogether unlike that of medieval Europe when Latin was still the official language of the court, the church, and literature. Classical Arabic, like Latin, is an inflected language, whereas the Arabic dialects are not. The spoken vernaculars of different Arab countries may differ as much as one Romance language from another.

3. Gen. 11:8.

4. See Jud. 12:6.

5. Because there is no *p* in Arabic, most Arabs pronounce it *b* when speaking a foreign language.

6. This laryngal consonant which is absent from European languages is not pronounced by Ashkenazi Jews, but is read as a silent letter like *alef*.

7. See Chapter 2, above.

8. Rashi script is a form of cursive Hebrew that developed in Spain. It is popularly called after the great French Bible and Talmud commentator Rashi, whose commentaries were printed in this script to set them off from the sacred texts as a form of italics. See M. M. Spitzer, "Typography," *EJ* 15, col. 1480; and S. A. Birnbaum, "Alphabet, Hebrew," *EJ* 2, col. 741.

9. That is, one sews from right to left.

10. For medieval examples of Jewish communities putting pressure on foreign bachelors in their midst to marry, see the examples from the Cairo Geniza documents cited in S. D. Goitein, *A Mediterranean Society III: The Family* (Berkeley and Los Angeles, 1978), p. 48.

11. The word used by Romanelli for "cheek" (audacity) is the Heb. *meṣaḥ* (lit. "forehead"), a contraction of the phrase *ʿazzūt meṣaḥ*.

12. Child marriage was common in Morocco well into the present century. The Alliance Israélite Universelle was particularly active in combatting the practice. See, e.g., Louis Brunot and Elie Malka, *Textes judéo-arabes de Fès* (Rabat, 1939), 330, n. 5 and the sources cited there; also David Ovadia, *La Communauté de Sefrou* III (Jerusalem, 1975), 73–74 [Heb.], where the problems that frequently resulted from such marriages

are discussed; and Norman A. Stillman, *The Language and Culture of the Jews of Sefrou*, 28, 127–30.

13. The first of the 613 commandments specifically mentioned in the Torah is "Be fruitful and multiply" (Gen. 1:22).

14. Gen. 8:21.

15. See BT Qiddushin 29b, where it is R. Ḥisdā who makes the statement. Romanelli, who surprisingly seems not to know or to have forgotten this well-known passage, cites R. Hisda's remark in Hebrew, rather than in the original Aramaic.

16. Heb. *Ba-yōm, Ḥasīd, Ūva-layla Rāshā͑*.

17. BT Yevamot 62a.

18. This is simply not true. Islam, unlike Judaism, permits coitus interruptus. See G.-H. Bousquet, *L'éthique sexuelle de l'Islam* (Paris, 1966), 176–83.

19. The image is from Deut. 29:17.

20. This pressure placed upon a foreign bachelor to marry was very real. See the example from the Cairo Geniza documents cited by Goitein, *A Mediterranean Society III: The Family*, 48.

21. Paraphrasing Isa. 22:18.

22. This is a particularly Jewish cry. See L. Brunot and E. Malka, *Glossaire judéo-arabe de Fès* (Rabat, 1940), 143, s.v. "*wób*." For the Muslim expressions, see W. Marçais, *Textes arabes de Tanger* (Paris, 1911), 501, s.v. "*ueil*." The lamentations described here by Romanelli remained unchanged into modern times. See, e.g., Elie Malka, *Essai d'ethnographie traditionnelle des Mellahs, ou croyances, rites de passage et vieilles pratiques des Israélites marocains* (Rabat, 1946), 123. Even in Israel today, one frequently sees North African Jewish women keening and scratching their faces.

23. Deut. 14:1.

24. I Kings 18:28.

25. Since *their custom* refers to the prophets of Baal, it is Gentile practice (Heb. *ḥuqqat ha-Gōy*) and ought not to be followed. See Meir Ydit, "Ḥukkat ha-Goi," *EJ* 8, cols. 1061–62.

26. Jer. 5:7 (wrong context); 16:6; 41:5; 47:5.

27. Romanelli is slightly mistaken here. The quotation is from Nahum 2:8. It is not the gashing that he is referring to here and in the following verses, but to the beating of the breast and the cries of woe.

28. Amos 5:16.

29. Mishna Tractate Mōʿēd Qāṭān 3:8.

30. Marçais, *Textes arabes de Tanger*, 437–438, s.vv. "*gežder*," and *g˘zdūr*, where it is noted that this is particularly a Jewish women's custom.

31. Ruth 2:4.

32. The traditional day of mourning for the destruction of both the First and Second Temples and other calamities in Jewish history. Concerning visits to the graves of relatives and other Moroccan customs associated with this day, see J. Goulven, *Les mellahs de Rabat-Salé* (Paris, 1927), 89.

33. Ps. 94:20.

34. We have never come across this particular superstition either in the literature—indigenous or ethnographic—or in our field work among Moroccan Jews in Morocco and Israel.

35. This great veneration of the beard goes beyond even the traditional Jewish respect for it and is probably due to the great influence of the Lurianic Kabbala in Morocco. Luria is reported to have refrained from even touching his beard, lest a hair should fall. See *Bā'ēr Hētēv* (Commentary in the Margins of the *Shulḥān ʿArūkh*), *Yōre Dēʿa* 181:5.

36. The belief in the curative powers of spittle is widespread in traditional Morocco. See, for example, Westermarck, *Ritual and Belief* I, 71, 93–94, 156, 158, 197, 203.

37. BT Bava Mesiʿa 107b: "Ninety-nine (die) from the evil eye for every one by natural causes." For parallel Arab proverbs, see Yedida K. Stillman, "The Evil Eye in Morocco," in *Folklore Research Center Studies* I, ed. D. Noy and I. Ben-Ami (Jerusalem, 1970), 82.

38. One can avoid having to spit by reciting an appropriate blessing when praising or admiring. See Y. K. Stillman, "The Evil Eye in Morocco," 90–91.

Chapter 5

1. Paraphrase of Isa. 24:4.

2. Gen. 35:2.

3. The image is from Isa. 1:25.

4. Paraphrase of II Kings 17:9. Romanelli is following the traditional interpretation of this difficult biblical passage. See, for example, Rashi's commentary on this verse.

5. This refers to the act known in Heb. as *qinyān*, by which a person acquires certain rights from another. Engagement agreements are formalized by the prospective bridegroom and the bride's representative, each taking hold of a kerchief (*qinyān sūdar*). See Shalom Albeck, "Acquisition," *EJ* 2, cols. 216–21 and the sources cited there.

6. Even in recent times, it was not customary for Moroccan Jewish

women to call their husband by name, but by such expressions as "O he" (Ar. *yā huwa*) or "O he who answers" (Ar. *yā wāzeb*). See Brunot-Malka, *Textes judéo-arabes de Fès*, 359, n. 5; and Malka, *Essai d'ethnographie*, 79. This is done both as a mark of respect and in order to ward off any ill omen.

7. In Jewish tradition, the "deadly woman" (Heb. *qaṭlānīt*) is one who has had two or three husbands die on her, not just one. See BT Yevamot 64b, where Rabbi Judah ha-Nasi says that such a woman may not marry a third time, and Rabbi Simeon b. Gamliel says she may not marry a fourth time. See also Rashi's commentary to ibid., 26a, where the term "deadly woman" is actually used.

8. The custom Romanelli is describing here, like much of what follows in his detailed description of the drawn-out wedding festivities, was still practiced well into this century with only minor variations. Compare, for example, R. Tadjouri, "Le mariage juif à Salé," *Hespéris* 3:3 (1923), 393–420. What Romanelli has omitted mentioning here is that the ox or cow was festooned with scarves, jewelry, ribbons, and flowers (ibid., 398). This would explain his otherwise obscure reference to see the Spanish verb *pintar* (which is also used in Moroccan Judaeo-Arabic, *penter*). The usual meaning of the word is "to paint," but it can also mean to decorate an animal. See, for example, Martín Alonso, *Enciclopedia del Idioma* III (Madrid, 1958), 3284, s.v. (We owe this last reference to our colleague Professor Richard Kerr.)

For other descriptions of Moroccan Jewish weddings, see Félix Nataf, "Le mariage juif à Rabat," *Revue des Traditions Populaires* (1919), 197–208; Issachar Ben-Ami, *Le Judaïsme marocain: études ethno-culturelles* (Jerusalem, 1975), 9–103, where a very extensive survey of the literature is given.

9. For "a swift or a wryneck," see Jer. 8:7. These ululating old women who play such an important role at family celebrations are known as *zghrātaṭ*. Concerning them, see Brunot-Malka, *Textes judéo-arabes de Fès*, 288–89, n. 4.

10. These ribbons that wrap the hair are known as *sfāyef* (sing. *sfīfa*) in Moroccan Arabic. In the cities of North Morocco where Romanelli was living, skeins of wool or silk, called *mdāyez* (sing. *mdedja*) were plaited into the hair and wrapped around it to form a braid. For an illustration of this, see Rackow, *Beiträge*, Tafel XX.

11. For examples of such facial decorations, see Illus. 8 and also *Hayyē ha-Yehūdīm be Mārōqō*, Israel Museum Cat. 103, pp. 99, 190, 191, 193, 207.

12. Romanelli is referring to the Shroud of Turin preserved in the

Cathedral of St. John the Baptist in Turin and believed by Catholics to be Jesus' burial shroud.

13. Hebrew liturgical or devotional songs. These are sung by Moroccan Jews on many different occasions. The art of writing *piyyūṭīm* has remained very much alive among the Jews in Morocco until very recently. For an extensive survey of the subject, see Haïm Zafrani, *Etudes et recherches sur la vie intellectuelle juive au Maroc de la fin du 15e au début du 20e siècle II: Poésie juive en Occident musulman* (Paris, 1977).

14. Amos 6:5. Romanelli is punning on the Hebrew words *pōreṭīm* ("strum") and *perūṭa* ("a small coin") which are both from the root *p-r-ṭ*.

15. Isa. 41:7.

16. In Romanelli's time, Mecklenburg consisted of two independent duchies in Northeastern Germany on the Baltic Coast. There, as elsewhere in Germany, post riders blew on a horn to announce their arrival in town.

17. Romanelli's philological intuition is correct here.

18. To this very day, these large metal castanets, known as *qrāqeb*, are used exclusively by the Gnāwa, black dancers of Guinean origin, who perform in the public squares of many of the major cities of Morocco and who are frequently pictured in tourist posters and brochures.

19. Romanelli is talking here about the style of vocal improvisation and not dancing as Schirmann had thought. See his edition, 56, n. 73.

20. This is rather typical of the style of Moroccan love songs. See Norman A. Stillman and Yedida K. Stillman, "The Art of a Moroccan Folk Poetess," *ZDMG* 128:1 (1978), 65–89.

21. See Chapter 1, above.

22. Hos. 3:4.

Chapter 6

1. Isa. 11:4. The belief that holy men are endowed with such powers is common among both Jews and Muslims in Morocco. See Norman A. Stillman, "Ṣaddīq and Marabout in Morocco," in *The Sephardi and Oriental Jewish Heritage: Studies*, ed. I. Ben-Ami (Jerusalem, 1982), 489–500.

2. See Jud. 19:16–18.

3. Continuing to paraphrase ibid.:20.

4. This sort of ritualized humiliation of non-Muslims was common throughout the Islamic world from the later Middle Ages to early modern times. It was in accordance with the injunction to humble the unbeliever.

See Stillman, *Jews of Arab Lands*, 20, 26–27, 63, 68–69, 83–84. The discriminatory regulations and ritualized humiliations imposed upon Jews in Morocco (there were no other native non-Muslims) were among the most rigorous in the Islamic world. The French captive Germaine Mouette, who was in Morocco a century before Romanelli, noted that the Jews "are subject to suffering the blows and injuries of everyone, without daring to say a word even to a child of six who throws stones at them" (trans. ibid., 304).

5. Paraphrasing Gen. 4:10.

6. Jer. 15:12.

7. The first blessing is recited at all holidays and joyous occasions, and upon experiencing some good thing for the first time. The second one is said when coming into the presence of someone who is a great Torah sage.

8. A parody of the well-known Hebrew proverb "The jealousy of scholars increases wisdom" (BT Bava Batra 21a).

9. He means, of course, the ability to write in Latin characters.

10. Ps. 55:15.

11. Isa. 25:1.

12. Prov. 1:6.

13. The text under discussion deals with the four primary causes of injury, and hence, damages and liability. Romanelli only mentions three of four (the last being the outbreak of fire). The talmudic discussion is based upon Mishna Bava Qama 1:1. The discussion Romanelli now proceeds to cite is found in BT Bava Qama 3b. However, he has reversed the speakers, attributing Samuel's opinion to Rav and vice versa.

14. Obad. 1:6.

15. Isa. 21:12.

16. Jer. 48:11.

17. Paraphrasing Job 10:8.

Chapter 7

1. We have seen several Moroccan synagogues in Morocco and in Israel that fit this description, with the reader's table on the ground level near the entrance. Most, however, have a raised pulpit either at the wall opposite the ark, or in the center of the sanctuary.

2. Most Moroccan synagogues did not have a women's gallery. Those women who came to services stayed in the courtyard and listened from the doorway.

3. Mal. 1:10.

4. Romanelli, for the sake of his parallel, is interpreting the verse from Malachi as if it meant that the open doors are letting light in upon the altar.

5. Ez. 41:22 and 44:16.

6. Isa. 62:9.

7. Zech. 3:7.

8. Neh. 8:16.

9. Ps. 84:11.

10. Ibid.

11. Romanelli is making a pedantic note here.

12. Paraphrasing Prov. 18:18. In Jewish civil cases oaths were administered where the evidence was insufficient for a judgment. If the defendant refused to take the oath, a *ḥerem*, or ban which was the Jewish equivalent of excommunication, was placed upon the individual for thirty days. See H. H. Cohn, "Oath: Talmudic Law," *EJ* 12, cols. 1298–302. The Talmud describes the court of Second Temple times as arranged in a semicircle. The students of the judges sat facing them in three straight rows. The students sat on the ground and the judges on benches. See BT Sanhedrin 36b (Mishna Sanhedrin 4:3) and the commentary of Rashi there.

13. *Sokhra* in Moroccan Arabic is corvée labor (Cl. Ar. *sukhra*). But it is also a commission carried out by soldiers or government officials who are called *msakhkhreyya*. See Louis Brunot, *Textes arabes de Rabat II: Glossaire* (Paris, 1952), 364–65, s.vv. *sohra* and *msahhrē*. In Moroccan Judaeo-Arabic, the word *skhra* has come to mean (rather understandably) "housework." See Brunot-Malka, *Glossaire judéo-arabe de Fès*, 60, s.v. Many writers mention the Jews having to do corvée labor. See, for example, the description of Mouette in Stillman, *Jews of Arab Lands*, 304. In 1864 the Sultan Mūlāy Muḥammad issued a decree at the request of Sir Moses Montefiore which put an end to this and other oppressive practices. However, the document became a dead letter soon after Sir Moses' departure. See ibid., 100 and 371–72, where the text of the decree is given in translation.

14. During the central prayer of the service known as the *ʿamīda*, or "standing prayer," the individual plants his two feet together and does not move them until the prayer is completed.

15. Isa. 64:11.

16. The Prophet Jeremiah.

17. Jer. 29:7. On the basis of this passage, Jews in each country to this day pray for the government under which they live.

18. Gen. 19:14.

19. BT Menaḥot 85a. The Hebrew equivalent of "carrying coals to New-castle."

20. Paraphrasing Ps. 27:11.

21. Apparently what he had prepared was not appropriate because of the wedding party, and so now he had to make an impromptu sermon.

22. See I Sam. 18:7.

23. This particularly Maghrebi form of humiliation remained in force until the late nineteenth century. See Norman A. Stillman, "L'expérience judéo-marocaine: un point de vue revisionniste," in *Judaïsme d'Afrique du Nord aux XIXe-XXe siècles: Histoire, société et culture,* ed. M. Abitbol (Jerusalem, 1980), 17; and idem, *Jews of Arab Lands,* 83, 304.

24. According to the English military physician William Lempriere, whose visit to Morocco overlaps with Romanelli's stay there, neither the Moroccan armed forces nor the country's defenses were any good. See his *A Tour from Gibraltar to Tangier, Sallee, Mogodore, Santa Cruz, Tarudant; and thence over Mount Atlas to Morocco,* 2nd ed. (London, 1793), 245, 261.

25. Romanelli probably has in mind the Cynic Diogenes, who is reputed to have eschewed most material comforts, wearing little clothing, eating coarse food, and sleeping in a tub.

26. Such as the *farajiyya, fūqiyya, čāmir,* or *jabadūlī.* For a general survey of Maghrebi dress, see Yedida K. Stillman, "Libās ii—The Muslim West," *EI²* V, 742–47.

27. Called *sirwāl.* These half-length pantaloons have the general appearance of a sack with two apertures below for the legs. This is why Romanelli says that few people wear pants as such.

28. Called *ḥāyk* or *ksa.* See Y. K. Stillman, "Libās," *EI²* V, Pl. XLV, no. 16, where the manner in which it is draped is illustrated.

29. The turban goes by various names (*'immāma, rezza, shedd*) and takes a variety of forms. The higher red caps are the *shāshiyya* and *ṭarbūsh.* The simple skullcap is the *ṭāqiyya.*

30. Called *belgha* or *bābūshāt.*

31. Called *silham.*

32. These *sirwāl* were more recognizably pantslike than the Muslim men's. For an example of the pants that came down almost to the ankle, see the nineteenth-century engraving in *Ḥayyē ha-Yehūdīm be-Mārōqō,* Israel Museum Cat. 103, 92, illus. 147, where a Jewish family of Tetuan or Tangier is depicted.

33. Romanelli's contemporary, the English surgeon Lempriere, describes the Jewish man's cloak as being of black wool and covering all of

the clothing beneath. See Lempriere, *A Tour from Gibraltar*, 2nd ed., 202. For one example—somewhat different from Romanelli's description—of how it might be slung over the shoulder, see *Ḥayyē ha-Yehūdīm be-Mā-rōqō*, 212, illus. 410.

34. For an example of this, see *Ḥayyē ha-Yehūdīm be-Mārōqō*, 213, unnumbered Pl.

35. Lempriere, *A Tour from Gibraltar*, 2nd ed., 202, also mentions this. The requirement for the Jews to wear black outer garments was a specifically Moroccan version of the traditional Islamic laws of differentiation (Ar. *ghiyār*). See Stillman, *Jews of Arab Lands*, 83.

36. This actually was a separate breastpiece, called by various names, such as *uzba* and *ktef* in Arabic, and *punta, peto*, and *bousdida* in Ladino. See Yedida K. Stillman, "The Costume of the Jewish Woman in Morocco," *Studies in Jewish Folklore*, ed. F. Talmage (Cambridge, Mass., 1980), 350, 365, Pl. 10, and 366, Pl. 11.

37. This is not a single dress, but a composite outfit, which when put together and joined with a belt, looks like a single dress. This festive dress which in recent times came only to be worn for weddings and special occasions is known in Arabic as the *kiswa l-kebira* ("the grand costume") and in Ladino as the *Traje Berberisco* ("the native Dress"). It has been described by many European travelers (as for example, Lempriere, *A Tour from Gibraltar*, 2nd ed., 203) and has been captured in several paintings and drawings by Delacroix and other artists. There are many illustrations of it in *Ḥayyē ha-Yehūdīm be-Mārōqō*, and it is described in detail in Y. K. Stillman, "The Costume of the Jewish Woman in Morocco," 350–52. The outfit is derived from sixteenth-century Spanish prototypes. See idem, "Hashpaʿōt Sefardiyyōt ʿal ha-Tarbūt ha-Ḥomrīt shel Yehūdē Marōqō," [Spanish influences on the Material Culture of Moroccan Jews], *Mōreshet Yehūdē Sefarād veha-Mizrah: Mehqārīm*, ed. I. Ben-Ami (Jerusalem, 1982), 359–66 and Pls. 1–4, where the prototypes and their derivatives are compared.

38. Romanelli has here Heb. *karpas*, which in the Book of Esther 1:6 and elsewhere is usually understood to mean "white cotton." However, since these skirts were invariably dark in color (deep red, green, dark blue, purple, or black) and usually of velvet, we have chosen to translate it as the latter.

39. The skirt is called *giraldeta* in Ladino. Its various Arabic names, such as *jaltēta, zentīta, faltīta*, are all derived from it. The embroidered belt is called in Arabic *hizām*, and in Ladino *cuchaca*.

40. Called in Arabic *sebniyya*, and in Ladino *panuela de manilla*.

41. For a nineteenth-century depiction of this headdress, see Oscar Lenz, *Timbouctou: Voyage au Maroc, au Sahara et au Soudan* (Paris, 1886), 393; reproduced in *Hayyē ha-Yehūdīm be-Mārōqō*, 200, illus. 389.

42. For examples of these large earrings, see *Ḥayyē ha-Yehūdīm be-Mārōqō*, 226–27, illus. 427–30; also Paul Eudel, *Dictionnaire des bijoux de l'Afrique du Nord: Maroc, Algérie, Tunisie, Tripolitaine* (Paris, 1906), 106–107.

43. BT Yoma 54a.

44. For an illustration of this style of veiling, see Y. K. Stillman, "The Costume of the Jewish Woman in Morocco," 364, Pl. 8.

45. Mishna Tractate Shabbat 6:6.

46. Isa. 3:19.

47. Cant. 5:7.

48. Romanelli is probably referring to the leggings (Mor. Ar. *ṭrābaq*) worn by peasant women in Northern Morocco. See Rackow, *Beiträge*, Tafel XLIII.

49. To this day, it is common to see women carrying infants and very young children tied to their back with a towel or cloth. The "bundle of filthy rags" is probably the enormous belt (Ar. *kurziyya*) which is wrapped around the waist innumerable times creating a huge bulge front and back. See Rackow, *Beiträge*, Tafel XL and XLVII.

50. This huge, enveloping wrap was until a generation or so ago the principal outdoor covering for women. It is now becoming rare in the major towns and cities. See Rackow, *Beiträge*, Tafel XXVII-XXIX, where the manner of draping it is shown step by step.

51. Cant. 8:6.

52. See Chapter 3, above.

53. BT Nedarim 49a.

54. BT Bava Qama 59a–b. Eliezer wore black shoes as a token of mourning for the destruction of Jerusalem, which Romanelli takes as an example of a local custom.

55. Isa. 32:18.

Chapter 8

1. That is because it is connected with the root *regel* meaning "foot." For *rōgēl* as laundryman, see Rashi's commentary to Josh. 15:7. This association is an ancient one since the Targum translates *rōgēl* with Aramaic *qaṣrā* ("fuller").

2. Romanelli notes here: The Arabs, like other Muslims, do these

things in secret, as it would seem from the memoirs of the Marquis d'Argens, 113. (The book he is referring to is: *Mémoires de Monsieur le Marquis d'Argens avec quelques lettres sur divers sujets* [London, 1735], where the Marquis accuses Turks of similar transgressions.)

3. Gen. 9:25. Islam adopted the tradition from Jewish and Christian legend that Ham became black as a result of his father's curse. See G. Vajda, "Hām," *EI²* III, 104–105; and Bernard Lewis, *Race and Color in Islam* (New York, 1971), 66–67.

4. Actually, this is the noun of unity (i.e., "auctions" in general). A single auction is *dlāla*. See Brunot, *Textes arabes de Rabat* II, 280, s.v.

5. Romanelli is referring to the Arabic emphatic /ḍ/ which is indeed related to Hebrew /ṣ/. However, in this instance he is off the mark because *delāl* is written with the non-emphatic /d/.

6. Hab. 3:16.

7. *Dellāl* in Moroccan Arabic is the crier, or auctioneer. Romanelli does not use the word here, only saying "he is," but the reference is obviously to him. In Morocco, the *dellāl* goes through the marketplace with an item for sale, accepting bids as he goes along. Concerning this profession, see Roger Le Tourneau, *Fes avant le Protectorat* (Casablanca, 1949; repr. New York, 1978), 306–314. For a contemporary example of the *dellāl*'s function in the jewelry trade, see Yedida K. Stillman, "A Moroccan Jeweler and His Art: Continuity and Change," *Pe'amim* 17 (1983), 98–99 [Heb].

8. Dan. 3:4.

9. Joseph: Gen. 37:27–36; Laws of Slavery: Ex. 21:2–11, Lev. 25:44–46, et passim.

10. This identification of the Berbers with the Philistines goes back to medieval Hebrew usage. See, for example, in the poetry of Samuel ha-Nagid, in *Divan Shmuel Hanagid*, ed. Dov Jarden (Jerusalem, 1966), p. 17, l. 14; p. 53, l. 16; p. 97, l. 12; and p. 112, l. 30; or in the poetry of Judah ha-Levi in Hayyim Schirmann (ed.), *Ha-Shīra ha-'Ivrīt bi-Sfārād ūve-Prōvanz*, II (Jerusalem, 1961), p. 479, l. 1. They were still called "Philistines" in the Hebrew of North African Jews in modern times. See, for example, Joseph Ben Naim, *Malkhē Rabbānān* (Jerusalem, 1931), 44b. This designation ultimately harkens back to legends connecting the Berbers with the Canaanites, concerning which see Hirschberg, *History of the Jews in North Africa*, I, 40–48.

11. Isa. 60:7.

12. The Targum of Jonathan is a midrashic Aramaic translation of the Bible. Why Romanelli should mention Jonathan here is not clear, since the translation "Arabs" (Aram.'arāvā'ē) is also in the standard Targum of

Onqelos. For this simile of being "black like a cooking pot," see BT Megilla 11a.

13. Isa. 6:6. This interpretation is quite imaginative. *Sharīf* in Arabic means a "noble," but has the special meaning of "a descendant of the Prophet Muhammad." In the verse quoted from Isaiah, the Seraph (whose name resembles sharif) performs an action that reminds Romanelli of a ritual performed by the priests in the Sanctuary which involved the taking of live coals from the altar for the burning of incense. See Lev. 16: 12, and many descriptions in the Mishna, as for example, Mishna Tractate Yoma 4: 3–4.

14. See the commentary of Tosafot to BT Menahot 110a. Here again the angels are depicted in a priestly role.

15. Paraphrasing Prov. 6:13. The local Jews were probably terrified out of their wits at Romanelli's lack of discretion, for which they might have to bear the consequences. The sharifs wielded tremendous power in Morocco during the sixteenth through nineteenth centuries, which are referred to in fact as the Sharifan period. For this period in general, see Charles-André Julien, *History of North Africa*, 213–72. On its implications for the Jews of that country, see Stillman, *Jews of Arab Lands*, 84–85.

16. Jews played a dominant role in the minting of coins and in gold and silversmithing in Morocco because of Maliki Muslim distaste for these professions. See, for example, Haïm Zafrani, *Etudes et recherches sur la vie intellectuelle juive au Maroc de la fin du 15e au début du 20e siècle I: Pensée juridique et environnement social, économique et religieux* (Paris, 1972), 164–65, where sources on Jewish predominance in this profession are cited for as far back as the fourteenth century; also Jane S. Gerber, *Jewish Society in Fez, 1450–1700* (Leiden, 1980), 150–51; Lempriere, 2nd ed., *A Tour from Gibraltar*, 199. For a photograph of the kind of dies used by the Jewish minters, see *Ḥayyē ha-Yehūdīm be-Mārōqō*, Israel Mus. Cat. No. 103, p. 134, illus. 277.

17. The Moroccan monetary system was a complicated affair. Both native and foreign coins circulated throughout the country. There was considerable fluctuation in the value of the native coins, and a number of the coins had more than one name. There were also monies of account. For a good survey on the subject, see Zafrani, *Etudes et recherches* I, 150–56; also Gerber, *Jewish Society in Fez*, 198–201.

18. According to Lempriere, *A Tour from Gibraltar*, 2nd ed., 199, note, the *ūqiya*, or "ounce," was equal to about five English pence at that time.

19. Prov. 4:26.

20. That is, the Bible uses the verb *pallis* here, which Romanelli is connecting with the small coin *fils*, to emphasize small details.

21. There is no word *zalīḥ*. Romanelli is apparently referring to the *qīrāṭ* (from the same Greek root as English "carat"), which was usually half a *fils*. See Zafrani, *Etudes de recherches* I, 151; also Gerber, *Jewish Society in Fez*, 199. The word given by Romanelli looks like a corruption of an Arabic word, perhaps *sellīkh*. *Sellīkha* in later Tangerine Arabic indicated "a flat, slippery stone." See Marçais, *Textes arabes de Tanger*, p. 336, s.v. This word (albeit with a different meaning) was transcribed *zalea* in sixteenth-century Spanish. See Reinhart Dozy, *Supplément aux dictionnaires arabes*, I (Paris and Leiden, 1967), 672, s.v.

22. The Heb. word *perūṭa* could indicate either the *fils* or the *qīrāṭ*. Sometimes the term *perūṭa gedōla* ("big prūṭa") was used to distinguish the *fils* from the smaller *qīrāṭ*. See Zafrani, *Etudes de recherches* I, 151; Gerber, *Jewish Society in Fez*, 199. Both *perūṭa* and the abbreviated form *prūṭ* are still used in Moroccan Judaeo-Arabic. See Moshe Bar-Asher, "'Al ha-Yesōdōt ha'Ivriyyīm ba-'Aravīt ha-'Medubberet shel Yehūdē Marōqō," *Leshonenu* 42:3–4 (1978), 182, para. 31.

23. He was the *dayyān* (chief Jewish judge) of Rabat, a noted talmudist, and a court banker to Sīdī Muḥammad. See D. Corcos, "Avila, de," *EJ* 3, col. 969. The d'Avila family which had its origins in the Spanish city from whence they took their name produced a number of noted scholars and communal leaders. See also Maurice Eisenbeth, *Les Juifs de l'Afrique du Nord: Démographie et onomastique* (Algiers, 1936), 117, s.v. "Dabila."

24. BT Shabbat 84b–85b.

25. Paraphrasing Ps. 139:6.

26. Deut. 5:19.

27. Ex. 20:2–14.

28. *Bina la-'Ittim* by the Italian scholar Azariah Figo (d. 1647). See Chaim R. Rabinowitz, "Figo (Picho), Azariah," *EJ* 6, col. 1274.

29. In the passage under discussion, the four plants used in the Sukkot ritual (i.e., the palm branch, myrtle, willow, and citron) are interpreted as symbolizing the three dimensions of rain (length, breadth, and height) and the dimension of the earth beneath (area). See Azariah Figo, *Bina la-'Ittim* (Lemberg, 1858), 51b, Sermon 15, para. 8. The text is also given by Schirmann in his edition of Romanelli, 72, n. 86.

30. Jud. 7:15.

31. Paraphrasing Isa. 28:7.

32. Supererogatory fasting was a common pietist practice throughout the Jewish world, especialy on Mondays and Thursdays, which were popular for such fasting since rabbinic times (see BT Ta'anit 12a). This ascetic practice of fasting for a full six days and nights, however, seems to have been a custom particular to Morocco. It was called in Hebrew *ta'anīt*

ḥafsāqa (hence the name of these people *baʿalē ḥafsāqa*), and in Judaeo-Arabic *settiya* (the sixer). The pious ascetic Rabbi David Abihaṣera is reported to have been a devotee of this practice. See Ben Naim, *Malkhē Rabbānān*, 27b, col. a. Zafrani mentions that he personally knew people who undertook this difficult fast. See Haïm Zafrani, *Mille ans de vie juive au Maroc: Histoire et culture, religion et magie* (Paris, 1983), 71–72, 276.

33. Ezra 9:9.

34. Isa. 57:15.

35. Isa. 38:16.

36. Neh. 9:6.

37. Num. 12:12.

38. Gen. 30:1.

39. BT Nedarim 64b, where the leper and the childless are also included.

40. I Sam. 25:37.

41. See Gen. 22:1–9.

42. See II Sam. 12:16–24.

43. II Sam. 19:1.

44. See II Kings 8–37.

45. II Sam. 12:23.

46. Lam. 5:3. According to an ancient tradition, the Prophet Jeremiah is the author of the Book of Lamentations. See the introduction to the Targum of Lamentations. In the Septuagint, and hence in the Christian canon, Lamentations is in fact appended to Jeremiah.

47. I Sam. 30:1–4.

48. A play on Prov. 2:15.

49. Gen. 6:9.

50. Ex. 32:16.

51. Paraphrasing Isa. 2:3.

52. This image is based upon the following talmudic citations. It should be recalled that Moses smashed the first set of tablets when he discovered that the Israelites had been worshiping the Golden Calf during his absence. Both the fragments of this first set of tablets and the second set of tablets were placed together in the ark (which in Hebrew also means a coffin).

53. BT Menaḥot 99a–b.

54. This is not from BT Pesaḥim, but from BT Bava Batra 14b and also BT Berakhot 8b.

55. Prov. 20:1.

56. Literally, "There is a thorn in every [sheep's] fat tail." See BT Rosh ha-Shana 17b.

57. Eliahu Levi was one of Sīdī Muḥammad's principal Jewish agents.

He appears in an intelligence report outlining the Moroccan court by Franz von Dombay (Haus-, Hof- und Staatsarchiv, Marokko Karton 3, No. 3, Lit e, dated June 22, 1789). Seven names are listed in the report under the heading "Sekretäre so Juden sind," with Eliahu Levi's name first. He may be the same as Liao Levi, whose name appears in a number of Italian documents from 1784 as a representative of the Sultan (for example, H. H. S. Marokko Karton I, fols. 37–38, A–C).

58. Apparently Lempriere was also struck by the good looks of the Jewish women of Tetuan. See Lempriere, *A Tour from Gibraltar*, 2nd ed., 432: "Their women are remarkable for their clearness of complexion, and the beauty of their features."

59. Isa. 1:22.

60. Pope, *Essay on Man*, Essay II, l. 220. The famous passage begins with the verse "Vice is a monster" (l. 217).

61. January/February. Three months have passed since the aborted summons to Meknes.

62. Lempriere, *A Tour from Gibraltar*, 2nd ed., 200, describes him this way: "Jacob Attal, the late emperor's Jewish and favorite secretary, had more influence with his royal master, and did more mischief by his intrigues and address, than all the other ministers put together. This young man, who was a native of Tunis, and who was tolerably well acquainted with the English, Spanish, Italian, French, and Arabic languages, was of an active and enterprising mind, and had so well informed himself of the natural disposition of the Moors, and particularly of that of Sidi Mahomet, that he had gained an entire ascendency over the emperor."

Chapter 9

1. From what follows below, it is apparently Tangier.

2. As opposed to Haketia, the Judeo-Spanish dialect of North Morocco.

3. The Moroccan monetary system, which had been reformed by Sīdī Muhammad in 1766, was based mainly on foreign coins, with those of Spain being the most popular. The piastre, which was known in Arabic as *dūrō bū medfa'*, was a Spanish silver coin worth one sixteenth of a gold dubloon. In 1799 it was equal to 10 *ūqiyas*, or 1 *mithqāl*. See Chapter 8, above. For a good survey of the system and its equivalences, see J.-L. Miège, *Le Maroc et l'Europe (1830–1894)*, III (Paris, 1962), 97–99.

4. Although Spain expelled its Jews in 1492 and did not normally even allow Jewish visitors thereafter, some Jews did enter Spain from time to time on diplomatic missions for various Moroccan rulers. See Y. H.

Yerushalmi, "Professing Jews in Post-Expulsion Spain and Portugal," *Salo Wittmayer Baron Jubilee Volume*, ed. S. Lieberman and A. Hyman (Jerusalem, 1975), 1023–58; also N. A. Stillman, *The Jews of Arab Lands: A History and Source Book* (Philadelphia, 1979), 82. Eliahu Levi's name, however, does not appear among the major deputations sent to Spain. See Vicente Rodríguez Casado, *Política Marroquí de Carlos III* (Madrid, 1946), passim.

5. Paraphrasing Ps. 17:3.

6. Jews normally walked in public in an humble and inconspicuous manner in accordance with their *dhimmī* status and the stipulations of the so-called Pact of ʿUmar, which in Morocco from the later Middle Ages to early modern times was interpreted in the strictest possible fashion. See Stillman, *Jews of Arab Lands*, 84–87, 304–305.

7. Concerning the requirement for Jews to walk barefoot through the streets of the imperial cities and everywhere in front of a mosque, see above, Chapter 7, n. 23.

8. Paraphrasing Job 20:7.

9. See Isa. 5:14.

10. Ezra 7:26.

11. Dan. 2:5.

12. Heb. *megilla ʿāfa*—literally, "a flying scroll" (cf. Zech. 5:1). Schirmann suggests that it might mean here "an urgent letter" (*iggeret deḥūfa*), but this is not really required by the context (see *Massāʾ*, 79, n. 60).

13. Jacob Attal. Concerning him, see above, Chapter 8, n. 62.

14. Romanelli came to London sometime during the 1780s and remained there until 1787. (See Introduction, above.)

15. This is probably the same friend mentioned in Chapter 3.

16. The prisoner is apostrophizing here.

17. The Jewish community of Gibraltar, which was first established around 1713, consisted mainly of Jews of Maghrebi origin. See H. Z. Hirschberg, *A History of the Jews in North Africa*, II (Leiden, 1981), 277–78. A considerable number of Gibraltar's Jews was involved in trade with North Africa, including members of the distinguished Cardozo family. See Stillman, *Jews of Arab Lands*, 367.

18. Cf. Job 21:6.

19. Paraphrasing Gen. 4:11.

20. Ps. 119:78.

21. Literally, "in Etzion Geber," a biblical Red Sea port near modern Eilat and Aqaba.

22. Romanelli is apparently referring to Baron (later Viscount) Sydney, who was British Home Secretary from 1783 to 1789. See *Dictionary of National Biography*, XIX (London, 1937–38), 1058, s.v., "Townshend, Thomas."

23. Romanelli is referring here to the epic poem *Shīrē Tiferet* of the German maskil Naphtali Herz Wessely (1725–1805), concerning which, see Waxman, *A History of Jewish Literature*, III, 108–14.

24. Moroccan Jews are indeed extremely fond of *piyyūtīm* (Hebrew liturgical poetry). Even today, it is not uncommon to have such poems recited—and often composed extemporaneously—when an important personage is called to the Torah. Romanelli's harsh judgment of this poetry is purely subjective. He himself was an accomplished poet who wrote according to the stylistic and thematic conventions of Italy. For a detailed treatment of Moroccan Hebrew poetry, see Haïm Zafrani, *Etudes de Recherche sur la vie intellectuelle juive au Maroc de la fin du 15e au début du 20e siècle II: Poésie juive en Occident musulman* (Paris, 1977).

25. "Poeta nascitur, non fit."

26. Muslim brides were traditionally brought to their husband's house in this manner. The box or container which covered her is known in Tangier as an ʿammāriyya. For a detailed description of this procession, see Edward Westermarck, *Marriage Ceremonies in Morocco* (London, 1914), 165–92.

27. The ritual dinner held on the first two evenings of Passover when the Exodus from Egypt is retold.

28. A play on Isa. 54:10.

29. Dan. 12:7 (see also Dan. 7:25).

30. Romanelli is saying in a playful way that these unexplained and divergent practices will continue until the coming of the Messiah. According to ancient folklore, at that time the Prophet Elijah will come and settle disputes. See Mishna Tractate ʿEduyyot 8:7; and BT Menahot 45a.

31. That is, the second evening of passover.

32. Romanelli seems to have related this custom primarily to make this *bon mot*. The custom he is describing is unknown to us.

33. Romanelli is referring here to the Mimouna festival, concerning which, see Issachar Ben-Ami, *Le Judaïsme marocain: études ethnoculturelles* (Jerusalem, 1975), 139–52 [Heb.]. The Mimouna has become a major holiday in Israel in recent years.

34. Isa. 61:11. The Mimouna does indeed have intimate associations with good luck and fertility. The traditional blessing exchanged on the holiday is *terbaḥu u-tsaʿadu* ("Be prosperous and fortunate").

35. Paraphrasing Micah 6:8.

Chapter 10

1. In the voice from the whirlwind. See Job 38–41.

2. Romanelli's argument here in favor of the rational nature of Jewish

law is based upon a long tradition of Jewish philosophy going back to the medieval Islamic world. See, for example, Saadia Gaon, *The Book of Beliefs and Opinions*, trans. Samuel Rosenblatt. Yale Judaica Series, I (New Haven, 1948), Treatise 3; and Moses Maimonides, *The Guide of the Perplexed*, trans. Shlomo Pines (Chicago, 1963), Part III, Chaps. 25–49. On the ability of prophets to philosophize, see Maimonides, *Guide*, Part II, Chap. 38. Many Jews in Romanelli's hometown of Mantua had studied philosophy, and the city produced a number of Jewish philosophers. See Shlomo Simonsohn, *History of the Jews in the Duchy of Mantua* (Jerusalem, 1977), 582–84 and 626–29.

3. See Chapter 9, above.

4. The sultans of Morocco spent part of each year in each of the imperial cities as well as other places.

5. Isa. 45:2.

6. BT Megilla 12a.

7. This word, derived from the Arabic word for *circle*, is still used throughout North Africa to designate nomadic and seminomadic encampments consisting of a circle of tents or huts, often surrounded by a corral of brushwood. For a detailed depiction of such camps, accompanied by photographs, see Budgett Meakin, *The Moors: A Comprehensive Description* (London and New York, 1902), 148–52.

8. Jud. 8:11.

9. Isa. 13:20.

10. Romanelli and the Genoese had either no beard or very short ones.

11. The image is from Prov. 30:27.

12. Ez. 27:20. Romanelli is playing here on the literal meaning of *bigdē ḥofesh* in this biblical verse, which is understood in Jewish tradition to mean "luxury clothes." Cf. the Targum and the commentary of Rashi to this verse.

13. El Qsar (Ar. al-Qaṣr al-Kabīr) lies 50 miles south of Tangier by the direct overland route. The easier coastal route is almost 80 miles.

14. Romanelli is referring here to the popular pietistic practice and not to the five daily formal prayers. The shrine is probably a *qubba*, or saint's tomb.

15. Romanelli is referring here to the famous battle that took place on August 4, 1578, which is known in Europe as the Battle of the Three Kings and in Moroccan historiography as Battle of the Wād al-Makhāzin. In this battle King Sebastian of Portugal and his ally, the deposed Sultan Muḥammad al-Mutawakkil were drowned in the Wād Makhāzin, while trying to break out of a trap. At the same time, the victorious Sultan ʿAbd

al-Malik died of an illness. Hence the name the Battle of the Three Kings. See Julien, *History of North Africa*, 227–28.

16. Concerning the humiliating regulation, see above, Chapter 7, n. 23.

17. The Moroccan sultans allowed monks (usually Franciscans) to minister to the spiritual needs of the Christian slaves who had been taken prisoner by the Barbary corsairs. Their convent was usually located near the prison. See for example, Gaston Deverdun, *Marrakech des origines à 1912* I (Rabat, 1959), 450.

18. The second sultan of the Alawid dynasty, he reigned from 1672–1727. He was a great builder. He turned Meknes, a small insignificant town into an imperial capital. For an eyewitness description of the palace shortly after it was built, see *Mémoire de J.-B. Estelle* in Pierre de Cenival (ed.), *Les Sources inédites de l'histoire du Maroc. Deuxième Série: Dynastie filalienne: Archives et bibliothèques de France*, IV (Paris, 1931), 688–90.

19. The mellāh (Jewish quarter) of Meknes mentioned here is today the Old Mellāh which is located just outside the Medina. See *Les Guides bleus: Maroc* (Paris, 1978), 242, map.

20. Concerning this custom, see I. Ben-Ami, "Le mariage traditionnel chez les Juifs marocains," in his *Le Judaïsme marocain*, 15, and the sources cited in n. 29.

21. Concerning this opera by Sallieri, see Chapter 1, above, n. 17.

22. Romanelli is referring to the common practice in his native Italy and other Catholic countries of parading through the streets with holy images on saints days.

23. The meaning of this may be taken two ways. Either Eliahu is referring to his former disgrace, or he is referring to his private affairs in general.

24. See BT Berakhot 58a, where Josh. 10:12 is cited in a cataloging of miracles alluded to in the liturgy. Where this particular interpretation is found, however, is a mystery.

25. In the concluding chapter to the introduction (known as *Eight Chapters*, or *Shemonah Perāqīm*) to his commentary on the mishnaic tractate Avot, Maimonides states that since everything goes according to the laws of nature, scholars were forced to the conclusion that all suspensions of those laws (i.e., miracles), both past and future, were already willed during the six days of creation. See *Mishna 'im Pērūsh Rabbēnū Moshe b. Maymōn: Māqōr ve-Tirgūm. Sēder Nezīqīn*, ed. and trans. Joseph David Qafih (Jerusalem, 1964), 399.

26. A play on Prov. 17:10.

27. Prov. 6:26.

28. Paraphrasing Job 15:23.

29. That is, Jacob Attal's brother who had accompanied Cardozo from Tangier. See Chapter 9, above.

30. Jacob Attal.

31. See Chapter 9, above.

32. See Chapter 8, above.

33. Paraphrasing Prov. 13:12.

34. For a picture of these tools used by Moroccan silversmiths, see Yedida K. Stillman, "A Moroccan Jeweler and His Art: Continuity and Change," *Pe'amim* 17 (1983), 108, illus. 3 [Heb.]. For a photo of the crucible on the hearth in the workshop, see ibid., 109, Pl. 8.

35. Romanelli is quoting from an aria in Metastasio's "Demofoonte," Act I, Scene 3, which in the Italian text reads:

e la necessitá gran cose insegna.
Per lei fra l'armi—dorme il guerriero;
per lei fra l'onde—canta il nocchiero;
per lei la morte—terror non ha.
Fin le piú timide—belve fugaci
valor dimostrano,—si fanno audaci,
quand'è il combattere—necessitá.

36. Until very recently, fatness was a mark of female beauty among the urban Jews of North and Central Morocco. Among the more popular folk remedies are those for fattening up women who are considered too thin (along with aphrodisiacs and cures for barrenness). On several occasions during our field work in the town of Sefrou, women offered Yedida potions to make her more pleasingly plump by their standards.

37. See Chapter 5, above.

38. Paraphrasing Gen. 44:16.

39. Literally, "These are the sons of Noah" (Gen. 10:1). In Hebrew *no'ah* means "rest." The entire paragraph that follows plays upon the Hebrew roots of the opening words "rest and relaxation."

40. Eccl. 1:8.

Chapter 11

1. Gen. 4:3.

2. Gen. 32:14.

3. Gen. 43:15.

4. Gen. 43:34.

5. Jud. 3:17.

6. I Sam. 9:8.

7. II Sam. 8:2 and 6.

8. I Kings 5:1.

9. II Kings 5:1.

10. II Kings 17:3.

11. II Chron. 17:11.

12. II Chron. 27:5.

13. Isa. 39:1.

14. Ps. 72:10.

15. Ps. 45:13.

16. Ps. 68:30.

17. I Sam. 10:27.

18. II Kings 17:4.

19. Ex. 23:15.

20. There are a number of depictions of such audiences by nineteenth-century artists including the famous Eugène Delacroix who accompanied a diplomatic mission to Meknes. See, for example, his painting of ʿAbd al-Rahmān, Sultan of Morocco, surrounded by his court, in the Musée des Augustins, Toulouse, reproduced in Bernard Lewis (ed.), *Islam and the Arab World* (New York, 1976), 337, Pl. 1. See also the engraving reproduced in Stillman, *The Jews of Arab Lands*, Illus. 27, opposite 392.

21. Job 41:17.

22. II Sam. 6:6–8.

23. Paraphrasing Esth. 4:11.

24. Mūlāy ʿAbd Allāh was an unpopular ruler who was deposed as many as five times between his accession to the throne in 1729 and his death in 1757. Concerning his reputation for cruelty, see Chénier, *The Present State of the Empire of Morocco*, II, 94–97; also Henri Terrasse, *Histoire du Maroc des origines à l'établissement du Protectorat français*, II (Casablanca, 1950; repr. New York, 1975), 282–86.

25. Romanelli has a note here explaining that he is using the Hebrew verb ʿāṣar twice in this sentence, first in the meaning of "to reign" (as in I Sam. 9:17) and second in the more usual meaning "to keep in check."

26. That is the Genoese representative of the merchant in Gibraltar.

27. As a Christian on a mission to the court, he did not have to make this gesture of humility, but to make a greater impression (and at Eliahu's advice) he did so nevertheless.

28. I Kings 10:22, where it is the Tarshish fleet of Solomon and Hiram that brings these exotic items.

29. Isa. 34:14; 35:9.

30. It is, of course, forbidden in Judaism to travel on the Sabbath. Eliahu had no choice since to disobey the Sultan's order would have been fatal. Where life is at stake, Jewish law permits such a violation. His family, however, was not under such a threat and therefore could wait until night-fall when the Sabbath ended to set out.

31. Paraphrase of Gen. 39:6.

32. Romanelli is playing on the Hebrew verbs *hit'abberū* (meaning both "to burn" and "to be impregnated") and *hōlīdū* (meaning "to beget," "to engender," and "to result in").

33. Literally, "His face went and he let me rest," paraphrasing Ex. 33:14.

34. The cities of Rabat and Salé face each other from either side of the outlet of the Bou Regreg River.

35. This is the famous Qasbat al-Wadaya (Kasba des Oudaïa in the familiar French transcription) which in 1627 was the capital of the pirate Republic of the Bou Regreg founded by Moriscos from Spain. See Terrasse, *Histoire du Maroc*, II, 220–23. The fortress stands on the southern bank which is on the right side if one faces it from the sea.

36. The reference is to the famous Tour Ḥassān, the monumental Al-mohad minaret which towers to a height of 44 meters and is over 16 meters in circumference.

37. Paraphrase of Prov. 31:29.

38. The imagery is from Job 15:27.

39. See Gen. 30:14–16.

40. Paraphrase of II Kings 9:30.

41. In a document from the archive of Romanelli's former employer Dombay, there is a copy of a letter from Sīdī Muḥammad to the king of Denmark expressing his thanks for some birds sent him as a gift and promising to send some Moroccan birds in return. See N. A. Stillman, "The Dombay Papers," *Bulletin of the John Rylands University Library* 57:2 (1975), 473, No. 41. Concerning Danish commercial and diplomatic relations with Morocco at this time, see Ramon Lourido Diaz, *Marruecos en la segunda mitad del siglo XVIII: El sultanato de Sīdī Muḥammad b. ʿAbd Allāh (1757–1790)*, 104, 116. In addition to the gift, the Danes paid a large annual tribute in cash. See Pierre Grillon (ed.), *Un chargé d'affaires au Maroc: La correspondance du consul Louis Chénier, 1767–1782*, II (Paris, 1970), 922, 1001.

42. Concerning this important seaport on the southeastern Moroccan coast, see Author's Introduction, above.

43. Romanelli is describing here the popular *istisqā'* rituals which are still practiced in Morocco and some Muslim countries. The formula cited

here is part of longer ones still used. See Westermarck, *Ritual and Belief in Morocco*, II, pp. 254–65; also Edmond Doutté, *Magie et religion dans l'Afrique du Nord* (Algiers, 1909), pp. 590–96. The official orthodox *salāt al-istisqā'* (prayer for rain) is alluded to in the beginning of this passage but is not described.

44. Romanelli's irony is based upon Elijah's taunt to the priests of Baal in I Kings 18:27.

45. The Jews were regularly included in the *istisqā'* prayers, and indeed their prayers were considered particularly efficacious. See Westermarck, *Ritual and Belief in Morocco*, II, 255; and Doutté, *Magie et religion dans l'Afrique du Nord*, 592. The ancedote about the Jews' stench is already reported by John Windus, *A Journey to Mequinez* (London, 1725), 62–63, and is repeated by Chénier, *The Present State of the Empire of Morocco*, I, 345–46.

46. Romanelli is referring here to the Spanish cult of San Isidro Labrador, the patron saint of farmers and agricultural workers in Spain. To this day, in Spain, South America, and the American Southwest, images of San Isidro are brought out into the fields in time of drought and to ensure the crops at the time of planting. See A. O'Malley, "Isidore The Farmer, St.," *New Catholic Encyclopedia*, VII (New York, 1967), 672, 673 (illustration and caption).

47. Ps. 75:5.

48. Literally, "calamity upon calamity," Ez. 7:26.

49. Literally, "with broken loins," Ez. 21:11.

50. Job 2:13.

51. Esth. 4:16.

52. Prov. 1:23.

53. Jud. 3:22.

54. Jer. 14:8.

55. Ps. 55:14.

56. For this town on the northwestern coast of Morocco, see Chapter 1, above, n. 26.

57. A small fortress and fishing village actually called Qaṣbat Mahdiyya about 25 miles north of Rabat at the edge of the Mamora Forest.

58. The Shleuh (Ar. *Shlüḥ*) are Tashelhīt-speaking Berbers of the Moroccan south. The term has the double meaing of "uncouth people," and thus is translated by Romanelli here by Heb. *benē beliyaʿal*.

59. I Kings 21:19.

60. The text has Mogador, but this is clearly a misprint.

61. This contradicts what has just been said about M. Barré.

62. This incident is also related by James Grey Jackson, *An Account*

of the Empire of Morocco and the Districts of Suse and Tafilelt, 3rd ed. (London, 1814; repr. London, 1968), 263–265. According to Jackson, the other European consuls made some protest, but the British Consul's inaction caused Great Britain a loss of face among the Moroccans.

Chapter 12

1. This was a M. du Rocher, who came to Morocco in 1786, four years after the previous French Consul, Louis Chénier, had been expelled from the country. See Lourido Díaz, El Sultanato de Sīdī Muḥammad b. ʿAbd Allāh (1757–1790), 115.

2. See Chapter 8, above.

3. See Lev. 22:24.

4. Eccl. 10:19.

5. Al-Baḥḥār in Arabic means "the seaman," hence his Spanish surname—de la Mar.

6. Cf. II Kings 17:9. Romanelli's etymology here is off. The qasba of Mansuriyya which lies about 60 km. south of Rabat takes its name from al-Manṣūr ("He who is made victorious by God"), the title of the sixth Sultan of the Saadian dynasty Aḥmad al-Manṣūr al-Dhahabī (1549–1603). Prosper Ricard, Maroc, Les Guides Bleus, 7th ed. (Paris, 1950), 236, merely mentions Mansuriyya (Mansouria) as an "ancienne kasba (53 hab.)." The 1978 edition of the Guide Bleu omits any notice of it altogether.

7. Again a false etymology. The word is derived from Makhzen, the term for the Moroccan central government. Makhazniyya means "government troops."

8. Dār al-Bayḍā is the Arabic name for Casablanca, which in Romanelli's day was just a small village. His explanation of "a dwelling the color of an egg" is based upon the Hebrew cognate words.

9. See Chapter 10, above.

10. The town of Azemmour lies 81 kms. southwest of Casablanca. Between 1541 and 1749, it was the major base for the Holy War against the Portuguese in neighboring Mazagan. We can only imagine the reasons for the severity of Romanelli's judgment of its inhabitants.

11. Mazagan lies 96 kms. south of Casablanca. A Portuguese fortress built on the spot in 1502, was called by the Arabs l-Brīja j-Jdīda, which means "the new fort" and not "rib." It is from this that the modern shortened name of El Jadida is derived.

12. The Portuguese built the town of Mazagan alongside their original fortress in 1506. The town came under Spanish control between 1580 and

1640 and then passed back to Portuguese rule. In 1739, only about thirty years before Romanelli visited, it was finally abandoned by the European colonists.

13. The description of the Muslim's prayer is essentially correct. See Edward William Lane, *The Manners and Customs of the Modern Egyptians* (London, 1923), 77–80. The curse upon the Christians and Jews is not an actual part of the prayer, but was the Arab's own addition.

14. Romanelli here is punning on the name of Jesse the Bethlehemite (I Sam. 16:18).

15. This cavernous vaulted cistern, which measures 34 by 33 meters, is to this day one of the principal sights in the town. See Les Guides Bleus, *Maroc* (Paris, 1978), 299–301.

16. Isa. 34:12.

17. Romanelli has a note here: The poet Tasso. He is referring to Torquato Tasso's epic *Gerusalemme liberata*.

18. This province is named after a confederation of Berber tribes inhabiting the vast triangle enclosed by the Atlantic Ocean, the Wad Tensift, and the Wad Umm al-Rbīʿ.

19. Paraphrase of II Kings 7:1. All of the Hebrew editions, including Schirmann's (p. 108, l. 121), have *ma'tayim se'orīm* for *sā'tayim se'orīm*.

20. The English military physician William Lempriere was in fact treating the women of Sīdi Muhammad's harem at this very time. See Lempriere, *A Tour from Gibraltar*, Chapter 12, which recounts his experience in the harem.

21. This is quite the opposite of recent times as anyone who has ever visited Morocco can attest. The reason is that in Romanelli's day, few weak or diseased Moroccans survived infancy.

22. Parody of Jer. 8:22.

23. Romanelli has a note here: The scholar Azulai. He is apparently referring to a remark in the writings of R. Hayyim Joseph David Azulai, who at this time lived in Italy. The reference is probably to blessings such as "Blessed art Thou, o Lord our God. . . . Who varies the aspect of Thy creatures" (*meshanne ha-beriyyōt*), which is said when beholding a person of abnormal appearance.

24. Imagery based upon I Sam. 18:6.

25. Imagery and part of the phrasing from Esth. 8:17, inspired by R. Mordechai's biblical namesake.

26. Hos. 10:12.

27. Ps. 107:42.

28. See Chapter 8, above.

29. Mishna Tractate Shabbat 1:3. Romanelli is probably alluding to the

southern Moroccan usage of *ḥazzān* ("cantor" in European Jewish usage) which mans a rabbi, and in Marrakesh and Mogador it has the special connotation of headmaster of a yeshiva and is therefore parallel to the mishnaic usage he is citing. See Louis Brunot and Elie Malka, *Glossaire judéo-arabe de Fès* (Rabat, 1940), 32, s.v. *ḥazzān*. According to Professor Haim Zafrani (oral communication), Bekka is a nickname for Mordechai and that the individual referred to here is the courtier Mordechai Shriqi, who is known from other sources.

30. Like Eliahu.

31. Jews had begun to join Freemason lodges in Europe in the generation preceding Romanelli. See art. "Freemasons," *EJ* 7, col. 122.

32. Gen. 49:6.

33. Ezek. 7:11. This is a difficult biblical assage. Romanelli is probably understanding it according to the commentaries of the medieval and Renaissance commentators, and we have translated here accordingly.

34. Paraphrase of Prov. 13:19.

35. Literally, "Behold, Commander!"

36. For a description of this gala exercise in horsemanship, which can still be observed today at festive gatherings, see Mercier's appendix to ʿAly Ben ʿAbderraḥman Ben Hodeïl El Andalusy, *La parure des cavaliers et l'insigne des preux*, tr. Louis Mercier (Paris, 1924), Appendix VI, 412–13.

37. Literally, "Take care," or "Watch out." It is the equivalent of the sentry's challenge in English, "Halt, who goes there?"

38. The text does not make sense in Arabic or Berber. It may stand for something like Tashelhit, *Iuwa, ssūfegḥ.*

39. Parody of Prov. 11:14.

40. Interpretive playing on Prov. 21:5.

41. Josh. 1:3; also Deut. 11:24.

42. See Jud. 6–7. Actually, the test of the fleece and dew involve God directly (Jud. 6:36–40). The angel appears in Jud. 6:11–24, where a sacrificial test is involved.

43. *Zohar*, Portion Lekh Lekha, Gen. 15:1.

44. BT Berakhot 40a mentions an "empty vessel," but does not have this dictum. Romanelli apparently had confused this passage with an Aramaic statement in the Zohar chapter he had just cited above (cf. n. 43) that blessings "do not rest upon an empty vessel or an empty place."

45. Jud. 6:25.

46. I Sam. 16:2.

47. I Kings 9:5.

48. See I Sam. 9:15.

49. Paraphrasing Ps. 90:17.

50. See Isa. 19:3.

51. Jer. 39:9ff.

52. Jer. 39:13.

53. Esth. 8:9. This is not actually a personal name, but the word for "satraps."

54. The reference is to Charles Rollin's *Histoire ancienne* (1730 and 1738), widely read in the eighteenth and early nineteenth centuries.

55. See the Commentary of R. David Kimhi to Jer. 38:7. Rashi and earlier commentators understood Ebed Melekh literally as being "the King's servant." However, most translations take it as a personal name.

56. Absalom means "my father is peace," not "servant of peace."

57. "Qādir" means "all-powerful," not "ability" (Ar. *qadr*). The author of the Thirteen Articles of Faith is Maimonides. Romanelli is probably referring to his *The Guide of the Perplexed*, Book 1, Chapter 53, which deals with God's attributes of power, knowledge, and will (119–23, in the translation of S. Pines, Chicago, 1963).

58. Ibn Ezra makes the observation not in his commentary on Ecclesiastes, but in his grammatical treatise *Sāfa Berūra*. See the edition of M. Wilensky in *Devir* 2 (1924), 286.

59. Romanelli is confusing the Arabic forms ʿabd and ʿābid with a non-existent *abd*. In any case, all of these compound theophoric names in Arabic that he has been discussing take only the element ʿabd.

60. I Sam. 17:9.

61. Paraphrase of Joel 2:23–24.

62. See Chapters 11 and 12, above.

63. See Jer. 25:28 and I Sam. 9–10.

64. Paraphrase of Jer. 48:29.

Chapter 13

1. Paraphrase of Prov. 24:31.

2. For Heb. *tekhūnātō* as "the treasure He has prepared," see the Targum of Nahum 2:10, as well as the commentaries of Rashi and Ibn Ezra.

3. Isa. 29:1.

4. Romanelli is mistaken in both of these etymologies.

5. It was a time-honored custom for children to throw pebbles at non-Muslims in many parts of the Islamic world. Though bothersome, it was rarely dangerous, since the act was more symbolic than malicious.

See N. A. Stillman, *Jews of Arab Lands*, 84, and the sources cited there in n. 64.

6. See Chapter 11, above.

7. Romanelli is slightly confused here. ʿĪd al-Saghīr (also called ʿĪd al-Fiṭr) comes at the end of Ramadan. Although it is called the Minor Festival, it is celebrated with greater festivity than the Great Festival (also called ʿĪd al-Adhā) which is the sacrificial festival at the end of the Ḥajj. Muhammad's birthday, called Mawlid (Mūlid in Morocco) is a noncanonical festival which is very popular in Morocco. Concerning the holidays in Islam, see G. E. von Grunebaum, *Muhammadan Festivals* (London, 1976).

8. The eighth and ninth months of the Muslim calendar.

9. This is the additional service performed on Sabbaths, New Moons, and holidays in Judaism.

10. Unlike in Judaism, where no labor is performed on Sabbaths and holidays ordained by the Torah.

11. I Sam. 23:8, The Arabic root *j-m-ʿ* is not, however, cognate to the Hebrew *sh-m-ʿ*.

12. This is correct.

13. Safi (Ar. Asfī) is an important port on the Atlantic coast of Morocco, 146 km. south of Mazagan and about 130 km. north of Mogador. Among its major edifices in Romanelli's time were a fourteenth-century *ribāṭ* (Muslim fortified convent) and a sixteenth-century Portuguese fortress.

14. Romanelli's employs here a concatenation of images from Jonah 2:7, Ps. 68:16, and Isa. 9:17.

15. Romanelli's interpretation is clever, but mistaken. Gibraltar derives from Ar. *Jebel Ṭāriq* (Ṭāriq's Mountain) and is named after the Berber commander of the Muslim forces that invaded Spain in 711.

16. Ps. 11:1.

17. Josh. 13:5.

18. Schirmann in his edition understands Heb. *qedōshīm* to mean "prayers of thanksgiving" (*tefillōt hōdāya*). See his edition p. 117, note to l.41. However, it is more likely here that Romanelli is referring to the saints or holy men who form such an integral part of popular religion in Morocco. See Chapter 3, above. Moroccan Jews still use the Heb. term *qādōsh* to designate a saint. It is still common for Moroccan Jews and Muslims to call upon their saints aloud in times of stress.

19. Reading *ʿōverīm* (as in the edition of Warsaw, 1926, p. 82) instead of *ʿōvedīm* (workers).

20. Romanelli probably understands Heb. *seʾelim* according to the medieval exegetes. See, for example, Rashi's commentary to Job 40:21.

21. This name with /s/ is given by Prosper Ricard in his *Maroc*, 7th

ed., Les Guides Bleus (Paris, 1950), 196, but is not repeated in later editions. The name *al-Ṣuwayra*, which in Moroccan is pronounced *Ṣwīra* (officially transcribed as Essaouira), and means "panorama," is the more commonly used Arab form. See, for example, al-Nāṣirī, *Kitāb al-Istiqṣā li-Akhbār Duwal al-Maghrib al-Aqṣā,* VIII (Casablanca, 1956), 24, 30, 32, et passim. See also above, n. 1.

22. Ps. 18:30.

23. I Chron. 4:39. This, of course, is totally fanciful.

24. This important port on a large bay is situated at the junction where the High Atlas and Sus Plain meet at the Atlantic, 173 km. south of Mogador. It was founded by the Portuguese in 1505 and named Santa Cruz del Cabo de Aguar. Its trade was indeed diverted to Mogador and it only returned to prominence in recent years. See R. Le Tourneau, "Agadir-Ighir," *EI²* I, 244–45.

25. The city was in fact laid out and designed by the Avignonnais architect Cournut and added to by an English Renegado. See Terrasse, *Histoire du Maroc,* II, 298–99. For a plan of the old city of Mogador, (Essaouira), see *Maroc,* Les Guides Bleus (Paris, 1978), 369.

26. Romanelli is referring here to the *qaṣba* (see plan cited in the preceding note).

27. For the medina of Mogador, see the plan cited in n. 25, above.

28. These were the principal exports of Mogador at this time; however, Romanelli has chosen his sequence of words on the basis of Gen. 43:11. Cf. Lempriere, *A Tour from Gibraltar,* 2nd ed., 88, where Mogador's exports are listed as follows: "To Europe, Morocco leather, hides, gum arabic, gum sandaric, ostrich feathers, copper, wax, wool, elephants' teeth, fine mats, beautiful carpeting, dates, figs, raisins, olives, almonds, oil, etc."

29. The argan tree (*Argania spinosa*) grows widely in the Sus. Its olivelike fruit is eaten by goats and is also the source of a highly prized edible oil.

30. Cf. Lempriere's list of imports: "In return they import timber, artillery of all kinds, gunpowder, woolen cloths, linens, lead, iron in bars, all kinds of hardware and trinkets, such as looking-glasses, snuff-boxes, watches, small knives, etc., tea, sugar, spices, and most of the useful articles which are not otherwise to be procured in this empire." (Lempriere, *A Tour from Gibraltar,* 2nd ed., 88.)

31. Concerning this family, see Moritz Kayserling, *Biblioteca Española-Portugueza-Judaica* (Strasbourg, 1890), 56–57.

32. The Gedalyas, or Ben Gedalyas, (sons of Gedalya), are well known from eighteenth- and nineteenth-century European and American sources. See, for example, the testimony of an American sea captain in Stillman,

Jews of Arab Lands, 368. Some members of the family were transplanted in England. From this branch came Haim Guedalla, the philanthropist, who was married to the niece of Sir Moses Montefiore. See G. Kressel, "Guedalla, Haim," *EJ* 7, cols. 957–58.

33. Concerning this famous Sephardi family, see Z. Avneri and D. Corcos, "Abudarham," *EJ* 2, cols. 180–81.

34. Concerning the famous ancestor of this family, see "Akrish, Isaac Ben Abraham," *EJ* 2, cols. 503–504.

35. A play on Eccl. 12:9.

36. I Kings 18:21.

37. Romanelli is referring to the penitential prayers (*selīḥōt*) recited in Morocco according to the Sephardi tradition for a forty-day period from the beginning of Elul to the Day of Atonement.

38. The period between Rosh ha-Shana and the Day of Atonement.

39. Romanelli's etymology is correct. For *ḥazzan* as "rabbi," see Chapter 12, above, n. 29.

40. Paraphrasing Ps. 16:6.

41. Paraphrasing Gen. 41:9.

42. The image is a paraphrase of Prov. 18:10 combined with I Kings 2:50 and I Kings 2:28.

43. The custom referred to here is known as *ʿār* (literally "shame"). It is a conditional curse to the effect that "shame will come to him who ignores the petitioner's request. It is frequently accompanied by a propitiatory offering to the spirits (Mor. Ar. *jnūn*—called here by Romanelli, Azazael). Concerning the various aspects of the *ʿār*, see Westermarck, *Ritual and Belief in Morocco*, I, 518–569. Seeking refuge at the Sultan's stable or by grasping one of his cannons were typical forms of *ʿār*. For the former, see Simon Ockley (ed.), *An Account of South-West Barbary* (London, 1713), 65–66; for the latter, see G. Salmon, "Le 'droit d'asile' des canons," *AM* 3 (1905), 144–53.

44. Ex. 15:2.

45. Paraphrasing Esth. 7:7.

46. Va-Yishlaḥ = Gen. 32:4–36:43. In his commentary, Abravanel writes: "Just as Jacob had grown to fear Esau, so his descendants had grown to fear Esau's descendants and their wickedness. And just as Jacob prepared himself for prayer, for gift-giving, and for war, so it has befallen us in each generation that we must try to save ourselves from Esau and his posterity, first by means of prayer and supplication to the God of Jacob, and next by gifts and bribery. . . . " See Don Isaac Abravanel, *Pērūsh ha-Tōrah* I, fasc. 2 (Warsaw, 1862), 11b.

47. See Judah ha-Levi, *The Kuzari*, Bk. II, para. 26; where referring to

the sacrificial offerings made to God, the Rabbi states: "The purpose of these commandments was to create a workable system in order that the King could 'sit enthroned' there, in the sense of the distinction of the place. . . ."

48. The Spanish word *commercio* for officially recognized commercial activity in Mogador appears in eighteenth-century Moroccan Arabic documents. Cf. N. A. Stillman, "The Dombay Papers," *Bulletin of the John Rylands Library* 57:2 (1975), 474, no. 187.

49. Prostitution continued to be a problem in the Moroccan Jewish community into the twentieth century. See André N. Chouraqui, *Between East and West: A History of the Jews of North Africa* (New York, 1973), 240–41.

50. Tarudant, the ancient capital of the Sus lies 254 km southeast of Mogador and 83 km east of Agadir.

51. The English doctor is none other than William Lempriere, whose book has been cited here so frequently in the footnotes. However, either the governor of Mogador or Romanelli has somewhat confused the details of the visit. Lempriere was invited to Morocco from the British naval base in Gibraltar to treat Mūlāy ʿAbd al-Salām, who in return promised to release some English seamen who had indeed been shipwrecked off the coast of Africa. See Lempriere, *A Tour from Gibraltar*, 2nd ed., 1–3.

52. Neh. 5:7.

53. The Genoese Consul in Mogador at this time was Giuseppe Chiappe, the brother of Francesco Chiappe, the doyen of the European consular corps in Morocco. Giuseppe was also the Consul of the United States of America in Mogador, which is probably why he was chosen to test Romanelli's knowledge of English. See Chapter 1, above, n. 26. See also Enrico de Leone, "Mohammed ben ʿAbdallâh e le repubbliche marinare," *Il Veltro* 7 (1963), 697; idem, "Veneziani e Genovesi nel Marocco nella seconda meta del secolo XVIII," *Levante* 10 (1963), 10–11.

54. Paraphrasing Eccl. 8:4.

55. The phrase is actually *lā ilāh illā*. . . . However, many Moroccans, especially in Tangier and Tetuan where Romanelli had spent some time, pronounce /n/ for /l/ in certain contexts, and perhaps he had heard someone doing that here.

Chapter 14

1. Paraphrasing Job 26:14.
2. See Chapter 12, above.

3. Paraphrasing Job 33:10.

4. I Kings 5:18. The context is Solomon's planning to build God's House in the biblical passage. Romanelli is, of course, referring to a house for himself.

5. Ps. 132:14.

6. The image is taken from Hos. 10:14 and 12:12.

7. A play on the first of the Four Questions in the Passover Haggada— "Why is this night different from all other nights?"

8. The director of the Ben Gedalyas' yeshiva and rabbi of their family synagogue. See Chapter 13, above.

9. Ben Gedalya brothers.

10. Paraphrasing Deut. 28:56.

11. The senior Ben Gedalya.

12. Another Ben Gedalya brother.

13. Micah 7:2.

14. Jud. 17:6, 21:25.

15. Paraphrasing Obad. 1:14.

16. Paraphrasing Isa. 6:11.

17. The merchant whom Romanelli met in Gibraltar and convinced him to come with him on business to Morocco. See above, Chapter 1.

18. Play on Job 3:3.

19. Paraphrasing Lam. 3:12.

20. Paraphrasing II Sam. 1:20.

21. Paraphrasing II Sam. 20:15.

22. Isa. 53:11.

23. Literally, "Do not awaken those asleep."

24. Ez. 9:2

25. Actually, it is the Audience Hall. The word is often used to designate the government administrative building. See R. S. Harrell, T. Fox, and M. Abu-Talib, *A Dictionary of Moroccan Arabic: Arabic-English* (Washington D.C., 1966), 88.

26. Paraphrasing II Kings 2:16.

27. Image based upon Job 16:13.

28. A similar description of the Sultan's death is given by Lempriere, *A Tour from Gibraltar*, 2nd ed., 440–42.

29. Deut. 24:6. According to Lempriere, *A Tour from Gibraltar*, 2nd ed., 442, he was buried within the royal palace in Rabat.

30. Ps. 107:29.

31. Image from Prov. 26:18.

32. See Chapter 3, above.

33. All of whom, it will be recalled, were Jews since Europeans had been banned from living in Tetuan. See Chapter 1, above.

34. Slight paraphrasing of Ps. 78:31. Romanelli is probably interpreting the passage in this way (*baḥūrē* = "choicest") following the medieval and later commentaries. See, for example, the commentary of Rashi on this verse.

35. Although Romanelli has modeled his conversation here on Gen. 18:25, the story of this Muslim intercessor seems to be essentially factual. It is also reported by the contemporary Moroccan Jewish chronicler Judah b. ʿŌvēd Ibn ʿAṭṭār in his *Zikkārōn livnē Yisrāʾēl*, edited text in David Ovadia (ed.), *Fās ve-Ḥakhāmēhā: Krōnīqōt Meqōriyyōt*, I (Jerusalem, 1978/79), 63–64. For an English translation of the passage, see H. Z. Hirschberg, *A History of the Jews in North Africa*, II (Leiden, 1981), 294.

36. II Sam. 24:17.

37. Job 1:11.

38. This well-known Hebrew proverb is based upon BT Nedarim 64b. The qāḍī in Ibn ʿAṭṭār's version also says that if the Sultan takes their money "they are as good as dead." See Ovadia, *Fās ve-Ḥakhāmēhā* I, 64.

39. Back to Job 1:11.

40. I Sam. 15:9.

41. Isa. 51:20.

42. Jos. 8:20.

43. The eyewitness account of R. Abraham Koriat's son which Romanelli repeats here coincides well with other contemporary accounts. See, for example, Norman A. Stillman, "Two Accounts of the Persecution of the Jews of Tetouan in 1790," *Michael*, V (1978), 131–42, where in addition to the two previously unpublished sources edited and translated there (one a report by Romanelli's former employer Dombay), most of the published accounts are cited in the notes. Romanelli composed a lament on the death of R. Judah (R. Abraham Koriat's father). See Ḥayyim Schirmann, "A Manuscript Collection of Poems by Samuel Romanelli," *Tarbiz* 35 (1966), 382, no. 52 [Heb.].

44. The entire image here is from Ez. 2:10.

45. Paraphrasing Num. 10:35.

46. Paraphrasing Ez. 16:55.

47. Paraphrasing Ez. 7:26.

48. Paraphrasing Ex. 1:10.

49. Jud. 17:6 and 21:25.

50. See Chapter 13, above.

51. Image from Num. 14:9.

52. Slight paraphrasing of Jer. 51:31.

53. Slight paraphrasing of Jud. 11:2.

54. The son-in-law of the patriarch of the Ben Gedalya clan. See Chapter 13 above.

55. Lempriere, *A Tour from Gibraltar*, 2nd ed., 450, notes that during this period "Mogadore was saved by being so well fortified, and the great exertions of the governor and inhabitants."

56. Reading *sheqer ʿānū bō* as in the earlier editions. The line is misprinted in Shirmann's edition, 136, l. 264.

57. According to Lempriere, *A Tour from Gibraltar*, 2nd ed., 465: he was "suspended from a cord passed through the tendons of the lower part of the legs, with his head downwards; in which situation, without any sustenance, he continued alive for near four days, when the emperor ordered his head to be taken off, by way of relieving him from his misery." Lempriere refers to the poor wretch's offense as perhaps "imaginary."

58. Imagery from Deut. 32:42.

59. Lempriere, *A Tour from Gibraltar*, 2nd ed., 466, describes Jacob Attal's end as follows: " . . . the unfortunate Jew was forced off his mule, stripped of his dress, and in an old Moorish frock and with a cord about his neck, was driven on foot with whips to Tetuan. Upon his arrival, he was immediately conducted to the emperor, who ordered both his hands to be cut off, in which state he continued three days in the greatest misery, and then he was decapitated." (This passage is not included in the 1st edition.)

60. Ibn ʿAṭṭār also mentions the plundering of El Qsar in his chronicle. See the Hebrew text in Ovadia (ed.), *Fās ve-Ḥakhāmēhā*, 64, and the English translation in Hirschberg, *Jews in North Africa*, II, 295.

61. Esth. 7.7.

62. Paraphrasing I Sam. 20:3.

63. Fez is the ancient religious capital of Morocco and site of the great Qarawiyyin academy. It lies about 240 kms. southeast of Larache. It appears, based upon a lawsuit brought in a Moroccan rabbinical court several years later by one of Eliahu Levi's wives, that he did not die in Fez as Romanelli reports (probably on the basis of hearsay), but survived and eventually was able to escape across the sea with another wife. Hence the lawsuit by the abandoned spouse. See Haim Bentov, "The Ha-Levi Ibn Yuli Family," *East and Maghreb*, II, ed. E. Bashan et al. (Ramat Gan, 1980), 141–43 [Heb.].

64. Concerning him, see Chapter 8, above.

65. Gen. 14:23.

66. A play on Jer. 1:11.

67. A slight paraphrasing of Ps. 78:49–50.

68. Concerning him, see Chapter 12, above.

69. I Sam. 20:30.

70. Romanelli is referring here to the gold brocaded silk belts worn by Moroccan Jewish women which are known as *kosākāt* (sing. *kosāka*) in Arabic and *cuchacas* in Ladino. They were, in addition to being articles of clothing, used as banners or hangings to decorate the sukka and the room for a circumcision. See Louis Brunot and Elie Malka, *Glossaire judéo-arabe de Fès* (Rabat, 1940), 115–16. For an illustration of such a belt, see *Ḥayyē ha-Yehūdīm be-Mārōqō*, Israel Museum Catalogue No. 103 (Jerusalem, 1973), 148, Pl. 303.

71. Actually, "May God make him victorious." This phrase is still used in its Classical Arabic form (*nassarahu 'llāh*) when the King is mentioned on news broadcasts in Morocco. Romanelli is interpreting on the basis of the Hebrew cognate *nāsar* which means "to protect."

72. Romanelli mentioned these two Spanish traders and their artillery in Chapter 12, above. Lempriere, *A Tour from Gibraltar*, 2nd ed., 452–54, also mentions this incident. According to Lempriere, the Spaniards only had a single gun, "an old twelve pounder."

73. R. Mordechai de la Mar (al-Baḥḥār), Romanelli's kind patron in Mazagan, for whom he went to work after leaving Eliahu Levi.

74. Concerning him, see above Chapter 13.

75. R. Nahum, the Palestinian tanna, was afflicted with terrible crippling ailments and sores. He himself had prayed for these to expiate a sin for which he would have to suffer far worse torments in the World to Come. When his disciples said to him, "Woe unto us that we must see you in such a state," he replied to them, "Woe unto me if you did not see me in such a state." See BT Ta'anit 21a. For Schirmann's somewhat different interpretation of this allusion, see his note on p. 141 of his edition.

76. Cit. Job 19:27. Literally, "My kidneys were consumed."

77. Isa. 51:8.

78. The Andalusian Fennish family of Salé produced a number of important officials during the reigns of Sīdī Muḥammad and Mūlāy Yazīd. The most frequently mentioned are 'Abd al-Ḥaqq and his son al-Ṭāhir. We have not found the names of this Sīdī Aḥmad and his brother in any of the sources.

79. Interpretive paraphrase of Ps. 125:3.

80. Esth. 9:1.

81. This interpretive use of *le-'ēt mesō* from Ps. 32:6 would later be adopted by modern Hebrew writers in the late nineteenth and early twentieth centuries. See Abraham Even-Shoshan, *ha-Millōn he-Ḥadāsh*, V (Jerusalem, 1981), 2021, s.v., and note the literary examples cited there.

82. See Chapter 13, above.

83. Romanelli has taken a passive biblical expression and has made it active. Cf. II Sam. 16:21.

84. Job 24:17.

85. II Sam. 1:9.

86. Imagery from Ps. 68:31.

87. See Ex. 23:8.

88. Romanelli has made a very elegant and multilayered literary pun here, recalling the passages Isa. 5:14 and 57:4.

89. Paraphrasing Esth. 4:14.

90. Job 16:2.

91. Prov. 17:1.

92. This entire image is from Ez. 12:18 and 4:16.

93. Ps. 13:6.

94. See God's blessing to Abram in Gen. 15:14.

95. See Ex. 12:36.

96. Here Romanelli has the following note: The communal leaders who have subscribed to this book's publication know—and in particualr the Gentleman F. [i.e., David Friedlaender] and the Bachelor Euchel [i.e., Isaac Abraham Euchel]—that the writing of this book was completed on the 19th of Adar (= March, 1792) prior to the reports that have appeared in the gazettes. Concerning Friedlaender and Euchel, see the Introduction, above.

97. June 13, 1790.

98. August 18, 1790.

99. Ps. 77:5.

100. Ps. 68:5.

101. This uncharacteristically pious note sets the tone for the final didactic paragraph which is in rhymed prose in the Hebrew and the closing sonnet.

102. Paraphrasing Ps. 139:6.

103. Romanelli has here the following linguistic note: *Yafū'aḥ* (literally, "blows," but translated here "fills") and *yanū'aḥ* (literally, "rests," but translated here "at rest") appear similar in form, but are different etymologically.

104. Job 41:12. Here Romanelli has another linguisitc note: The use of the form *yabba'* here for *yabbi'a* is like the use of *yassa'* for *yassi'a* in Ps. 78:26. (That is, it is an apocopaic form.)

105. Prov. 27:17. Romanelli notes here that he has used *yaḥad* here meaning "together," whereas in the following line he uses it to mean "sharpens."

106. Paraphrasing Ps. 121:1.

107. Romanelli uses this epithet for the Jewish people that is found so frequently throughout Lamentations to designate very appropriately the Jews of Morocco.

This sonnet consists of two verses of four lines each and four verses of three lines. It is a so-called double-tailed sonnet because of the two extra three-line verses. Each line is fourteen syllables. The rhyme scheme is: abab/abab/cdc/ede/eff/fgg.

Abbreviations of Journals
and Encyclopedias

AM	*Archives Marocaines*
Ben Chananja	*Ben Chananja. Wochenblatt für jüdische Theologie*
BIHM	*Bulletin de l'Institut d'Hygiène du Maroc*
EI[1]	*Encyclopaedia of Islam*, first edition
EI[2]	*Encyclopaedia of Islam*, second edition
EJ	*Encyclopaedia Judaica*, new English edition
Hespéris	*Hespéris. Archives Berbères et Bulletin de l'Institut des Hautes-Etudes Marocaines*
Leshonenu	*Lěšonénu: A Journal for the Study of the Hebrew Language and Cognate Subjects* [Hebrew]
MGWJ	*Monatsschrift für die Geschichte und Wissenschaft des Judentums*
Michael	*Michael: On the History of the Jews in the Diaspora*
Pe'amim	*Pe'amim: Studies in the Cultural Heritage of Oriental Jewry* [Hebrew]
Tarbiz	*Tarbiz. A Quarterly for Jewish Studies* [Hebrew]
ZDMG	*Zeitschrift des Deutschen Morgenländischen Gesellschaft*
ZHB	*Zeitschrift für Hebräische Bibliographie*

Selected Bibliography

Abravanel, Don Isaac. *Pērūsh ha-Tōrah*. Vol. 1. Warsaw: 1862.

Addison, Lancelot. *The Present State of the Jews in the Barbary States (more particularly to those in Barbary)*. London: 1665.

Adler, Marcus Nathan, ed. and trans. *The Itinerary of Benjamin of Tudela*. London: 1907.

Albeck, Shalom. "Acquisition." *EJ*. Vol. 2.

Alonso, Martín. *Enciclopedia del Idioma*. Vol. 3. Madrid: 1958.

ʿAly Ben ʿAbderrahman Ben Hodeïl El Andalusy. *La parure des cavaliers et l'insigne des preux*. Translated into French by Louis Mercier. Paris: 1924.

Anon. "Akrish, Isaac Ben Abraham." *EJ*. Vol. 2.

Anon. *Qin'at Adōnāy Ṣevāʾōt*. Jassy: 1852.

Argens, Marquis d'. *Mémoires de Monsieur le Marquis d'Argens avec quelques lettres sur divers sujets*. London: 1735.

Avneri, Z., and D. Corcos. "Abudarham." *EJ*. Vol. 2.

Bar-Asher, Moshe. "ʿAl ha-Yesōdōt hā-ʿIvriyyīm bā-ʿArāvīt ha-Medubberet shel Yehūdē Marōqō." *Leshonenu* 42: 3–4 (1978): 163–89.

Ben-Ami, Issachar. *Le Judaïsme marocain: études ethnoculturelles*. Jerusalem: 1975.

Benjamin of Tudela. *The Itinerary of Benjamin of Tudela*. Edited and translated by Marcus Nathan Adler. London: 1907.

Bennarroch, C. "Ojeada sobre el judeoespañol de Marruecos." *Actas del Primer Simposio de Estudios Sefardies*. Edited by I. M. Hassan, et al. Madrid: 1970.

Ben Naim, Joseph. *Malkhē Rabbānān*. Jerusalem: 1931.

Benoliel, José. *Dialecto judeo-hispano-marroqui o hakitia*. Madrid: 1977.

Bentov, Haim. "The Ha-Levi Ibn Yuli Family." *East and Maghreb: Re-*

searches in the History of the Jews in the Orient and North-Africa. Vol. 2. Edited by E. Bashan, A. Rubinstein, and S. Schwarzfuchs. Ramat Gan: 1980 [Hebrew].

Birnbaum, S. A. "Alphabet, Hebrew." *EJ.* Vol. 2.

Bousquet, G. H. *L'éthique sexuelle de l'Islam.* Paris: 1966.

Brignon, Jean, et al. *Histoire du Maroc.* Casablanca: 1967.

Brunel, R. *Essai sur la Confrérie religieuse des Aissaoua au Maroc.* Paris: 1926.

Brunot, Louis. *Textes arabes de Rabat II: Glossaire.* Paris: 1952.

Brunot, Louis, and Elie Malka. *Textes judéo-arabes de Fès.* Rabat: 1939.

———. *Glossaire judéo-arabe de Fès.* Rabat, 1940.

Cenival, Pierre de, ed. *Les Sources inédites de l'histoire du Maroc. Deuxième Série: Dynastie filalienne: Archives et bibliothèques de France.* Vol. 4. Paris: 1941.

Chénier, Louis. *Recherches historiques sur les Maures et histoire de l'empire du Maroc,* 3 vols. Paris: 1787.

———. *The Present State of the Empire of Morocco.* London: 1788.

Chouraqui, André N. *Between East and West: A History of the Jews of North Africa.* New York: 1973.

Cohn, H. H. "Oath: Talmudic Law." *EJ.* Vol. 12.

Corcos, D. "Avila, de." *EJ.* Vol. 3.

de Leone, Enrico. "Mohammad ben ʿAbdallâh e le repubbliche marinare." *Il Veltro* 7 (1963): 665–98.

———. "Veneziani e Genovesi nel Marocco nella seconda meta del secolo XVIII." *Levante* 10 (1963): 3–13.

Delitzsch, Franz. *Zur Geschichte der judischen Poesie vom Abschluss der heiligen Schriften des Alten Bundes bis auf die neueste Zeit.* Leipzig: 1836.

della Torre, Lelio. "Samuel Romanelli und seine Schriften." *Ben Chananja* 5:4 (1862): 626–28.

Deverdun, Gaston. *Marrakech des origines à 1912.* Vol. 1. Rabat: 1959.

Dombay, Franz von. *Geschichte der Scherifen.* Agram: 1801.

———. *Grammatica Linguae Mauro-Arabicae.* Vienna: 1800.

Doutté, Edmond. *Magie et religion dans l'Afrique du Nord.* Algiers: 1909.

Dozy, Reinhart. *Supplément aux dictionnaires arabes.* 2 Vols. 3rd ed. Leiden and Paris: 1967.

Dukes, Leopold. "Literarische Anzeigen: Die Reisebeschreibung des R. Petachiah aus Regensburg." *Ben Chananja* 4:49 (1861): 423–24.

Eisenbeth, Maurice. *Les Juifs de l'Afrique du Nord: Démographie et onomastique.* Algiers: 1936.

Eisenstein, J. D., ed. *Ozar Massaoth: A Collection of Itineraries by Jewish*

Travelers to Palestine, Syria, Egypt and Other Countries. New York: 1926; reprinted Tel Aviv: 1969 [Hebrew].

Elon, Menachem. "Minhag." *EJ*. Vol. 12.

Eudel, Paul. *Dictionnaire des bijoux de l'Afrique du Nord: Maroc, Algérie, Tunisie, Tripolitaine*. Paris: 1906.

Even-Shoshan, Abraham. *Ha-Millōn he-Ḥādāsh*. 7 Vols. + Supplement. Jerusalem: 1981.

Fahn, Reuben. "Shemū'ēl Romanelli: Ṣūrātō ha-Sifrūtīt ve-Tōledōtāv," *Mizraḥ u-Maʿarav* 5 (1932): 337–50.

Figo, Azariah. *Bīna la-ʿIttīm*. Lemberg: 1858.

Frances, Jacob. *Kol Shīrē Yaʿaqōv Fransēsh*. Edited by P. Naveh. Jerusalem: 1969.

Friedberg, Ḥayyim Dov. *Tōledōt ha-Defūs ha-ʿIvrī*. 2nd ed. Tel Aviv: 1955/ 56.

Freimann, A. "Typographisches: Die hebraïsche Druckerei in Fez im Jahre 1516–21." *ZHB* 14 (1910): 79–80 and 15 (1911): 180–81.

Geiger, Ludwig. "Ein italienischer Jude als Vermittler deutscher Geisteswerke." *Allgemeine Zeitung des Judentums* 67 (1903): 9–11.

Gerber, Jane S. *Jewish Society in Fez, 1450–1700*. Leiden: 1980.

Goitein, S. D. *A Mediterranean Society III: The Family*. Berkeley and Los Angeles: 1978.

Goulven, J. *Les mellahs de Rabat-Salé*. Paris: 1927.

Greenberg, Moshe. "Urim and Thummim." *EJ*. Vol. 16.

Grillon, Pierre, ed. *Un chargé d'affaires au Maroc: La correspondance du consul Louis Chénier, 1767–1782*. Vol. 2. Paris: 1970.

Harrell, R. S., T. Fox, and M. Abu-Talib. *A Dictionary of Moroccan Arabic: Arabic-English*. Washington, D.C.: 1966.

Hirschberg, H. Z. (J. W.) *A History of the Jews in North Africa*. 2 Vols. Leiden: 1974–1981.

———. "Francos." *EJ*. Vol. 7.

Höst, Georg. *Efterretninger om Marokos og Fes*. Copenhagen: 1779; German trans. 1781.

Israel Museum. *Ḥayyē ha-Yehūdīm be-Mārōqō*. Israel Museum Catalogue No. 103. Jerusalem: 1973.

Jackson, James Grey. *An Account of the Empire of Morocco and the Districts of Suse and Tafilelt*. 3rd ed. London: 1814; repr. London: 1968.

Judah ha-Levi. *Judah Hallevi's Kitab al-Khazari*. Translated by Hartwig Hirschfeld. Rev. ed. London: 1931.

Julien, Charles-André. *History of North Africa: Tunisia, Algeria, Morocco: From the Arab Conquest to 1830*. Translated by J. Petrie. New York and Washington: 1970.

Kaufmann, David. "Shīr R. Shemū'ēl Romanelli ʿal Mōt Ben Menaḥem." *Hā-Asīf litqūfat ha-Shāna* 4 (1887): 189–90.

Kayserling Moritz. *Biblioteca Española-Portugueza-Judaica.* Strasbourg: 1890.

Klausner, Joseph. *Hīstōreya shel ha-Sifrūt hā-ʿIvrīt ha-Ḥadāsha.* Vol. 1, 3rd ed. Jerusalem: 1960.

Korkut, Besim. *Arapski Dokumenti u Državnom Arkhivu u Dubrovniku: Dokumenti o Odnosima Dubrovnika i Maroka.* Sarajevo: 1960.

Kressel, G. "Guedella, Haim." *EJ.* Vol. 7.

Lane, Edward William. *The Manners and Customs of the Modern Egyptians.* London: 1923.

Lempriere, William. *A Tour from Gibraltar to Tangier, Sallee, Mogodore, Santa Cruz, Tarudant, and thence over Mount Atlas to Morocco: including a particular account of the Royal Harem.* London: 1791; 2nd enlarged ed. 1793.

Lenz, Oscar. *Timbouctou: Voyage au Maroc, au Sahara et au Soudan.* Paris: 1886.

Le Tourneau, Roger. "Agadir-Ighir." *EI².* Vol. 1.

———. *Fès avant le Protectorat.* Casablanca: 1949; repr. New York: 1978.

Levi, Gabi. *The Jewish Community in Meknes.* Tel Aviv: 1982 [Hebrew].

Lewin, A. "Geschichte, Geographie und Reiselitteratur: Samuel Romanelli." *Die judische Litteratur Seit Abschluss des Kanons.* Vol. 3. Edited by J. Winter and A. Wünsche. Berlin: 1897.

Lewis, Bernard, ed. *Islam and the Arab World.* New York: 1976.

———. *Race and Color in Islam.* New York: 1971.

Loewenberg, A. *Annals of Opera.* Vol. 1, 2nd ed. Geneva, 1955.

Lourido Díaz, Ramón. *Marruecos en la segunda mitad del siglo XVIII: El Sultanato de Sīdī Muḥammād b. ʿAbd Allāh (1757–1790).* Cuadernos de Historia del Islam, Serie Monográfica-Islamica Occidentalia, No. 2. Granada: 1970.

Maimonides, Moses. *The Guide of the Perplexed.* Translated by Shlomo Pines. Chicago: 1963.

Malka, Elie. *Essai d'ethnographie traditionnelle des Mellahs, ou Croyances, rites de passage et vieilles pratiques des Israélites marocains.* Rabat: 1946.

Marçais, William. *Textes arabes de Tanger.* Paris: 1911.

Marsak, Leonard M., ed. *The Achievement of Bernard le Bovier de Fontenelle.* The Sources of Science, No. 76. New York and London: 1970.

Mathieu, J., R. Baron, and J. Lummau. "Etude de l'alimentation au Mellah de Rabat," *Bulletin de l'Institut d'Hygiène du Maroc* 3–4 (1938): 99–153.

Metastasio, Pietro. *Opere.* Vol. 3. Edited by Fausto Nicolini. Bari: 1914.

Michon, J.-L. "'Īsāwā." *EI²*. Vol. 4.

Miège, J.-L. *Le Maroc et l'Europe (1830–1894)*. Vol. 3. Paris: 1962.

Morag, Shelomo. "Pronunciations of Hebrew," *EJ*. Vol. 13.

al-Nāsirī. *Kitāb al-Istiqsā li-Akhbār Duwal al-Maghrib al-Aqsā*. Vol. 8. Casablanca: 1956.

Nataf, Félix. "Le mariage juif à Rabat." *Revue des Traditions Populaires* (1919): 197–208.

Norsa, Jedidiah Solomon. *Minhat Shay*. 4 Vols. Mantua: 1742–44.

Ovadia, David, ed. *Fās ve-Hakhāmēhā: Krōnīqōt Meqōriyyōt*. Vol. 1. Jerusalem: 1978/79.

Ovadia, David. *La Communauté de Sefrou*. Vol. 3. Jerusalem: 1975 [Hebrew].

Petahya of Regensburg. *Sibbūv ha-Rāv Rabbī Petahyāh mē-Regenspūrg*. Edited by L. Gruenhut. Jerusalem: 1905.

Pope, Alexander. *The Poetry and Prose of Alexander Pope*. Edited by Aubrey Williams. Boston: 1969.

Rabinowitz, Chaim R. "Figo (Picho), Azariah." *EJ*. Vol. 6.

Rackow, Ernst. *Beiträge zur Kenntnis der materiellen Kultur Nordwest-Marokkos: Wohnraum, Hausrat, Kostüm*. Wiesbaden: 1958.

Ravenna, Alfredo. "Impressioni marocchine di un viaggiatore ebreo italiano del settecento." *Rassegna Mensile di Israel* 18:5 (May, 1952): 222–29 and 19:6 (June, 1953): 281–86.

Ricard, Prosper. *Maroc*. Les Guides Bleus. 7th ed. Paris: 1950.

Richelieu, Maréchal Duc de. *Mémoires du Maréchal Duc de Richelieu*. Vol. 1. London: 1790.

Rodríguez Casado, Vicente. *Política Marroquí de Carlos III*. Madrid: 1946.

Romanelli, Samuel. *'Alōt ha-Minha ō Hāvēr Me'ushshār*. Vienna: 1793.

———. *Grammatica ragionata italiana ed ebraica con trattato, ed esempj di poesia*. Trieste: 1799.

———. *Haqqōlōt Yehdālūn ō Mishpat Shālōm*. Berlin: 1791.

———. *Ketāvīm Nivhārīm: Massā' Ba'rāv, Leqet Shīrīm, Qetā'īm mittōkh Mahazōt*. Edited by Hayyim Schirmann. Jerusalem: 1968.

———. *Massā' Ba'rāv: Hū' Sēfer ha-Qōrōt asher Histāregū 'Alū 'alay veha-Massā' asher Hāzītī bi-Gelīlōt Ma'arāv, Darkām ve-'Alīlōtām Huqqēhem ū-Mishpetēhem bēn ha-Yehūdīm bēn hā-'Arāvī'īm ha-Melekh ve-Sārīm ve-'Am hā-Āres*. Berlin, 1792.

———. *Massā' Ba'rāv: Hū' Sēfer ha-Qōrōt . . . etc*. Warsaw: 1926.

———. *Massa Ba'arab sive Samuelis Aaronis Romanelli Mantuani itineris sub finem saeculi decimi octavi per Mauretaniam facti descriptio*. 5th Hebrew ed. Edited by Salomo Marcus Schiller-Szinessy. Cambridge, London, and Leipzig: 1886.

————. *Ossia Raccolta di inni ed odi*. Trieste: 1802.

Roth, Cecil. *The Jews in the Renaissance*. Philadelphia: 1977.

Saadia Gaon. *The Book of Beliefs and Opinions*. Translated by Samuel Rosenblatt. Yale Judaica Series, Vol. 1. New Haven: 1948.

Saisset, Pascale. *Heures juives au Maroc*. Paris: 1930.

Salmon, G. "Le 'droit d'asile' des canons." *AM* 3 (1905): 144–53.

Samuel ha-Nagid. *Divan Shmuel Hanagid*. Edited by Dov Jarden. Jerusalem: 1966.

Schereschewsky, Benzion. *Family Law in Israel*. 2nd ed. Jerusalem: 1967 [Hebrew].

Schirmann, Ḥayyim Jefim. "A Manuscript Collection of Poems by Samuel Romanelli." *Tarbiz* 35 (1966): 373–95 [Hebrew].

————. "Marini, Shabbethai Ḥayyim." *EJ*. Vol. 11.

————. *Shemū'ēl Rōmmānēllī: ha-Meshōrēr veha-Nōdēd*. Jerusalem: 1968.

————. *Ha-Shīra ha-ʿIvrīt bi-Sfārād ūve-Prōvanz*. 2 vols. (in 4 pts.). 2nd ed. Jerusalem and Tel Aviv: 1961.

Scholem, Gershom. "Magen David." *EJ*. Vol. 11.

Servi, F. "Samuel Romanelli." *Corriere Israelitico* 30 (1882): 87–88.

Silberschlag, Eisig. *From Renaissance to Renaissance: Hebrew Literature from 1492–1970*. New York: 1973.

Simonsohn, Shlomo. *History of the Jews in the Duchy of Mantua*. Jerusalem: 1977.

Slousch, N. "Le Maroc au dix-huitième siècle. Mémoires d'un contemporain." *Revue du Monde Musulman* 9 (1909): 452–66, 643–64.

Spitzer, M. M. "Typography." *EJ*. Vol. 15.

Steinschneider, Moritz. "Die italienische Literatur der Juden," *MGWJ* 42–44 (1898–1900).

Stephen, Sir Leslie, and Sir Sidney Lee, eds. *The Dictionary of National Biography*. Vol. 19. London: 1937–38.

Stillman, Norman A. "A New Source for Eighteenth-Century Moroccan History in the John Rylands University Library of Manchester: The Dombay Papers." *Bulletin of the John Rylands University Library of Manchester* 57:2 (Spring, 1975): 463–86.

————. "L'expérience judéo-marocaine: un point de vue revisionniste." *Judaïsme d'Afrique du Nord aux XIXe-XXe: Histoire, société et culture*. Edited by M. Abitbol. Jerusalem: 1980.

————. "Muslims and Jews in Morocco: Perceptions, Images, Stereotypes." *Proceedings of the Seminar on Muslim-Jewish Relations in North Africa*. New York: 1975, pp. 13–27.

————. "Ṣaddīq and Marabout in Morocco." *The Sephardi and Oriental Jewish Heritage: Studies*. Edited by I. Ben-Ami. Jerusalem: 1982.

————. *The Jews of Arab Lands: A History and Source Book*. Philadelphia: 1979.

————. *The Language and Culture of the Jews of Sefrou, Morocco: An Ethnolinguistic Study*. JSS Monograph Series, No. 11. Manchester, 1988.

————. "Two Accounts of the Persecution of the Jews of Tetouan in 1790." *Michael* 5 (1978): 131–42.

Stillman, Norman A., and Yedida K. Stillman. "Magic and Folklore, Islamic." *Dictionary of the Middle Ages*. Vol. 8. New York: 1987.

————. "The Art of a Moroccan Folk Poetess." *ZDMG* 128:1 (1978): 61–84.

————. "The Jewish Courtier Class in Late Eighteenth-Century Morocco as Seen Through the Eyes of Samuel Romanelli." *The Islamic World, Classical and Medieval, Ottoman, and Modern—Essays in Honor of Bernard Lewis*. Edited by C. E. Bosworth, Charles Issawi, Roger Savory, and A. L. Udovitch. Darwin Press: Princeton: 1988.

Stillman, Yedida K. "A Moroccan Jeweler and His Art: Continuity and Change." *Pe'amim* 17 (1983): 96–111 [Hebrew].

————. "Attitudes Toward Women in Traditional Near Eastern Societies." *Studies in Judaism and Islam Presented to Shelomo Dov Goitein on the Occasion of his Eightieth Birthday*. Edited by S. Morag, I. Ben-Ami, and N. A. Stillman. Jerusalem: 1981.

————. *From Southern Morocco to Northern Israel: A Study in the Material Culture of Shelomi*. Haifa: 1982 [Hebrew].

————. "Hashpa'ōt Sefardiyyōt 'al ha-Tarbūt ha-Ḥomrīt shel Yehūdē Marōqō." *Mōreshet Yehūdē Sefarād veha-Mizraḥ: Meḥqārīm*. Edited by I. Ben-Ami. Jerusalem: 1982.

————. "Libās." *EI²*, Vol. 5.

————. "The Costume of the Jewish Woman in Morocco." *Studies in Jewish Folklore*. Edited by F. Talmage. Cambridge, Mass.: 1980.

————. "The Evil Eye in Morocco." *Folklore Research Center Studies*. Vol. 1. Edited by D. Noy and I. Ben-Ami. Jerusalem: 1970.

Tadjouri, R. "Le mariage juif à Salé." *Hespéris* 3:3 (1923): 393–420.

Terrasse, Henri. *Histoire du Maroc des origines à l'établissement du Protectorat français*. Vol. 2. Casablanca: 1950; repr. New York: 1975.

Vajda, G. "Ḥām." *EI²*. Vol. 3.

von Grunebaum, G. E. *Muhammadan Festivals*. London: 1976.

Waxman, Meyer. *A History of Jewish Literature*. Vol. 3. South Brunswick, New York, London: 1960.

Weikert, Thomas A., ed. *La Merope, Tragoedia Illustrissimi Poetae Veronensis Marchionis Francisci Scipionis Maffei quam ex Italico Sermone in Linguam Sacram Classicam Convertit Celeber Poeta Mantuanus Samuel Aaron Romanelli.* Rome: 1903.

Wensinck, A. S. "Ṣalāt." *Shorter EI.*

Westermarck, Edward. *Marriage Ceremonies in Morocco.* London: 1914.

―――. *Ritual and Belief in Morocco.* 2 Vols. London: 1926; repr. New Hyde Park: 1968.

―――. *Wit and Wisdom in Morocco: A Study of Native Proverbs.* London: 1930.

Wilensky, Michael. "Ṣāfa Berūra le-Rabbī Avrāhām Ibn ʿEzra." *Devir* 2 (1924): 274–302.

Windus, John. *A Journey to Mequinez.* London: 1725.

Ydit, Meir. "Ḥukkat ha-Goi." *EJ.* Vol. 8.

Yerushalmi, Y. H. "Professing Jews in Post-Expulsion Spain and Portugal." *Salo Wittmayer Baron Jubilee Volume.* Edited by S. Lieberman and A. Hyman. Jerusalem: 1975, pp. 1023–58.

Zafrani, Haïm. *Etudes et recherches sur la vie intellectuelle juive au Maroc de la fin du 15e au début du 20e siècle I: Pensée juridique et environment social, économique et religieux.* Paris: 1972.

―――. *Etudes et recherches sur la vie intellectuelle juive au Maroc de la fin du 15e au début du 20e siècle II: Poésie juive en Occident musulman.* Paris: 1977.

―――. *Mille ans de vie juive au Maroc: Histoire et culture, religion et magie.* Paris: 1983.

―――. *Pédagogie juive en terre d'Islam: L'enseignement traditionnel de l'hébreu et du Judaïsme au Maroc.* Paris: 1969.

Zedner, J. *Auswahl historischer Stücke.* Berlin: 1840.

Index